SOCIAL-CULTURAL ANTHROPOLOGY

About the Author

Dr. Gaya Pandey (b.1954) is a Senior faculty in the Department of Anthropology, Ranchi University, Ranchi (Jharkhand). Ever since his joining as a faculty in the Department in February 1985, he is fully dedicated and committed to the teaching and Research assignments. As a result he has to his credit two and half dozen articles in Journals of national and international repute. Besides research papers, he had published nine books under co-authorship and eleven books as self-authored. The books have been in Hindi and English medium covering different branches of anthropology. All books have been written covering syllabus which are taught under different Indian Universities to cater the needs of the students, scholars and candidates who are interested in the study of anthropology. Some recent publications are:

- Developmental Anthropology
- Bio-cultural Evolution
- Jaivik-Sanskritic Udavikas
- Bhartiya Pragaitihasik-Puratatwik Manavshastra
- Sampreshanatmak Manavshastra
- Chikitsatmak Manavshastra (Medical Anthoropology)
- Neo Anthropological Theory

SOCIAL-CULTURAL ANTHROPOLOGY

Gaya Pandey

CONCEPT PUBLISHING COMPANY PVT. LTD.
NEW DELHI-110059

ISBN-13: 978-93-5125-261-0 (HB)
ISBN-13: 978-93-5125-262-7 (PB)

First Published 2017

Published and Printed by

Concept Since 1974

Concept Publishing Company Pvt. Ltd.
Regd. Office: A/15-16, Commercial Block, Mohan Garden,
New Delhi-110059 (INDIA)
Phones : 25351460, 25351794, *Fax* : 091-11-25357109
E-mail : publishing@conceptpub.com
Website: www.conceptpub.com

Cataloging in Publication Data—DK Courtesy: D.K. Agencies (P) Ltd. <docinfo@dkagencies.com>

Pandey, Gaya, 1954- **author.**
Social-cultural anthropology / Gaya Pandey.
pages cm
Includes bibliographical references and index.
ISBN 9789351252610 (HB)
ISBN 9789351252627 (PB)

1. Ethnology—India. 2. Ethnology. I. Title.

GN635.I4P36 2017 DDC 305.800954 23

DEDICATED TO

I dedicate this book to my family members:
Mother Smt. Anasuiya Devi,
Wife Smt Indu Devi,
Daughters—Sudha, Suman, Sarita and Anu
Son—Shekhar, Grand sons—Kushagra and Harshit
with all kinds of respect and gratitude
who took every care during the period of my
long illness and provided thereby a second life to me.

Preface

The book entitled, '*Social-Cultural Anthropology*' is an outcome of sincere labour, dedication and commitment of the Author. Ever since man entered in the stage of civilization, he is continuously trying to write books to preserve the knowledge on particular topic for future generations. A good number of books have been written by various scholars and anthropologists on social-cultural anthropology. But all topics which are taught under it are not found in a single book. This book has been written to cater the needs of the students and candidates who opt Anthropology as an optional paper in various competitive examinations. The purpose of writing the book is purely contextual. The author does not claim to have something contributed new which cannot be found in the writings of the others. Sometimes, others' expressions have also been followed in word by word in toto. This have been done to bring all materials of syllabus on social-cultural anthropology under one cover for the benefit of the students. The simple English language may help students and scholars of anthropology to understand subject matter of social-cultural Anthropology.

The book could achieve its completion with the support of colleagues, students, family members, well-wishers and others who have extended their help at different stages of writing the book. Now it is my pious duty to express some words for their help extended to me.

First of all I extend my sincere gratitude to those writers whose contributions have played significant role in the completion of the book. I express my thanks to all colleagues of the Department of Anthropology who encouraged me to complete the book as early as possible. I am also thankful to the students of the department and candidates of competitive exams, who always demanded to write a book in English medium on social-cultural Anthropology, whenever they came for suggestions. Non-teaching staff of the Department also deserve special thanks who extended help of different types when I remained engaged in writing in the Department.

I am deeply indebted to my family members, mother Smt. Anasuiya Devi, wife Smt. Indu Devi, daughters—Sudha, Suman, Sarita and Anu, son—Shekhar, and grandsons—Kushagra and Harshit for their contributions in taking my every care as a patient of heart and diabetic and who allowed me to complete the book under their care.

No less thankful I am to Shri Ashok Kumar Mittal and his team of Concept Publishing Company Pvt. Ltd., who printed the hand written manuscript of the book with meticulous care.

Last but not the least, I would like to extend thanks to all those, collectively and individually, who extended their cooperation in completion of the book.

Gaya Pandey
Department of Anthropology
Ranchi–834008 (Jharkhand)

Contents

Chapter 1

Anthropology and its Main Branches

Definition

Etymologically, the term Anthropology is composed of two Greek words—(i) Anthropos and (ii) Logous. The meaning of 'Anthropos' is man and the meaning of 'Logous' is study. Thus, etymologically the meaning of Anthropology is study of man. The one meaning of the term 'logous' is science, too. So, we can also say that Anthropology is science of man. In other words, we can say that Anthropology is scientific study of man. There is no doubt that Anthropology is science of man or study of man. But it is study of man in totality. It makes study of man in whole a totality right from his origin on earth to societies in which he had lived in different periods of time and living to-day. The wholistic study of man requires an understanding about his social-cultural, physical-biological, pre-historical-archaeological and linguistic features in time and space. Thus, anthropology is a science which deals with study of man as a social-cultural, physical-biological, prehistorical-archaeological and linguistic being in time and space.

Nature of Anthropology

Different anthropologists have attempted to deal with nature of anthropology in different ways. The different views expressed by anthropologists regarding its nature are as follows:

- Anthropology is a science
- Anthropology is a social science
- Anthropology is an applied social science
- Anthropology is normative science
- Anthropology is an art.

Anthropology is a Science: Any science is a science because of application of scientific methods to deal with cause-effect relationship. Physics, chemistry, geology and other are science because they use scientific methods to establish cause-effect relationship. Anthropology also makes use of scientific methods to establish cause and effect relationship. Therefore, we can say that Anthropology is a science. The scientific methods on the basis of which cause and effect relationship is established are as follows:

- Observation
- Recording
- Verification
- Generalisation

Observation: Science begins with observation. That is why science makes use of observation. This is the first step of scientific method. Observation is systematic viewing of seen phenomenon. Systematic viewing of seen phenomenon helps us in understanding relationship between cause and effect. It establishes that effect is result of cause because for every effect cause is responsible. Observation establishes logic behind cause and effect relationship and finally leads us towards rationality. On the basis of rationality, we are able to discover facts which is ultimate goal of a science. Like natural and physical sciences, anthropology applies observation technique to find out facts, develop logic behind cause-effect relationship and arrive at rationality in discovering facts. In this way, anthropology fulfils the first step of a scientific method.

Recording: The second step of scientific method is recording. The scientists record their observation systematically. They record cause-effect relationship in very systematic manner. It is because scientific result is based on systematic recording. Error in recording of observation, brings error in final results. That is why a scientist takes reading of his observations very attentively. Anthropologists also record their observations paying due attention towards their observations. They record facts observed in very attentive and systematic manner. Without proper recording they cannot justify their observations dealing with truth.

Verification: After recording the next step of a scientific method is verification. Scientists believe in verification of their observation. According to scientists, the facts should be verifiable. It must be verified again and again before arriving at certain conclusion. That is why scientists verify their results again and again before reaching at final conclusion. Anthropologists also verify their results again and again. They make cross-verification of facts to arrive at a conclusion. Cross-verification of facts plays significant role in establishing a conclusion. In this way anthropology relies upon verifiability of data.

Generalisation: Generalisation is the last step of a scientific method which a scientist uses in his study or research. With the help of generalization the cause-effect relationship is established scientifically. On the basis of observation, recording, verification and cross-verification a final result or conclusion is drawn by the scientist. Based on final result or conclusion, the scientist is in a position to make a general statement regarding the outcome of his research. Anthropologists also make some general statement based on their conclusion of research.

From the above account, it is quite clear that Anthropology fulfils all steps of a science, therefore, Anthropology is a science. Like any natural and physical sciences, anthropological data are observable, recordable, verifiable and generalisable. On this ground, some anthropologists consider anthropology as a science.

Anthropology is a social science: An another opinion regarding the nature of anthropology is that anthropology is a social science. The followers of this opinion treat anthropology as a science but not as a Natural Science. Rather they put Anthropology under the category of social science.

As Anthropology is concerned with study of different types of human societies prevalent in the world, therefore, it should be placed under social sciences not under Natural Sciences. Thus, we can say that Anthropology is a social science which studies different institutions and systems prevalent in different societies of the world.

Anthropology is Applied Social Science: Some anthropologists are of opinion that Anthropology is a social science but it should be placed under applied social science. There is no doubt that Anthropology is a social science but it has applied value for the society too. Anthropological knowledge has value for the society. Therefore, anthropology is beneficial for the society in a number of ways. Keeping applied value in mind, Anthropology has been divided into nearly hundred branches and sub-branches. Each branch claims its special interest for the benefit of society. Thus, Anthropology is applied social science because its knowledge can be applied for the benefit of society.

Anthropology is Normative Science: Some anthropologists are of the opinion that Anthropology should be placed under the category of Normative Science. It is because Anthropology makes study of norms and value of society. As anthropology studies norms and value system of the society, therefore, Anthropology is a Normative Science.

Anthropology is an Art: Some anthropologists do not agree with views of other anthropologists who treat Anthropology as science, social science, applied social science or normative social science. According to them, Anthropology is not a science. Rather, it is an art. The art of Anthropology lies in problem-finding and solution-providing. As an artist anthropologists are well-versed in the art of problem-finding and solution-providing. Therefore, Anthropology is an art. It is also an art because it makes mental reconstruction of things and events.

Scope of Anthropology

The scope of Anthropology is very vast. It is not only limited to the study of simple societies of world. Rather complex societies also come under the scope of its study. Its scope covers not only non-literate societies of the past but also literate societies of present time. It studies not only industrial and global society of present time, but also non-industrial society of past. But initially the scope of Anthropology was confined only to following areas or branches:

- Social-Cultural Anthropology
- Physical-Biological Anthropology
- Prehistoric-Archaeological Anthropology
- Linguistic Anthropology
- Applied Anthropology

A detailed description about these areas of Anthropology is being presented below one-by-one under the sub-heading main branches of Anthropology.

Main Branches of Anthropology: As referred to earlier, now-a-days Anthropology is divided into nearly hundred interest groups, each claiming their applied role for the benefit of society. But here we are going to deal with only five main branches of Anthropology which were initially introduced in different universities to study and understand man in totality. These branches are as follows:

- Social-Cultural Anthropology
- Physical-Biological Anthropology
- Prehistoric-Archaeological Anthropology
- Linguistic Anthropology
- Applied Anthropology

Social-Cultural Anthropology

When Anthropology was introduced in Oxford University as a teaching subject in 1884 under the leadership of founder of British Anthropology E.B. Taylor, it was known as 'Science of Culture'. As it was established by Taylor, so it was also known as Mr. Taylor's science. In those initial days, it was confined basically to Cultural Anthropology. But in the last book of Tylor, 'Anthropology: An Introduction to Man and His Civilization' (1881) four-field wholistic approach of the subject Anthropology was advocated because there are chapters on cultural, prehistoric, physical and linguistic aspects of man.

The founder of American Anthropology in British Columbia University Franz Boas also advocated four-field wholistic approach for the subject Anthropology. He was of opinion that Anthropology can be understood in totality by such branches as Cultural Anthropology, physical anthropology, prehistory and linguistics and folklores.

In the beginning there was no distinction between Cultural and Social Anthropology. Cultural Anthropology was basically also a social Anthropology. But with the emergence of A.R. Radcliffe-Brown and his supporters in Britain, distinction between the use of Social Anthropology and Cultural Anthropology began. Radcliffe-Brown and his supporters were in favour of establishing a separate branch of Anthropology under the title, 'Social Anthropology'. They wanted to isolate social Anthropology from cultural Anthropology. According to them the term culture is not confined only to social institutions. Rather it is related to physical, prehistoric and linguistic aspects of man, too. But Social Anthropology as a separate branch of Anthropology should be confined only to study of social institutions in the maintenance of whole community. However, the use of cultural

Anthropology never became out of scene in America because Franz Boas did not prefer to use the term Social Anthropology in place of Cultural Anthropology. When Social Anthropology was gaining momentum in Britain with the support of A.R. Radcliffe-Brown and his supporters, Franz Boas and his students were devoting their time in study of relation between culture and personality and also between language and culture. In this way Franz Boasians discarded the scope of Social Anthropology in America.

In France, Levi-Strauss and his supporters took a middle way to resolve the conflict between social and cultural Anthropology. They preferred to use the term, 'Social-Cultural Anthropology, in place of using them Social Anthropology or Cultural Anthropology separately. This middle way to resolve the conflict was adopted by all and since then the term Social-Cultural Anthropology is used together.

Social-Cultural Anthropology makes study of ideas and ways of life of man which is known as culture. This branch of Anthropology makes study of art, magic, religion and science besides economic and political organizations. The main scope of Social-Cultural Anthropology are as follows:

- Basic concepts like culture, society, community, civilizations, institution, association, folk-ways, mores, norms, values, band, tribe, group, social-structure, social organization, social change, cultural change, ethnology, ethnography, social stratification.
- Family, marriage and kinship
- Art, Magic, Religion and Science
- Economic organization of simple society
- Political organization of simple society
- Language and culture of simple society

Physical-Biological Anthropology

Physical-biological Anthropology is that branch of Anthropology which makes study of origin and evolution of diverse forms of species Homosapiens. The Physical-biological Anthropology takes help of primatology, Palaeontology and Genetics to understand properly and systematically origin and evolution of diversified forms of species

Homosapiens. The main scope of Physical-Biological Anthropology is as follows:

- Position of Man in Animal Kingdom
- Fossil Apes and Fossil Man
- Hominids
- Australopithecus
- Homoerectus
- Early Homosapiens
- True Homosapiens
- Human Genetics
- Anthropometry
- Ethnology
- Biometry
- Living primate behaviour
- Anthropology of sports
- Forensic Anthropology
- Applied Physical-Biological Anthropology
- Nutritional Anthropology
- Medical Anthropology

Prehistoric-Archaeological Anthropology

It is that branch of Anthropology which makes study of culture of prehistoric man. Prehistoric-archaeological anthropologists make study of human activities depicted through artifacts found from a place on the surface or a site excavated by the scholar. They take help of geologists, botanists, zoologists and historians. Development of literacy was a dividing line between prehistory and history. The main scope of prehistoric-archaeological Anthropology is as follows:

- Origin of Earth and Emergence of Man
- Pleistocene and its main features
- Eolithic man and culture
- Lower Palaeolithic man and culture
- Middle Palaeolithic man and culture
- Upper Palaeolithic man and culture
- Mesolithic man and culture
- Neolithic man and culture

- Chalcolithic man and culture
- Bronze age man and civilization
- Iron age man and civilization
- Methods of dating
- Tool techniques and tool types

Linguistic Anthropology

It is that branch of Anthropology which deals with origin, history, nature, structure, function, change, plurality and diffusion of human languages spoken and written in different parts of the world. Since, his origin on earth, man is a speaking animal, but became a writing animal when he reached in the stage of civilization as appears from his evidence of writing in river valley civilizations. The scope of linguistic Anthropology includes following:

- Meaning, nature and characteristics of Human Languages
- Theories of origin of Human languages
- Structure of Human languages
- Functions of Human languages
- Diffusion of Human languages
- Human language families
- Human communication
- Social context of Human languages
- Language and culture
- Language and linguistics
- Language and change

Applied Anthropology

Towards the end of 19th Century, a number of interest groups were created in each main branch of Anthropology. The creation of interest groups in each branch was based on the concept of applied value of Anthropology and anthropological knowledge for the benefit of society. Each interest group of Anthropology began to claim their own applied value for the benefit of society. As a result of this now we have nearly hundred interest groups, each forming a separate branch or sub-branch of Anthropology and claiming their own applied value for the interest of the society. The tradition of creation of branches and sub-branches of Anthropology on the basis of interest groups began in both places—Britain and America. This tradition led the foundation of a fifth branch of Anthropology known as Applied Anthropology. The branch provided occasion to anthropologists to get employment away from museums and Universities. Applied Anthropology provided anthropologists to serve as an expert in different committees and commissions of the Government and also as an adviser to Government during war and other critical situations. Some of interest groups of Anthropology claiming their applied value are as follows:

- Applied Social-Cultural Anthropology
- Applied Physical-biological Anthropology
- Applied prehistoric-archaeological Anthropology
- Applied Linguistic Anthropology
- Anthropology of children
- Anthropology of women
- Anthropology of Youth
- Anthropology of Aged
- Anthropology of Sports
- Anthropology of Disaster Management
- Medical Anthropology
- Nutritional Anthropology
- Theoretical Anthropology
- Demographic Anthropology
- Ecological Anthropology
- Psychological Anthropology
- Urban Anthropology
- Developmental Anthropology
- Anthropology of foreign relations
- Anthropology of Law
- Anthropology of Markets
- Anthropology of Religion
- Anthropology of Dalits
- Anthropology of Tribals
- Anthropology of Other Backward Classes
- Anthropology of Labour
- Gender Anthropology
- Communicational Anthropology
- Indian Anthropology
- Anthropology of SAARC Nations

- Anthropology of European Nations
- Anthropology of South-East Asian Nations
- Anthropology of Public Administration
- Anthropology of Human Resource Management

Some other Branches of Anthropology

It will be the fitness of things to present here a brief description of some other branches of Anthropology in the interest of readers and scholars interested in the study of some other branches of Anthropology. Here, we are going to deal with the following branches of Anthropology:

- Ecological Anthropology
- Medical Anthropology
- Urban Anthropology
- Developmental Anthropology

Ecological Anthropology: Ecological Anthropology is that branch of Anthropology which makes study of interactions between environment and organism particularly man. We all are aware of the fact that environment of the universe is not same everywhere. That is why in different types of environment, different kinds of species are found. In other words, we can say that organisms have to make adaptation with environment in order to survive in a particular environment. The science which deals with study of interaction between environment and organism is called ecology. Ecological Anthropology deals with the study of man and habitat-interactions and adaptations. The themes which come under the study of Ecological Anthropology are as follows:

- Ecology and Material Culture
- Ecology, Technology and Economy
- Ecology, Society and Religion
- Ecology and Demography
- Ecology, Health and Nutrition
- Ecology and Crime
- Ecology, Transportation and Communication
- Ecology and Industrial Development
- Ecology and Environmental Preservation

- Ecology and Disaster Management

Medical Anthropology: It is that branch of Anthropology which makes study of Pan historical and cross-cultural study of disease and health. This branch of Anthropology includes following themes under its scope:

- Beliefs related to disease and health
- Practices related to disease and health
- Disease and Food medicine
- Disease and Folk medicine
- Disease and medical systems
- Categorization of disease and medicine
- Disease and health education
- Nutrition and Health care
- Maternity and child health care
- Sexual health and sexually communicated diseases
- Social behaviour with patients suffering from leprosy, cancer and AIDS.
- Cattle disease and treatment
- Various health related programmes and their impact.

Urban Anthropology: It is that branch of Anthropology which makes study of process of urbanization and characteristics of complex urban society and culture. This branch of Anthropology includes following themes under its scope:

- Process of urbanization
- Urban society
- Urban culture
- Urban marriage
- Urban kinship
- Urban economy and occupation
- Urban religion
- Urban polity
- Urban administration
- Urban amenities
- Urban problems
- Urban planning

Developmental Anthropology: It is that branch of Anthropology which makes study of concepts, policies, planning, implementation, monitoring, evaluation and follow-up of development. This branch of Anthropology includes following themes under its scope:

- Concept and meaning of development
- Areas, parameters and indicators of development
- Factors supporting development
- Impediments to development
- Agencies of development
- Media and development
- Development policies and programmes
- Implementation, monitoring, evaluation and follow-up.
- Development, Displacement and rehabilitation
- Development and Social Justice
- Development and Human Rights
- Development and Women Empowerment
- Development and Communication

Psychological Anthropology

It is that branch of Anthropology which makes study of relationship between culture and personality. This branch includes following themes under its scope:

- Impact of culture on personality
- Impact of personality on culture
- Adaptation between culture and personality
- Basic personality type
- Modal personality type
- National character
- Socialization process
- Cross-cultural Analysis

Relation between Different Main Branches of Anthropology

It seems fitness of the things to present here relationship between main branches of Anthropology such as social-cultural and physical-biological Anthropology, Social-cultural and pre-historic archaeological Anthropology, social-cultural Anthropology and linguistic Anthropology.

Relation between Social-Cultural Anthropology and Biological Anthropology

Social-Cultural Anthropology and Biological Anthropology both study man. Therefore, both seem close to each other. In fact social-cultural Anthropology is an extension of Biological Anthropology. For becoming social and cultural some significant changes took place in man. For example erect posture, bipedal walk, freely opposable thumb, stereoscopic and chromatic vision, intelligent brain and creation of symbols. On account of such biological changes, man could become social-cultural animal. In this sense, social-cultural anthropology and biological Anthropology show close relation. But in themes of study and methods of research they differ profoundly. Social-cultural Anthropology studies social-cultural institutions of contemporary simple societies, whereas Biological Anthropology studies human palaeontology, human evolution, evolution of species Homosapiens, primatology and Human Genetics. Social-Cultural Anthropology uses ethnographic method, Biological Anthropology uses morphological and Genetic method.

Relation between Social-Cultural Anthropology and Pre-historical Archaeological Anthropology

Social-cultural Anthropology and prehistoric archaeological Anthropology both seem close to each other because both deal with study of culture of mankind. Both study social-cultural features of man. But in subject matters and methods of research they differ profoundly. Social-Cultural Anthropology studies social-cultural features of present-day simple societies, prehistoric-archaeological Anthropology studies social-cultural features of prehistoric man on the basis of evidences left in the form of artifacts. Social-cultural Anthropology uses ethnographic method of research, whereas prehistoric archaeological Anthropology uses exploration and excavation method of research.

Relation between Social-Cultural Anthropology and Linguistic Anthropology

Social-Cultural Anthropology and linguistic Anthropology seem very close to each other because they study human languages. Both study human languages as a system and both rely upon linguistics for analysis. But in subject matter and method of study both differ profoundly. Social-cultural Anthropology studies different inventories related to material and non-material cultures of contemporary simple society, whereas linguistic Anthropology studies nature, characteristics, meaning, structure, function and change in human languages spoken and written in different parts of the globe. Social-cultural Anthropology studies language as vehicle of culture, whereas Linguistic Anthropology studies language as a means of communication between two individuals or two groups. Social-Cultural Anthropology uses ethnographic method, whereas Linguistic Anthropology uses linguistic method.

Relation between Biological Anthropology and Prehistoric Archaeological Anthropology

Biological Anthropology and Prehistoric Archaeological Anthropology seem close to each other because both study human evolution and both take help of Palaeontology, i.e., Palaeo-botany and palaeozoology in order to know the origin of man and evolution of Homosapiens. But the subject matter and method of research of both Biological Anthropology and Prehistoric-archaeological Anthropology differ profoundly. Biological Anthropology studies both macro and micro evolution of man, but prehistoric archaeological Anthropology studies only macro evolution of mankind. Biological Anthropology studies human evolution to know the relation between primates and man and also diversified forms of Homosapiens. But prehistoric archaeological Anthropology studies macro evolution of man just to know the evolution of prehistoric culture of mankind. Biological Anthropology uses morphological and genetic methods of research, whereas prehistoric archaeological Anthropology uses exploration and excavation method of research.

Relation between Biological Anthropology and Linguistic Anthropology

Biological Anthropology and Linguistic Anthropology seem closer to each other because both make study of human evolution to know as to why man became a speaking and writing animal and why other animals did not become speaking, reading and writing animals. For becoming a speaking, reading and writing animal certain changes have taken place in physical features of man. These changes are erect posture, bipedal walk, freely opposable thumbs, stereoscopic and chromatic vision, large brain and creation of symbols. The erect posture made pharynx to move downward in man and it became the first resonator. Mouth cavity including teeth and tongue became second resonator and nasal cavity became third resonator. In this way, he became a speaking animal. The head in man became straight on neck. The brain size became enlarged which helped man to think and develop verbal symbols. Freely opposable thumbs helped man to draw his imagination on cave wall, ceiling and floor. Expression of non-verbal symbols in the form of drawing was first step of man in the direction of writing. When he reached in civilized stage he developed phonetic alphabet and writing. He gradually developed script and became a writing animal. Thus, both biological Anthropology and linguistic Anthropology study evolutionary processes of man. So, they show close relationship with each other. But in subject matter and method of research they differ profoundly. Biological Anthropology studies human genetics, Linguistic Anthropology studies human languages. Biological Anthropology uses morphological methods and genetic methods, linguistic Anthropology uses methods of linguistics.

Relation between Prehistoric-Archaeological Anthropology and Linguistic Anthropology

Prehistoric Archaeological Anthropology and Linguistic Anthropology both seem closer to each other because both attempt to deal with evolution of human languages and emergence of writing on the basis of prehistoric archaeological evidences. But this similarity does not show that they do not differ. Rather they differ profoundly in subject matter and method of study. Prehistoric-archaeological Anthropology studies evolution of writing, whereas Linguistic Anthropology studies origin and evolution of human languages. Prehistoric-Archaeological Anthropology uses exploration and excavation methods of research, whereas Linguistic Anthropology uses methods of Linguistics.

Relation of Social-Cultural Anthropology with other Sciences

Social-Cultural Anthropology shows close relationship with natural sciences, social sciences, earth sciences, life sciences, Medicine, Law,

Linguistics and Literature. It will be the fitness of the thing to present here in brief relationship between Social-Cultural Anthropology and other sciences one-by-one.

Relation between Social-Cultural Anthropology and Natural Sciences

Natural sciences like physics and chemistry show closeness with Social-Cultural Anthropology. Like physics and chemistry, Social-Cultural Anthropology uses observation as a main technique of research like physics and chemistry, social-cultural anthropology also makes recording, verification and generalization. In this way like natural sciences, Social-Cultural Anthropology makes use of scientific method. So, Social-Cultural Anthropology comes close to Natural Sciences. Like physical and chemical sciences, Social-Cultural Anthropology makes use of absolute methods of dating the artifacts in order to understand the past forms of culture of mankind. But similarity in application of scientific method does not reveal that both natural sciences and social-cultural anthropology have similarity in approaches and subject matters of teaching. Natural sciences adopt laboratory approach, whereas social-cultural Anthropology adopts ethnographic approach. Natural sciences study natural objects, whereas Social-Cultural Anthropology studies social-cultural institutions of simple society. Thus, both differ profoundly in their approach and subject matter.

Relation between Earth Sciences and Social-Cultural Anthropology

Social-Cultural Anthropology shows relation with earth sciences particularly Geography and Geology to some extent. Let us discuss relation of Social-Cultural Anthropology with Geography and Geology one-by-one.

Relation with Geography: Geography and Social-Cultural Anthropology shows relationship because both make study of culture and society in different types of environment of the world. Both studies demography, diseases, crime, resources, technology and economy in different areas of the globe. Thus, both Geography and Social-Cultural Anthropology show closeness and relationship. But this closeness does not indicate that both show similarity in their approaches and subject matter of study. Social-Cultural Anthropology follows ethnographic approach, whereas Geography follows land and density of population approach. Social-Cultural Anthropology studies Social-Cultural institutions of simple people, Geography studies relation of land with human population. In this way, both differ profoundly in their approaches and subject matter of study.

Relation with Geology: Both Social-Cultural Anthropology and Geology study nature of environments in different periods of time with a view to understand origin of earth, emergence of life, and finally man and his tools of existence. Both study sedimentary rocks to record fossils of living beings, tools and culture. In this way, both Social-Cultural Anthropology and Geology come together. But this closeness does not tell us that they show similarity in their approaches and subject matters of study. Social-Cultural Anthropology follows ethnographic approach and Geology follows uniformitarianism and catastrophism. Social-Cultural Anthropology studies social-cultural institutions of simple people, whereas Geology studies formation of sedimentary rocks to reconstruct Cosmic and Geological time scale.

Relation of Social-Cultural Anthropology with Biological Sciences. Biological sciences particularly Botany and Zoology show some closeness with Social-Cultural Anthropology. Botany and Zoology both studies plants and animal fossils to understand evolution of plants and animals on the earth. Social-Cultural Anthropology also studies plant and animal fossils to understand nature of past environment and evolution of man and his culture on the earth. Like Palaeo-Botany and Palaeo-Zoology Social-Cultural Anthropology also takes help of Palaeo-Anthropology to understand forms of lives, emergence of man and evolution of culture. Social-Cultural Anthropology also takes help of Ethno-Botany and Ethno-Zoology to understand behaviour related genetic counselling practiced by different ethnic groups. In this way, Social-Cultural Anthropology shows relationship with life sciences. But this similarity does not indicate that Social-Cultural Anthropology and life sciences have similar approaches and subject matters of study. They differ profoundly in their approaches and subject matters of study. Social-Cultural Anthropology follows ethnographic approach, life sciences follows laboratory approach. Social-Cultural Anthropology studies social-cultural institutions of simple society, whereas life sciences study taxonomy physiology of plants and animals.

Relation of Social-Cultural Anthropology with Medicine: Medicine as a science studies disease and health of people.

Social-Cultural Anthropology also studies disease and health of people. In this way both seem close to each other. But this relation does not tell that they are not different in their approach and subject matters of study. Medicine makes study of modern system of treating diseases and maintaining health, whereas Social-cultural Anthroplogy makes pan historical and corss-cultural study of treating diseases and maintaining health.

Social-Cultural Anthropology follows ethnographic approach to know treatment of diseases and maintenance of health, whereas medicine follows scientific approach for treatment of diseases and maintenance of health.

Relation between Social-Cultural Anthropology and Law

Social-Cultural Anthropology makes study of law of people and law also makes study of different types of laws of people. As both these subjects make study of nature and characteristics of laws, so they seem close to each other. But these closeness does not indicate that they do not differ. Rather they differ profoundly in approach and subject matter of study. Social-Cultural Anthropology follows ethnographic approach, whereas law follows modern Social Justice approach. Social-Cultural Anthropology makes study of nature and characteristics of primitive laws of simple society whereas law makes studies of nature and characteristics of modern laws formulated by states.

Relation of Social-Cultural Anthropology with other Social Sciences

The Social-Cultural Anthropology shows relation with other Social Sciences like History, Economics, Political Science, Home Science, Sociology and Psychology. Now it will be proper to discuss relation of Social-Cultural Anthropology with all these social sciences one by one.

Relation with History: Social-Cultural Anthropology and History show close relation because both study past Social-Cultural events, both make historical reconstruction and both follow chronology. In this way, Social-Cultural Anthropology and History show close relation. But this closeness does not reveal that they show similarity in their approaches and subject matter of study. Rather they show profound difference in their approaches and subject matters of study. History makes study of literate society and Social-Cultural Anthropology makes study of illiterate society. Social-Cultural anthropology makes study of prehistoric archaeological materials particularly artifacts, whereas history makes use of only historical archaeological matcrials like seals, inscriptions, coins etc. Social-Cultural Anthropology takes help of folkloric traditions for historical reconstruction, history takes help of written traditions to reconstruct history. Social-Cultural Anthropology follows both textual and contextual approaches whereas history follows only textual approach. Social-Cultural Anthropology uses ethnic periods for chronology such as savagery, barbarism and civilization, whereas history uses man made events to follow chronology such as Ancient, Medieval and Modern. Social-Cultural Anthropology studies human actions and behaviour, history uses individual action and behaviour in a particular period. Social-Cultural Anthropology follows ethnographic approach and history follows textual and historical archaeological approach. Thus, we see that approaches and subject matters of Social-Cultural Anthropology and history are quite different, but both deal with historical reconstruction. So, we can say that Social-Cultural Anthropology is a history but of another kind.

Relation with Economics: Social-Cultural Anthropology and Economics both show close relationship because both study economic institutions like production, consumption, distribution, exchange, trade and market. As both study economic institutions, naturally both show closeness with each other. But this closeness does not tell us that both follow similar approaches and subject matters in research and study. Social-Cultural Anthropology follows ethnographic approach, Economics follows econometric approach. Social-Cultural Anthropology pays attention on micro and macro both types of approaches, but Economics pays attention only on macro approach. Not only approaches, but subject matters of Social-Cultural Anthropology and Economics are also quite different. Social-Cultural Anthropology studies economic institution of primitive people or simple people, whereas Economics studies economic institutions of modern society. Social-Cultural Anthropology pays attention on primitive economy and economics pays attention on modern economy. Thus, we see that Social-Cultural Anthropology and Economies differ in their approaches and subject matter of study.

Relation of Social-Cultural Anthropology with Political Science

Social-Cultural Anthropology and political science both show relation and closeness with one another. Both study law, Judicial system, Government and State. Thus, both Social-Cultural Anthropology and political science make study of political institutions of human society. Naturally, they show relationship and closeness with one another. But this relationship and closeness does not tell us that they do not differ in their approach and subject matter. Rather they differ in their approach and subject matter to a great extent. Social-Cultural Anthropology follows ethnographic approach, whereas political science follows textual approach. Social-Cultural Anthropology makes study of law, justice, Government and State of primitive people, whereas political science studies political institutions like law, justice, Government and State of modern people. Social-Cultural Anthropology studies political institutions of simple society, whereas political science studies political institutions of modern complex society.

Relation of Social-Cultural Anthropology with Sociology

Social-Cultural Anthropology and Sociology show close relation. They are treated as sister discipline because both make study of social-cultural institutions and various forms of societies. But their closeness and relationship does not show that they are not different in their approaches and subject matter of study. Rather they differ profoundly in their approaches and subject matter. Social-Cultural Anthropology follows ethnographic approach, whereas sociology follows telescopic approach. Social-Cultural Anthropology makes study of Social-Cultural institutions of simple society, sociology makes study of Social-Cultural institutions of modern complex society. Social-Cultural Anthropology also makes study of prehistoric cultures and societies, whereas sociology does not make study of prehistoric societies and culture. Social-Cultural Anthropology makes study of characteristics of human languages, but sociology does not make study of human languages. Thus, we see that Social-Cultural Anthropology and sociology are sister discipline and show closeness and relationship with each other, but they also show differences in their approach and subject matter of study.

Relation with Psychology

Social-Cultural Anthropology and Psychology show closeness and relationship with each other. Both study personality, feeling, sentiments, belief, attitude, crowd leadership and adaptation process. Thus, both are concerned with individual and group behaviour of human beings. But this closeness and relationship does not reveal that they do not differ in their approach and subject matter. Rather they show a great difference in their approach and subject matter of study. Social-Cultural Anthropology follows ethnographic approach, Psychology follows experimental approach. Social-Cultural Anthropology studies Social-Cultural institutions of simple society, whereas psychology makes study of behaviour of individuals of different age, sex, caste, lingual and religious groups. Social-Cultural Anthropology makes study of plants, animals and other things as cultural objects, but psychology makes study of animal psychology.

Relation with Home Science

Social-Cultural Anthropology and Home Science show closeness and relationship with each other. Social-Cultural Anthropology studies family and Home Science also studies family. Because both are related to the study of family, therefore, they show relationship and closeness to each other. But this closeness does not show that both follow same approach and subject matter of study and research. Rather they differ in their approach and subject matter of study and research. Social-Cultural Anthropology uses ethnographic approach in their study and research, but Home Science uses survey approach in their study and research. Social-Cultural Anthropology studies Social-Cultural institutions of simple people, Home Science studies husband-wife relationship, marital success, marital happiness and cooking food in family.

Relation with Linguistics

Social-Cultural Anthropology and Linguistics show close relation with each other. It is because both study origin, characteristics, structure, function, diffusion and change of human languages spoken, read and written in different parts of the world. Both follow emic, etic, semantic and cognitive approaches. Social-Cultural Anthropology have taken clue from languages to describe culture and linguistics have taken clues from culture for the analysis of languages. Thus, Social-Cultural Anthropology and linguistics show close relationship with each other. But this relationship does not tell us that both follow same approach and study same subject matter. Rather they differ in their approach and subject matter of study. Social-Cultural Anthropology follows ethnographic approach, whereas linguistics follow phonological and morphological approaches. Social-Cultural Anthropology studies language as vehicle of culture and linguistics study language as means of communications. Thus, both show differences.

Relation with Humanities

Social-Cultural Anthropology and Humanities show close relation with each other because both study humanism. For both man is a creative animal. Both study and describe human creativity through a particular language and in a particular style. Thus, Social-Cultural Anthropology and Humanities are close to each other. But this does not show that both Social-Cultural Anthropology and Humanities follow same approach and have same subject matter of study and research. Social-Cultural Anthropology follows ethnographic approach, Humanities follows textual approach. Social-Cultural Anthropology studies and describes creation of Folk artists, which exists as oral tradition in the form of folklores, whereas Humanities presents a description and critical reviews of great poets, authors and other scholars concerned with humanities.

Chapter 2
Basic Concepts of Social-Cultural Anthropology

In this chapter attempts have been made to present some basic concepts which are taught under Social-Cultural Anthropology and which are used frequently in study and research of Social-Cultural Anthropology. These concepts are as follows:

- Society
- Association
- Groups
- Social Organization
- Norms
- Status
- Social Change
- Band
- Ethnology
- Culture
- Civilization
- Class system
- Social Stratification
- Community
- Institution
- Social Structure
- Social System
- Values
- Role
- Cultural Change
- Tribe
- Ethnography
- Caste System
- Jajmani System

Society

The term society is frequently used by anthropologists. It is because society is laboratory for an anthropologist. For collection of primary data he has to visit in a society and stay with people whom he wants to study. While in field he hears the term society frequently from informants in day-to-day life. Even layman says that our society is at top, our society has deteriorated, our society is progressive or our society is still conservative. This indicates that even a layman has the concept of society in his mind. But his concept of society is different from the concept of society developed by a social scientist or anthropologist.

For a layman society means aggregate or collection of people at a particular place. It refers to a group of people at a place. But for social scientists society is not only a group of people, but a group of people having interactions and activities for fulfilment of certain objectives. Thus, group of people standing on road, Railway Station, bus stand and ration shop is not society. For a layman society is understood as tangible object, but for social anthropologist society is intangible entity. It is a mental construct which we realize in everyday life but we cannot see it. For social anthropologist society is abstract system of social relationships. In society an individual is related to others through ties of kinship, marriage, family, neighbourhood, caste, occupation, religion, political party and peers (friend groups). In this way, an individual becomes part and parcel of several layers of groups through these different multiple relationships. These relationships do not occur at random. These are patterned. Therefore, Social-Cultural Anthropologists define society as a pattern of social relationships formed through interactions of its members.

Attributes of Society

Social-Cultural Anthropologists have identified certain attributes of society. According to them they are as follows:

- Likeness
- Interdependence
- Cooperation
- Conflict

• **Likeness:** It is the first attribute of society. No society can come into existence unless its member feel that they are like one another. It is because society is an aggregate of individuals who share the sense of likeness. Members of a family, lineage, tribe, caste and village generally have this feeling, i.e. the feeling of likeness. The first likeness is that of physiognomy. Man along with other animals cannot form a human society.

But likeness as attribute of society does not tell us that society does not have differences. The members of a society differ in terms of age, sex, education, occupation, mental status, religious status, political status, health status, personality, outlook and personal preferences. But these differences complement each other in such a way that stability in society is maintained. This principle is applicable in all types of societies whether small or big.

- **Interdependence:** It is another attribute of a society. The members of a society are interdependent on each other for its smooth functioning. In village society members of different caste groups depend on each other in everyday life. For example Brahmin, Washerman, Potter, Carpanter, Cobbler, Ironsmith, Sweeper, Shopkeeper are seen doing their own work but they are dependent upon each other. No individual can perform all functions alone or one's own. Therefore, individuals depend upon each other to live smoothly in society.
- **Cooperation:** It is also an essential attribute of society. Without cooperation no society can come into existence. For society, cooperation of members with each other is a must. In every kind of society cooperation of members is needed. For example, husband and wife need cooperation, neighbours need cooperation, caste groups need cooperation, occupational groups need cooperation and so on.
- **Conflict:** Conflict is also one of attributes of society. Society is characterized not only by cooperation but by conflict, too. In family one finds husband-wife conflict, father-children conflict, mother-children conflict, brother-brother conflict, brother-sister conflict, sister-sister conflict. Similarly, we have interfamily conflict, inter-caste conflict, inter-communal conflict and so on. But conflicts are also resolved in the society. Without resolution of conflict society cannot function smoothly.

Need of Society: Human beings need society for following reasons:

- Man is a social animal by nature.
- Man needs society for fulfilment of various needs.
- Man needs society for protection.
- Man needs society for acquiring culture.
- In order to observe law and order.

Community

Just above we have studied that society is an abstract notion, but community is a concrete entity. For Social-Cultural Anthropology, community can be defined as "whenever the members of any group—small or big—live together in such a way that they share not only this or that but the basic conditions of a common life, we call that group a community." Thus, community refers to a group of individuals living in a geographical area. They share the same physical environment and basic conditions of common living. A neighbourhood or a village is good example of a community.

Characteristics of Community

- Community is an aggregate of individuals.
- It is associated with a locality or a fixed territory.
- Members of community have strong community sentiment or we feeling.
- Community as a group of people is created spontaneously over a long period of time.
- Community is permanent.
- Community has a wider purpose.
- Each community has a specific name.
- Community has no legal status.

Similarity between Society and Community

- Both are spontaneously created social groups.
- Both serve wider ends.
- Members of both have a sense of we feeling.

Difference between Society and Community

The main points of differences between Society and Community are as follows:

- Society includes every relation which is established between people. It has no territorial boundaries. But community has a definite boundary.
- Society is universal but community is local.
- In society sense of belongingness is weaker, but in community sense of belongingness is stronger.
- Society is abstract mental construct, but community is a concrete entity.

- German scholars Gimmer Mann and Frampton in their book, "Family and Society" have used the term Gemenschaft for community and Gesellschaft for society.

Types of Community: Although there are many types of community but four significant types are as follows:

- Village/Rural Community
- City/Urban Community
- Nation Community
- World Community

Community Life in India

The soul of India resides in villages. The village/rural community in India is characterized by the following facts:

- Agricultural economy
- Peace and simplicity
- Tradition and custom
- Poverty and illiteracy
- Traditional Panchayat
- Caste based division of labour
- Jajmani system

Change in rural community: Westernization, modernization industrialization, urbanization and globalization processes have weakened the traditional community structures. Now, we feeling has been diluted to a large extent. The life of individuals is now not bound to customs and traditions. Village communities are now not in isolation. Even remote village is connected to globe through different channels of communication like media, transport and markets.

Association

An association is a group of people who come together for the purpose of fulfilment of certain specific goals. Sometimes, the number of goal is limited. For example, *Mahila Sudhar Samiti*, *Gram Sudhar Samiti*, *Navyuvak Sangh*, Family, School, College, Hospital, *Mahila Mandal*, Voluntary Organization, Music Club, Trade Union etc.

Characteristics of Association: An association has following characteristics:

- It consists of a group of individuals.
- The people are organized here.
- It has certain specific goals.
- The people are engaged in activities to attain the goals.
- There are certain rules and regulations for the conduct of people in association.
- The membership of association is essential.
- The association may be temporary or permanent.
- Association functions through written laws and rules.

Institution

Here, it is necessary to make a distinction between the general and the social anthropological meaning of the term institution. Thus, the concept of institution has two sets of meaning:

I. By institution, people generally mean an organization. For example, people generally call family, school, college and hospital as institutions.

II. But in Social-Cultural Anthropology the term institution has a different meaning. Here, the term institution is used to understand the ways of doing things.

In Social Cultural Anthropology the term institution refers to established codes of conduct for carrying out group activities. It refers to a set of rules and procedures which provide guidelines for human activities. Thus, institutions are blueprint for human action. Have you ever thought as to why you bow your heads before images in a temple or why you go to Church/Mosque/Gurudwara. We bow our heads before deities or we go to Temple/Church/ Mosque/Gurudwara because we follow codes of conduct of worship. We imbibe code of conduct of worship unconsciously because religious institutions have laid down in us such code of conduct from very beginning in the society. We do not see them but follow them unconsciously as what to do or what not to do.

In every organization there are certain usages, rules and procedures. These forms of procedures are called institutions. They are also reorganized and accepted by the society. Thus, they regulate the relations between individuals and groups. If rules and procedures are called institution, then individuals themselves belong to association. Thus, institution refers to rules of procedure, and association refers to human component.

Examples of Association and Institution both: There are some examples before us which are known as association and institution both. For instance, we can say family, school, college, hospital, club, church and others. They are known as institution as well as association. This happens so because we are members of association but we have to function according to rules established by the institution.

The family as an association consists of husband, wife and children. But each member of a family functions according to rules established by the institution of family. Usually, there is division of labour among the family members. The division of labour is based on age and sex. Usually, husband performs outside work, wife performs domestic works, children assist them, and aged persons look after kids, chicks, goat, thrashing field, houses etc. Each member of family maintains discipline and cooperate each other. In this way as the association, family has father-mother and children, but as the institution family has established procedure of code of conduct which every member has to observe.

The school as an association consists of students, teachers and some non-teaching staff. The school is established for the fulfilment of particular goal. That goal is imparting education to the children of society. But the school functions according to rules established by the institution. Students, teachers, headmaster, and non-teaching staff function according to rules set by the institution. They observe discipline and extend full support in the functioning of school.

Similarly, college as an association has students, professors, principal and non-teaching staff. It has a specific goal of imparting higher education among youth and to make them career-oriented. For this, students, teachers and non-teaching staff maintain discipline and function as per rules set by the institution. Every member has to perform his duties according to rules or code of conduct.

Likewise, hospital as an association has patients, nurses, doctors and other kind of staff. It has to fulfil a specific goal of curing diseases of patients. But as institution the hospital has code of conduct. Patients, nurses, doctors and all staff have to perform their duties according to rules of the hospital.

Similarly, as an association the club has members, officials and some staff. It has a specific goal of providing entertainment and amusement to its members. The club also fulfils some social purpose. These reveal associational aspects of the club. But rules, procedure and conduct by which members behave reveal institutional aspect of the club.

In the same way, church is an example of institution as well as association. As association, church has priest, officials and followers. Priest, officials, followers reveal associational aspects of the church. The church fulfils religious and some social purposes. But the priest, officials and followers have to observe certain rules. They function according to rules, procedures and code of conduct. These reveal the institutional aspects of the church.

Groups

Groups are those units of Society which possess all characteristics of the society. But groups are different from the society because they are concrete entities. We live in group such as family and we belong to groups like lineage, clan, moiety, phratry, caste, tribe, village and so on.

Some scholars have made comparison of groups with bricks. According to them as bricks build a building in the same way groups build a society.

Every human individuals is a member of one or more than one groups like family, lineage, clan, moiety, phratry, tribe, caste, neighbourhood, village, and peer group. Occupational group, religious group, linguistic group, club, political parties and the other.

Within each group human individuals interact with each other. Members of the group are aware of their activities and they share a common consciousness of their joint interaction.

A social group is a dynamic concept. It may be small or big. In a group new members join and old members leave. Thus, a group is changing. In most cases the goals of group remain diffused, but sometimes a group is formed for specific purpose. As soon as the purpose is fulfilled, the group is dissolved.

Characteristic of a Social Group

On the basis of above definitions and discussion, the following characteristics of a social group can be listed:

- *Number of Person*: At least two persons are required for the formation of a group. For example, couple, two friends.
- *Membership*: A group provides membership to its members. Therefore, every individual is membership conscious in a group.
- *Organization*: A group reveals an organized structure.
- *Meaningful and purposeful interaction*: Interaction between members takes place with definite meaning and purpose.
- *'We' feeling*: The members of a group possess 'We' feeling.
- *Common interest*: The members of a group possess common interest and work together to achieve the goal. For example, all members of a family work together to raise the family income, all members of a cricket club play together to win the match.
- *Group norms*: Each member of a group follows group norms strictly.
- *Relative permanency*: Each group reveals relative permanency.
- *Nomenclature*: Each group is known by a particular name.
- *Specific culture*: Each group has its own specific culture.
- *Reciprocal relation*: The members of a group maintain reciprocal relation with each other.

Types of Group

As referred to earlier, a society is made up of several groups. In other words, we can say that society consists of various types of groups. Some of them are similar, while others are dissimilar. It is also true that some groups are formed naturally, while some groups are formed artificially. For example, children acquire membership in family naturally, while an individual attains membership of a cricket club artificially. Again it is also true that same person is a member of various groups in a society.

Some scholars have emphasized upon the size as a criteria for classifying a group. According to them, even two persons can form a group, i.e. husband and wife or three persons can form a group, i.e. polygenous or polyandrous couple. The size of group may be very large, i.e. youth club and political parties. It may be as small as husband and wife. Family, lineage and clan fall within private social sphere of an individual, whereas club and political party form the public life of a person.

As referred to earlier, German scholars Gimmer Mann and Frampton have given the concept of two major groups: (1) Gemeinschaft (Community) and (2) Gesellschaft (Association).

The various types of groups are as follows:

- Formal group
- Informal group
- Primary group
- Secondary group
- Tertiary group
- Horizontal group
- Vertical group
- In-group
- Out-group
- Ephemeral group (chance group)
- Enduring group (peer group)
- Reference group
- Open group
- Closed group

Formal group: The group whose members follow formal rules in behaviour is called formal group. For example school.

Informal group: The group whose members follow informal rules in behaviour is known as informal group. For example family.

Primary group: The group whose members know each other by name and face is known as primary group. For example family.

The external features of Primary group are as follows:

- Small size
- Face to face relation and interaction
- Physical proximity

The internal features of Primary groups are:

- We feeling
- Goodwill for group members
- Known face and name
- Permanency
- Spontaneous growth
- Enduring character

- Relation as ends and as means
- Dominance of informal social norms
- Interpersonal relation with emotional bondage.

Secondary group: The group whose members do not have face to face relation is known as secondary group. For example, Political party, caste, trade union. The members of Secondary group show indirect relation.

The external characters of a Secondary group are as follows:

- Large size
- Indirect relation
- Goal oriented
- Impersonal relation
- Option of membership

Difference between Primary and Secondary Groups

Feature	*Primary Group*	*Secondary Group*
Size	Small	Large
Interaction	Permanent	Temporary
Proximity	Face to face	Not face to face
Interest	Diffused	Specific
Relation	Direct or personal	Indirect or impersonal
Existence	Rural society	Urban society

Tertiary Group: It is a group of groups whose members possess similar characters and have notional or theoretical interaction. For example federation of labour unions.

Horizontal group: The group whose members interact without giving any significance to hierarchy. For example a group of friends or peer group.

Vertical Group: The group whose members interact with sense of hierarchy is called vertical group. For example caste.

In-Group: The group whose members interact with a sense of unity is know as In-group. For example high castes, low castes, middle castes etc.

Out-Group: The group whose members interact with a sense of diversity is known as out-group.

Superiority and inferiority complex exists in out-groups and in-groups. Ethnocentrism is found in members of in-groups. In-groups are called as we-groups and out-groups are also known as they-group.

These two groups differ from each other on the basis of feeling. For example, upper castes and lower castes living in Indian villages are examples of in-groups in themselves. But for one another they become out-groups.

Ephemeral Group or Chance Group: A group which is formed by chance is called ephemeral group or chance group. Such groups are transitory in nature. For example group formed in travelling by bus, railway or aeroplane etc.

Enduring Group: The group which continues for a longer period of time is called enduring group. For example, the peer group.

Reference Group: The group which is referred to as model for action and behaviour is called as reference group. Reference group is contrast to membership group. For example in a village society land owners constitute a reference group for landless labourers. Similarly, for educated unemployed salaried class constitute a reference group.

Open Group: The group whose membership is open or voluntary and mobility of members is possible is called an open group. For example—a soccer club.

Closed Group: The group whose membership is not open and mobility is relatively difficult is called closed group. For example caste.

The group play significant role in shaping the personality of individuals.

Difference between Group and Society

Group	*Society*
A collection of human beings	A system of social relationship
An artificial creation	Spontaneous and natural growth
Group is organized	Society may be organized and unorganized
Group may be temporary	Society is permanent
Group is a concrete concept	Society is abstract concept
Marked by we feeling	Society has a sense of belongingness

Difference between Group and Institution

Group	*Institution*
Group is collection of people	Institution is set of rules and norms
Group may be temporary	Institution is always permanent
Group is created	Institution may be natural or artificial
Comparatively temporary	Comparatively permanent

Difference between Group and Community

Group	Community
Group is created	Community may be natural or created
Group has certain purposes	Community is for whole life of members
Comparatively temporary	Comparatively permanent
Group is a part of community	Community consists of many groups

Social Structure

You might have heard the term structure. You might be using this term frequently in your day-to-day life. For example, the structure of building, school, college, hospital, rest house etc. The structure is integration of different parts in an order. The parts of building are visible. But when we talk about social structure, an invisible concept comes into our mind. It is because social structure is an abstract concept. It refers to arrangement of social units in an order. A society is composed of different units. Each unit is known as a group. Within group social structure refers to institutionalized arrangement of persons. For example, on the basis of structure, a family may be nuclear, joint or extended. The structure of a caste reveals family, lineage, clan and sub-caste.

Characteristics of Social Structure

- Social structure is an abstract concept.
- Family, lineage, clan, sub-caste, caste, tribe, class etc. are concrete isolates of social structure.
- Social structure is arrangement of persons in institutional relationship.
- In social structure an individual is not only an organism, but he possesses a network of relationship.
- Social structure is dynamic concept
- Social structure can be divided into two parts:
  (i) Real social structure, and (ii) General social structure.
- Real Social structure is always under change because an individual is mortal. Old individuals die and new individuals are born as children.
- General social structure reveals continuity because it deals with institutional aspects of social structure. As institutions are immortal so social structure remains always continued.

- From the point of view of linguistic approach social structure is a mental construct. It appears as a model.

Concept of Social Structure

The term social structure was used for the first time by French sociologist Herbert Spencer in his book "Principle of Sociology" (1876). In this book Spencer attempted to understand social structure like the structure of an organism. He has dealt with similarity between social structure and organism structure. As the structure of an organism reveals ordered arrangement of parts, in the same way the structure of a society reveals ordered arrangement of its different units. As different parts of organism show functional relation and interdependence, similarly, different units of society reveal functional relation and interdependence. As different parts of body perform different functions to make organism dynamic, in the same way, different units of society perform different functions to make the society dynamic. Besides these similarities between different parts of units of organism and society, Spencer was also of opinion that as the evolution of organism has followed simple to complex form, similarly, the evolution of society had also followed simple to complex form.

The concept of social structure and function also appears in the book, "Division of Labour" (1893) written by an another French Scholar Emile Durkheim. In his book he opined that an organism has to divide labour among different parts in order to survive, similarly, the society makes division of labour among different members in order to fulfil different needs. The division of labour is an important social system which shows the structure of society on the basis of speciality. Persons having speciality perform special function in the society.

Being influenced by his mentor Emile Durkheim, British anthropologist A.R. Radcliffe-Brown had described social structure as arrangement of persons in institutionalized relationship in his book, "Structure and Function in Primitive Society" (1952).

An another British anthropologist E.E. Evance Pritchard in his book, "The Nuer" (1940) defined social structure as interrelation between two unit of society.

An another British anthropologist E.R. Leach in his book, "Political System of Highland Burma", (1954), had shown that social structure was not static, rather it was a dynamic concept. He attempted to deal with change in social structure by using 'conflict' as explanatory tool. According to him, conflict had brought changes in Shan society of Highland Burma.

Mayer Fortes, a British Social Anthropologist has also observed that social structure is not a static concept, rather it is a dynamic concept. In his book "Web of Kinship Among Tallency" (1945) he has shown that kinship relation is also changing with reference to time.

S.F. Nadel in his book "Theory of Social Structure" (1957) has observed social structure as a group in which different members perform their roles. In social structure every member appears as an actor and performs his role for need fulfilment in the society.

Raymond Firth in the book, "Elements of Social Organization" (1963) has attempted to make a distinction between social structure and social organization. According to him, social structure is arrangement of persons in a group and social organization is arrangement of activities of persons in a group.

French scholar Levi-Strauss in his book, "Structural Anthropology" (1963) has opined that social structure is a mental construct. It is a model of study not a reality. He has talked about two kinds of model of social structure—mechanical model and statistical model.

According to the book, "Notes and Querries in Anthropology", Social Structure is a complex network of relationship in which all members of a community are tied in relationship.

Chief Features of Social Structure

Social structure is created by inter-relationship of human beings within and outside the group. The purpose behind the creation of social structure is fulfilment of certain common objectives of society. For the fulfilment of certain objectives, social structure has to follow certain principles. These principles reveal chief features of social structure. These features are as follows:

Normative System: Normative system deals with norms and values prevalent in the society. Every society has its own norms and values. The members of society are expected to observe those norms and values. If a member does not follow them, he or she is not only subjected to severe criticism, but also to severe punishment. On the basis of norms and value, the difference in social structure of two or more societies appears frequently. For example, norms and values of Indian society is different from American and Western Society.

Position System: The social structure also deals with position system. In a social group different members occupy different position. Their positions reveal their status in the group and group members have to perform roles according to their status or position. As an individual possesses ascribed and achieved status, he or she has to perform roles according to both types of status. Again the same individual is member of more than one groups, so he or she possesses different status in different groups. He or she has to perform role in different groups according to different status.

Sanction System: Social structure has sanction system. There are two types of sanction—(i) Positive sanction, and (ii) Negative sanction. There are certain behaviours which have positive sanction of the society. For example, helping the aged, regarding seniors, loving juniors etc. But there are also certain behaviours which possess negative sanction. For example, thefty, dacoity, extra marital relation, rape, gang rape, murder etc. In a social group, an individual has to work following sanction system. Sanction system also reveals rewards and punishment. For observing positive social sanction, members are rewarded, but for observing negative sanction members are punished.

Anticipated Response System: Social structure possesses anticipated response system. Anticipated response system makes individuals to be dutiful and observe morality. Social structure works successfully on the basis of anticipated response system.

Social Organization

The concept of social structure embraces concept of social organization, too. In fact social structure is concerned with principal forms of social organization, i.e. types of groups, institutions and associations. Now let us try to understand the meaning of the term social organization. The term social organization means arrangement of activities of persons in a group, institution and association. Thus, family, lineage, clan, tribe, caste, village, church, club, play group, political parties are all examples of organization. They all reveal arrangement of activities of persons in group.

The organization may be of various kinds. A state is a political organization, a family is social organization, a church is religious organization, a factory is economic organization, a club is cultural organization, but they all are organizations of society. So, they are social organizations. The fulfilment of different kinds of needs gave rise to social organization. We may say that social organization is organization of human beings in the form of society for the fulfilment of various types of needs.

An American anthropologist Robert Lowie in his book, "Primitive Society" (1920) has described that Primitive Society is an excellent example of social organization. In primitive societies, members observed taboo, endogamy, exogamy in organized way. In these societies family, lineage, clan, moiety, phratry, sub-tribe, tribe are concrete isolates of organization.

The primitive societies lived together and worked together for fulfilment of various kinds of needs. His opinion reveals clearly that social organization is such a group of the society whose members live together and work together for satisfaction of various types of needs.

A British anthropologist Raymond Firth in his book, "Elements of Social Organization" (1961) has mentioned the following elements responsible for formation of organization in a society:

1. Age
2. Sex
3. Kinship
4. Locality
5. Status
6. Occupation
7. Religion
8. Magic
9. Totem
10. Political power
11. Voluntary organization

In this book he has opined clearly that social organization is a social system which establishes coordination of social relationship among different parts of society. Social organization makes a society to exist in a wnole.

In his another book, "Social Organization and Values" (1963) he opined that social organization is for maintaining social values in the society. In an organization every member possesses a status and perform roles observing the value associated with his/her status.

Further Firth has opined that social structure and social organization terms have been used interchangeably, but both terms possess basic difference. The hidden sense behind social organization is planned actions. Thus, social organization is a means by which a society fulfils its needs at a particular time.

An another British anthropologist A.R. Radcliffe-Brown in his book, "Structure and Function in Primitive Society" (1952) has defined social organization as system of activities of persons.

Characteristics of Social Organization

From above discussions, the following characteristics of Social Organization emerge:

- Social organization is a social system of activities by which members of a society fulfil their various kinds of needs.
- Groups, parties and associations are concrete isolates of social organization.
- Social organization embraces the hidden sense of planned activities.
- Social organization is meant for the fulfilment of needs.
- Sex, age, family, lineage, clan, sub-tribe, tribe, caste, place, religion, magic, occupation, entertainment are bases of social organization.

Difference between Social Structure and Social Organization

The followings are main points of differences between social structure and social organization:

- Social structure is arrangement of persons, whereas social organization is arrangement of activities of persons.
- The concept of social structure is abstract and the concept of social organization is concrete.
- Social organization asserts on coordination of social relationships, whereas social structure includes status and roles along with social relations.

- Changes take place in social structure but continuity is also maintained, while social organization is disorganized or reorganized with reference to time.
- Social structure is a model of social study, but social organization is a social reality.
- Social structure is a mental construct, but social organization is a means for fulfilment of needs.

Social System

In order to know the meaning of social system, it will be the fitness of the thing to know the meaning of the term system. When we talk of system, the underlying meaning is orderly management of constituent units. The followings are main features of a system:

- A system consists of different parts.
- All parts of system show systematic relationship.
- Orderly arrangement of these parts create a pattern.
- The parts of a system are functionally related.
- All parts create a new entity, when they are functionally related.

On the basis of above discussion we can say that social system is orderly arrangement of constituent social units. As a society consists of individuals, that is why social system consists of plurality of individuals. Each individual interact with others according to norms and meaning in a social system. That is why we may say that social system is orderly and systematic arrangement of social interactions. There are various sub-systems of a social system such as social, economic, political, religious, recreational etc.

Characteristics of Social System: The following are chief features of a social system:

- Social system is based on interaction of plurality of individuals.
- Interaction of plurality of individuals must carry a meaning.
- Social system consists of integration of parts.
- Parts of social system are functionally related.
- Social system is related to cultural system because it is culture which determines interrelation and interaction.

- Social system is also related to particular environment or ecology.

Elements of Social System: The followings constitute the elements of social system:

- *Belief:* A belief is any proposition about any aspect of the universe which is accepted as true. It is basis of social system.
- *Knowledge:* Any truth based on experience is called knowledge. Human knowledge is acquired on the basis of experience. Our knowledge is accumulated in the form of tradition and pass from one generation to the next. Social system works on the basis of knowledge.
- *Sentiment:* Sentiments are closely related to beliefs. It denotes what we feel about the world. Sentiments are product of experience and cultural training. It may be of various types, such as intellectual, ethical, religious, social, cultural. Social system is closely related to sentiment of individuals and the group.
- *Goal*: Goal is one of elements of social system. It determines nature of social system. Human beings are united to accomplish the basic needs of life, i.e. food, clothing and shelter. In this way goals or objectives create social system.
- *Norms*: In every social system there are norms according to which all members are expected to behave. Norms are standards for determining what is right and what is wrong or what is appropriate and inappropriate in social relationships.
- *Status and Role*: In a social system every individual possesses a status. The status may be ascribed or achieved. The achieved status is one which an individual achieves by his own efforts. But ascribed status is one which is conferred upon an individual by the society. It may be based on sex, age, caste. An individual's status on the basis of caste may be of Brahmin, Rajput, OBCs, Dalit, Tribals, Muslim etc., but he can achieve his status as Ward member, Mukhiya, Pramukh, Zilla Parishad Adhyaksha, MLA, M.P., Minister, Chief Minister, Prime Minister, President, Teacher, Professor, Doctor, Engineer, I.A.S., I.P.S., Clerk, Worker etc.

In social system, an individual has to perform certain roles according to his status in the society. In this way roles and status are interdependent and interrelated. In social system individuals may change but roles and status remain the same.

- *Ranks:* Rank includes the importance an individual has for the social system. An individual is given rank by the society on the basis of evaluation and norms of the system. For example in modern society, a business corporate executive enjoys higher rank than even a teacher. But in ancient time a teacher used to enjoy higher rank than even a king.
- *Power*: Power refers to capacity of an individual in a social system by which he controls or deprives other. State and policing system are the expression of such power.
- *Sanction*: It refers to reward and punishment given by members of social system. Sanction may be positive or negative. The negative sanction is death penalty for doing heinous crime. The positive sanction is rehabilitation of convict.
- *Facility*: Facility is a means to attain ends within social system. In order to perform roles efficiently an individual is given sufficient facilities to perform roles.

Norms and Values

Norms are standards of behaviour in a Society. They are means by which values are expressed in behaviour. For example, when a teacher enters the classroom, the students are expected to standup in respect. The students are expected to maintain discipline in school. Youngers are expected to respect olders, olders are expected to love youngers, one should not drink, children should obey their parents, etc. In social anthropology such behaviours are known as norms and values. Now let us discuss in detail about norms and values prevalent and practiced in society.

Norms: In every society there are a number of guidelines which direct the behaviour of individual and group in particular situation. They are correct and proper forms of behaviour. They are specific prescription of an individual's behaviour in consistent with values of contemporary society. Thus, norms are reflection of values. When students stand up at the time of entering a teacher in the class, this particular norm reflects the value of showing regard to teacher. All societies follow definite types of norms which have positive or negative sanctions.

A norm is a rule that governs our behaviour in social situation in which we act and live. We expect that a doctor should be calm, stable, sympathetic and responsible at all times. We do not expect such behaviour from other professionals. In this way norms are group shared expectations.

Such expectations are reflected in statements like good citizens always respect lives, drinking is bad for health and family, get up early in the morning, go to bed early.

Norms are unwritten laws. They determine, guide, control and predict human behaviour.

A distinction can be made between personal or private norm and social norm. Private norms are purely individual in character and they are concerned with individuals only. They influence only behaviour of an individual concerned. For example an individual can make some resolutions on the occasion of his birthday, New year day, Independence day. He may give up smoking and decide abide by it. Social anthropologists are more interested in social norms. In social anthropological terms, social norms are rules developed by a group of people that specify how people should and should not behave in various situations. For example children must seek permission of parents before going out.

Social norms have backing of social sanction. Social sanction may be positive or negative. In negative social sanction those who violate the social norms are punished, whereas in positive social sanction those who abide the social norms are rewarded. On this ground we can say that a sanction is a reaction of others towards the behaviour of an individual or a group.

Sanction may also be formal and informal. Formal sanction is found where there is formal agency to look after the behaviour of individuals or groups. For example police, courts and prison.

In formal sanction positive or negative are routine matters of a society. This includes reward or praise for positive sanction and punishment for negative sanction.

Associational norms are features of modern society. All organized groups have their own rules and regulations prescribed in black and white. For example, political parties have their own norms, trade union has its own norms, Colleges and Universities have their own norms, hostels have their own norms. These are examples of associational norms.

Characteristics of Norms: From the above discussion, the following characteristics of norms come into existence:

- Norms are generally known as correct or proper forms of behaviour.
- Forms are guidelines which direct individual and group to conduct in a particular social situation.
- Norms are group shared expectations.
- Norms are unwritten laws.
- Norms are means through which values are expressed in behaviour.
- Norms may be personal and social. Personal norms are concerned with individual, whereas social norms are concerned with the society.
- Social norms are always backed by social sanctions—positive or negative and formal and informal.
- In modern societies, we have a number of associational forms of norms.
- Norms are indispensable parts of our life.
- Norms govern the behaviour of individuals.

Above characteristics of norm also tell us about the importance of norms for individual and society.

Types of Norms

Social norms are numerous and varied. They assume different forms. They may differ in terms of severity and durability. Their influence on individuals and society have not been uniform. Here we are going to discuss three different kinds of norms namely, folkways, mores and customs.

Folkways: Folkways are behaviour pattern of everyday life. They arise generally unconsciously in a group. They are accepted ways of behaviour. For example, ways of bathing, washing, eating, cooking, talking, dressing, playing, walking, working etc. are all folkways. Wearing different types of dresses on different times and occasions, cooking different food on different times and occasions, taking bath regularly, offering worship to gods and goddesses, respecting elders, loving youngers etc. are different kinds of folkways. Thus, folkways are universal characteristics of all human societies. They contribute to the order and stability of social relations. They become a part of our personality through socialisation process.

Mores: Mores represent another category of norms. They denote behaviour patterns which are not only accepted but prescribed. In simple terms we can say that mores are those folkways which clearly represent the group standards, the group sense of what is right, appropriate and necessary for the well-being. Mores can be positive or negative. Positive mores represent ideal behaviour such as obeying elders, respecting aged, giving preference to women, speaking truth, and others. Negative norms represent those behaviour patterns which exist as a taboo for the benefit of society. For example, do not steal any thing, do not tell a lie, do not disobey, do not be undisciplined and so on. Mores always bring direct pressure on our behaviour. They mould our character and are regulator of our behaviour. They bind people in one cohesive group.

Customs: Customs are another kind of social norms. Customs are socially accepted ways in which members of a society observe practices together. They continue from generation to generation and thus, exist as traditions of a society. Our accepted practices of eating, meeting friends, relatives, elders, and youngers, playing, working, are called as customs. Customs preserve our culture and transmit it to the next generation. Customs have been reported in every part of the world in human communities. Thus, customs are effective means of social control. Customs provide the background for the formulation and establishment of rules. Customs become laws when the State enforces them as rules to be obeyed by the citizens.

Normlessness: Normlessness means detachment from the existing social norms or rules. Generally, society functions in an orderly fashion. A good number of people obey norms of their respective groups unconsciously. This maintains the society functioning smoothly. But such situations do not remain always. Sometimes, a situation arises when people feel detached from the norms of society and they began to behave individually. Now, they start caring for their own interest and do not care for the interest of other members of the society. In this situation, social norms become ineffective and the society moves towards disorganization. This situation is called anomie.

Values

Values are broad ideas regarding what is desirable, correct and good that most members of a society share.

Values define social preference, specify social choice and provide a vision for future action. Individual's values are strongly influenced by the culture.

Social structure, social organization, social institution, social interaction and social behaviour are all based upon values. Any changes in social structure and social institutions is generally followed by a change in social values. It also takes place sometimes *vice-versa*. No society is stable. Society is changing. By incorporating changes and making adaptation with changed situations we have modernized our values.

Importance of Values

For every individual and society values are important. Values are important due to following reasons:

1. Values provide stability in group interactions.
2. Values bring legitimacy to the rules that govern our specific activities.
3. Values bring some kind of adjustment between different kinds of rules.

Traditional and Modern Values

The Traditional Indian Society was organized on the principle of hierarchy, pluralism and holism system.

Hierarchy implies the ordering of units of a relation to whole in a superior-inferior gradation. For example in traditional Hindu society, the Brahmins occupied top most position and the Shudras had lowest position. There were some castes whose position was in the middle, i.e., in between the two—Brahmins and Shudras.

Hierarchy manifested itself not only in caste system and sub-caste stratification, but it was also related to occupation, life cycle, age, grade and moral duties. For example in traditional Hindu Society, Shudras were not allowed to take up the occupation of a priest and teaching. In this sense, hierarchy was related to inequality.

It was related to a fixed position of every individual and caste. But it was also related to assumed means of livelihood because no individuals or castes were allowed to adopt the occupation of another castes.

Pluralism: Pluralism as a value implies that one should be tolerant towards the lifestyle of others, while preserving one's own lifestyle. For example, Hinduism believe in existence of multiple paths leading to the same ultimate goal. Thus, faiths of other religions not only survived but also prospered for centuries in India. In spite of differences at the level of doctrines and rituals, the followers of different religions lived in relative harmony in India. In caste system, each caste had its own identity, but different castes were interrelated and interdependent socially and economically. *Jajmani* system was its best example.

Holism: Holism indicates relationship between individual and group in which the group has primacy over individual. In holism, individual is expected to perform his duty and claim his rights in the wider interest of the community. For example, in joint family system, children, aged, widow, unmarried, physically challenged all enjoy their rights and contribute according to their ability.

The above discussion reveals an idea about importance of value in traditional society. Now, let us discuss about the significance of value in modern society.

Modern values are embodied in the Constitution of India. These values are related to democracy, secularism and socialism. These values are western in origin but they have been applied to Indian context with the necessary adaptation and indigenization.

Democracy: This modern value has brought equal opportunity to all adult members of the community to participate in Government and decision-making process through voting rights.

Secularism: Secularism means respecting and tolerating the practices of other religious communities. India is a multi-religious nation. Each religious community has its own symbols, beliefs, rituals and values. One religious community is expected not only to regard its own value, but also to show equal respect to belief, ritual and symbol of other religious community.

Socialism: The word socialism means production, distribution and exchange of material resources of the community for the common good and interest of the people. It is opposed to the concentration of wealth in the hands of few individuals.

Value Conflict: Value is important for the society because they play significant role in all societies. It is also true that values have evolved through the ages. They are not static, rather they are changing. In changed situation one has to make an adjustment between traditional values and modern values. If there is no adjustment, conflict comes into existence. We may also say that value sets have conflict among them, but similarity among these sets is also possible.

We may say that there is no basic contradiction between the traditional value of pluralism and modern value of secularism because tolerance is found in both cases. But one finds a difference between the two also. Traditional pluralism was related to distinct tradition of each group, which provided legitimacy for special privileges. But secularism calls upon the advantaged groups not to handicap the less privileged group.

Hierarchy was an another value of traditional order. In hierarchy, allocation of resources and distribution of rewards was based on birth. For example, Brahmin enjoyed high status than other castes. In modern society, status is achieved on the basis of potential to contribute to the system.

The traditional principle of holism required that the individuals should stay away from self interest to pursue collective goal. Democracy on the other hand implies individuals to be autonomous entities to pursue their independent and self-interest often at the cost of collective interest. Thus, the principles of holism and individualism (democracy) are quite different. Here it is apparently clear that congruence between traditional and modern value is possible only in case of pluralism and secularism.

A synthesis between the traditional and modern value can be acquired. Traditionally castes emphasized the ritual dimension of status. In modern India castes are becoming secularized and they perform instrumental functions for their members. There are several caste associations. They open schools, colleges, institutes, establish financial agencies to provide funds for housing. They field candidates in election through political parties. These reveal secularization of castes in terms of functions in urban areas. The traditional caste purity is no more functional. But modern caste secularism is expanding which insists on material improvement of caste council member. In this way, the gap between traditional and modern values has been bridged.

Relation between Norms and Values

Value may be defined as a measure of goodness or desirability. They provide general guidelines for conduct. In this way, they are referred to as a higher order norms. But norms are given much more specific meaning. They define appropriate and acceptable behaviour in particular situations. Values are cherished only through the observance of norms. The example given will make clear the relation between the two. The society may cherish the value of privacy. This value provides only a guide to behaviour. Norms define as to how the value of privacy is translated into action in particular situation. Norms relating to privacy may insist that the letter of a person must not be opened without his permission.

Status

The term status implies social position. Each individual occupies a social position in a situation of interaction. For example, an individual may occupy the position of son, father, brother, grandfather, nephew, grandson, student, teacher, player, labourer, master, trader and several others depending upon the social situatio in which he/she is placed. With respect to each social position, an individual has to play a role. In this way, status refers to a position and role refers to the behaviour expected from that position.

The status may be of two types—ascribed and achieved status. An individual gets his ascribed status because of his/her birth. Because of birth individual may be son or a daughter or a Brahmin or a *dalit*. The position occupied on the basis of birth (caste and sex) is called as ascribed status.

The social position achieved by an individual on the basis of competition is called as achieved status. For example, if an individual competes civil service examination and becomes a civil servant, it is his/her achieved status.

In simple society, one finds predominance of ascribed status. But there are certain positions which are decided by competition. For example, the position of best hunter, best craftman and best gardener are examples of achieved status in simple society. Teacher, clerk, engineer, doctor, professor, Chief Minister, Prime Minister, MLA, M.P., President etc. are all examples of achieved status in complex society.

In complex society, social positions are largely achieved, but this does not mean that ascribed positions are completely ignored. In complex society too, ascribed positions are rather important in many situations. Ascribed positions often influence the achievement of a status. Being male brings several privileges in the society. A boy is allowed to go anywhere for study, but a girl is not allowed to do so. Therefore, males have more chances of achieving status than females.

Status is ranked, too. The principle of ranking differs from society to society, but in all societies one finds the existence of status group, i.e., a group of people occupying the same status because its members show similarity in their style of life. One status group is distinguished from another status group on the basis of lifestyle its members lead. The best example of status group is different castes.

On the basis of above discussions, following points may be mentioned as characteristics of status:

- Status reveals position of an individual in society.
- Status is enjoyed
- An individual occupies different status at the same time depending on social situation.
- An individual has to perform role according to his/her status.
- Status may be achieved or ascribed.
- The simple society has predominance of ascribed status and complex society has predominance of achieved status.
- Status may be high or low.
- Rights, duties and privileges are attached to status.
- Status groups are also found in society.
- Status conflict also comes into existence.
- Status is not static, rather it is changing according to situation and time.
- Status is related to prestige.
- Status is related to expectations.
- Change in role brings change in status.
- Status has physical, social, cultural, economic and political dimensions.

Determinants of Status

The following factors play significant role in determining status of an individual:

- *Birth*: Family, lineage, clan, sub-caste, caste etc.
- *Sex*: Male-female, boy-girl, husband-wife, father-mother, brother-sister, grandfather-grandmother, grandson-granddaughter etc.
- *Age*: Infant, child, adolescent, adult, old, elder-younger etc.
- *Caste*: High castes, low castes, middle castes.
- *Occupation: Purohit-Jajman*, *Malik-Mazdoor*, peasant, artisan labourer.
- *Class*: Forward castes, Backward castes, *Dalit* and *Adivasi*.
- *Religion*: Priest, *Guni*, *Ojha*, *Pahan*.
- *Wealth*: Landlord, landless, rich-poor.
- *Traditional Post*: Village head, inter-village head.
- *Modern Post*: Clerk, teacher, engineer, doctor, professor, MLA, M.P. and all achieved posts.
- *Education*: Literate, illiterate, matriculate, intermediate, graduate, post-graduate, technical.

Role

Role refers to the behaviour expected from a position occupied by an individual in society. Every status of an individual is related to a specific role. An individual has to perform several roles depending upon several status in several situations. Role is associated with duty and responsibility. It is also related to the expectations of the society.

Like status, role is also ascribed or achieved. Ascribed role is associated with ascribed status and achieved role is related to achieved status.

The role may also be positive or negative. Positive role brings organization and reorganization, whereas negative role brings disorganization. Positive role has social sanction, while negative role has no social sanction. Positive role is appreciated and negative role is criticized.

Role is changing according to change in status. Role has social, economic, political and religious dimensions.

Role is appreciated and criticized. Rewards and punishments are attached to the performance of roles. Role leads to success and failure of a status.

Status and Role

Status and role are not in isolation. Rather they are interrelated, interdependent and complement to each other. Without status, role has no existence and without role status cannot maintain its existence. Role is precondition for the existence of status and status is prerequisite for the existence of status. But in spite of all such interdependence, attempts have been made to deal with the differences between the two concepts. The main points of differences between status and role are as follows:

1. Status refers to a position, whereas role refers to behaviour expected from that position.
2. Role is performed, status is enjoyed.
3. Role is duty and responsibility, status is position occupied.
4. Role is related to reward and punishment, status is related to prestige and privilege.
5. Role may be positive or negative, status is not positive and negative, rather superior, inferior or equal.
6. Role has social sanction, status has social value.

Band

The earliest form of human organization subsisting on wandering economy with strong sense of group unity under leadership of a captain. During entire Palaeolithic and Mesolithic period man was living in band. When Neolithic revolution took place, the band began to lead a settled life and the concept of tribe developed. In the beginning, the band was endogamous but it became exogamous by observing group marriage later on. Similarly, the band was matriarchal in the beginning but it gradually changed into matri-patriarchal and finally patriarchal society. Man would have learnt living in a band from primates. The leader of the band used to redistribute materials obtained in gathering, hunting and collecting. The leader of the band was most respected person. He was obeyed. Every member of the band's worked for band solidarity. Uthalu Birhor, a section of Birhor tribe, still live in a band. They call their band as Tanda. They subsist on gathering and hunting. They used to wander from place to place in forest. They live in a particular place till the food materials are available. The leader of Birhor band is known as Naya. Birhor is one of scheduled tribes of Jharkhand.

Characteristics of Band

- Band is the most primitive form of social organization of mankind.
- Each band has a leader who is powerful and knowledgeable member of the group.
- The different bands call their leaders by different local names.
- The leader of the band is most respectable member. Other members do not disobey him.
- The band subsists on hunting and gathering in forests.
- The band has wandering economy.
- In band, every member works for the safety of band. For them security of band is more important than their lives.
- Members of band are always active for group solidarity.
- The members of band follow the rules of sexual behaviour strictly.
- The change of leader of the band is done on the basis of physical power. As soon as a leader of a band becomes weak, he is changed.

Tribe

Tribe is a greater social organization of mankind formed by the organization of several bands, clans, moiety and phratry. According to evolutionist anthropologists, it is second stage in the evolution of social organization of mankind. The social organization of mankind has passed through three successive stages—band, tribe and state. The social organization in the form of a tribe emerged after Neolithic revolution and settled village life.

Different scholars have attempted to define the term tribe in their own ways. But the facts gathered from their definitions reveal that tribe is a regional ethnic group whose members have same culture, language, occupation and political organization, but they are distributed into several exogamous clans and show strong sense of solidarity during warfare.

Nomenclature: Etimologically. the term tribe has its origin from the term triangle. Meaning of triangle is union of three parts. For Romans tribe was a political institution of several human groups. Its influenced area was limited to particular geographical regions.

Through this organization an attempt was made to control the human groups living in a particular region.

When nationalism developed in Europe, the term tribe was used for ethnic groups living in different definite regions of the world. The term tribe now got racial definition. It was used for those ethnic groups living in Asia, Africa, America and Australia who were far away from civilization and were residing in hilly, forested, coastal, desert and islands. The term tribe became British legacy during British period. All western scholars have used the term tribe in the same way as Britishers.

In anthropological literatures, we find a number of terms used as synonymic to the term tribe. For example, Native, Naive, Primitive, Aboriginal, Savage, Indigenous, original settlers, uncivilized, barbarous, simple people, folk society, preliterate society, pre-industrial society and little community.

One also finds nomenclature of tribe based on occupations they are practicing. For example, hunting tribe, gathering tribe, pastoral tribe, shifting cultivator tribe, settled agricultural tribe, artisan tribe etc.

On the basis of religion in which they are found living—For example—Santhal tribe.

On the basis of social characteristics they are termed as matriarchal tribe, patricarchal tribe, polyandrous tribe etc.

On the basis of religion we find the terms like Hinduised tribe, Christian tribe, Islamised tribe, etc.

On the basis of country and continents, they are termed as Indian tribe, Asian tribe, African tribe, Australian tribe, American tribe etc.

In Hindi we find the term Jana Jati, Aadivasi, Girijan, Vanavasi, Vanya Jati, Pahari and Aadim for the English term tribe.

In our textual tradition one finds the terms like Bhil, Kirat, Kol, Nishad, Das, Dasyu, Shudra, Asur, Rakshasas, Anarya, Kapi, Vanar, Gridha, Riksha, Savar, and Bhaksha widely used for the people living in hilly, forested, coastal and desert areas, but we do not find the term tribe or Jana Jati or Aadivasi used for them.

In India the use of the term tribe is also a British legacy and has racial connotation. Britishers used the term tribe for our those people who were living in hilly, plateau, forest, desert, coastal and island areas and were leading their lives on the basis of their traditional knowledge and were not part of *Hindu Varna Vyavastha.*

Indian administrators attempted to collect classified informations for the tribes. In the Census Report of 1891, the terms like *Charwaha* caste and *Vanya* castes appeared for them. In 1901 and 1911, they were termed as naturalistic. In 1921 Census Report they were termed as Pahari and Vanya Jana Jati. In 1931 Census Report they were termed as primitives.

In Indian Government Act 1935, they were termed as Backward castes and class. In 1941 Census Report, the term tribe appeared for them.

British administrators had also used the terms head hunting tribes, criminal tribe and excommunicated tribe. Indian anthropologist G.S. Ghurye called them backward Hindus. Verrier Elwin had suggested the National Park Theory for the tribes.

The term scheduled tribes is a Constitutional name for those tribes who have been scheduled as scheduled tribes by Hon'ble President as per article 342 of our Constitution. Now, we have 533 scheduled tribes in different parts of our country. In present day, the term tribe includes only scheduled tribes in our country.

In order to get status of a tribe as scheduled tribe, the following characteristics are taken into consideration:

- Traditional right over a definite geographical territory.
- Specific culture, language, customs, traditions, beliefs, arts and crafts.
- Subsistence on the basis of primitive economy.
- Lack of educational and technological development.

Among 533 scheduled tribes, 75 scheduled tribes of our country have got their status as Primitive Tribal Groups (P.T.Gs). Now-a-days they are also known as Particular Vulnerable Tribal Groups (V.T.G.s).

General Characteristics of Tribe: The following are general characteristics of tribe.

- Each tribe has a common name.
- Each tribe has a common residence.
- Each tribe has a common culture.
- Each tribe has its common social laws.
- Each tribe follows endogamous rule.
- Each tribe follows totemic clan exogamous rule.

- Each tribe has common gods, goddesses, festivals and specialist.
- Each tribe has its own traditional political organizations.
- Each tribe maintains social relation with relatives through reciprocity.
- Each tribe shows unity during warfare.
- It is a territorial organization.
- It is a greater social organization than band, clan, moiety and phratry.

Specific Characteristics of Tribe: The following are specific characteristics of tribe:

- We feeling
- Common interest
- Homogeneous culture
- Identity with a name
- Simple division of labour
- Importance of kin groups
- Prevalence of magic
- Own sacred specialist
- Simple technology
- Own village head and officials
- Oral traditions
- Own art and literature.

Difference between Band and Tribe

- The band is earlier in origin than the tribe.
- A tribe consists of several bands, clans, moiety and phratry.
- The band is smaller in size and the tribe is larger in size.
- The band has a head who is most powerful member of the group. But the tribe has own village head and inter-village head whose posts are hereditary.
- The members of band are ready to sacrifice their lives for the safety and security of the band, but the tribe has less such we feeling than the band.
- The economy of band is wandering based on food gathering and hunting, but the economy of tribe is based on agriculture, artisan and labour.

- Band is wandering in nature, but tribe is settled in nature.
- The captain of band performs magical and religious activities but the tribe has own religious head for magical and religious performances.
- The band follows exogamy rule, but the tribe follows endogamy and clan exogamy rule.

Social Change

The meaning of change is transformation in earlier form. In this sense the social change is earlier status or position of a society. No Society is static, rather society is dynamic. Changes in society occur according to time and situation. Because change is law of nature. In social-cultural anthropology, the meaning of social change includes those changes which bring changes in social relation, social customs, social values, social behaviour, social structure and social function. The impact of social change may be positive or negative both. But social change is a fact for a society in different periods of time.

Types of Social Change: Social change may be categorized into two types:

- Spontaneous/Natural social change
- Induced social change

When social change occurs spontaneously, it is known as spontaneous social change. For example, transformation of folk society into peasant society, peasant society into urban society, urban society into industrial society. These are examples of spontaneous social change.

When changes are induced into society through planned action and governmental interventions, it is known as induced social change. For example, Untouchability Act, Child Marriage Act, Dowry Act, Social, Occupational, Education and health upliftment programmes, planned urbanization and pianned industrialization have brought changes in Indian Society.

A number of factors are responsible for social change. For example, Geographical, Natural, biological, Technological, occupational, economic, political, religious and cultural factors.

Processes related to social changes are as follows:

- Sanskritisation, Hinduisation, Tribalisation, Islamisation, Charistianisation, Westernisation, modernization, urbanization, industrialization and globalization.

Characteristics of Social Change: Characteristics of social change are as follows:

- The nature of social change is social.
- Social change may be natural or induced.
- Social change is universal phenomenon.
- The motion of social change is unequal and comparative.
- Social change is concerned with structural and functional change in society.
- Social change brings changes in social values, customs, traditions, and behaviour
- There are a number of factors responsible for social change such as natural, biological, religious, political, technological, occupational, economic, and cultural.
- Social change brings changes in social system.
- Impact of social change is positive and negative both.
- Social conflict is also responsible for social change.

Cultural Change

British anthropologist and functionalist, B.K. Malinowski in his book, "Scientific Theory of Culture" (1944) has defined culture as a system, mechanism and means by which human beings satisfy their various kinds of need. According to time and place, new needs are created and in order to satisfy those needs human beings bring changes in culture. Form this opinion of Malinowski, it is quite clear that culture is dynamic not static. Thus, cultural change is universal reality. It brings changes in cultural system.

According to Malinowski, culture has two forms—material and non-material. Material culture includes house, cloth, ornaments, tools, furnitures, beds, utensils, musical instruments, war weapons, artifacts, basketry, crafts, Pictographs and writing. Non-material culture includes views, faiths, behaviour, tradition, customs, arts, language, knowledge, science, magic, religions etc.

One finds a phenomenon of cultural lag in cultural change. According to the concept of cultural lag, material culture changes faster than non-material culture. Change in different kinds of technology takes place frequently. But change in beliefs and faiths does not take place quickly. Due to this phenomenon, material culture changes faster than the non-material culture. This phenomenon is known as cultural lag. In his posthumous book, "Dynamics of Culture Change" (1945), Malinowski accepted the process of culture change. According to him, process of cultural change is related to institutional change. New inventions, technologies, methods, value, opinions and faith give rise a number of changes which are accepted by cultural institutions. Thus, cultural changes are brought through institutional change.

Process of Cultural Change: Process related to cultural changes are as follows:

- Evolution
- Diffusion
- Migration
- Acculturation
- Assimilation

Characteristics of Cultural Change: Followings are chief characteristics of cultural change:

- Culture change is related to change in cultural system.
- Cultural change is universal phenomenon.
- Cultural change is natural as well as induced.
- The result of culture change is not always positive.
- Culture change deals with changes in both forms of culture—material and non-material.
- New inventions bring changes in cultural institutions which ultimately reveal culture change.
- In culture change one finds the phenomenon of cultural lag.
- Evolution, diffusion, migration, degeneration, acculturation and assimilation are processes related to culture change.

Difference between Social Change and Culture Change

It is very difficult to make a distinction between the concepts of social change and culture change. Because both are two faces of the same coin of human life. Both are inter-related, inter-dependent. Both show co-existence. That is why the terms social change and cultural change are used interchangeably by different scholars. But in spite of such interdependency and interrelatedness, there are some scholars who have attempted to make a distinction between the concepts of social change and cultural change. For them both are different entities. Main points of difference between social change and cultural change are as follows:

- Social change is concerned with change in social system and cultural change is concerned with change in cultural system.
- Social change deals with change in social structure and social relation, whereas cultural change is concerned with changes in material and non-material aspects of culture.
- Social change is responsible for break in social relation or creation of new social relation, but cultural change is concerned with addition of new traits in tradition or modification of old traits.
- The phenomenon of social lag does not appear in social change, but the phenomenon of culture lag appears in culture change.
- Evolution, diffusion, migration, acculturation and assimilation are concerned with culture change, but Sanskritization, Hinduization, Islamization, Christianization, Tribalization, Westernization, modernization, secularization and globalization are concerned with social change.

Ethnology

The science which deals with the study of racial distribution and historical reconstruction of culture of mankind is known as ethnology. Ethnological studies in anthropology got momentum as soon as classical cultural evolutionists established their theory of cultural evolution and attempted to reconstruct the cultural history of mankind on the basis of their deductive approach and comparative method. They were criticized as arm chair anthropologists because they had deduced the historical stages of cultural evolution on the basis of study of reports, papers, books produced by travellers, businessman, traders and missionaries.

After establishment of classical evolutionary theory, school of diffusion, migration and culture area came into existence. They began to claim themselves as anti-evolutionists. But thcy were also ethnologists. They attempted to describe the geographical distribution, migration and movements of mankind and attempted to reconstruct history of particular races of mankind. In this way, they were also ethnologists.

Characteristics of Ethnology

- It is science of origin of human races and historical reconstruction of culture of mankind.
- It is concerned with movements, migration and diffusion of mankind and their culture.
- It uses historical and comparative methods for historical reconstruction of culture of mankind.
- It applies diachronic approache.
- It utilizes deductive approach.
- It is a sub-branch of Biological anthropology and cultural anthropology.
- Cultural evolutionists, diffusionists, migrationists and cultureareaists were ethnologists.

Ethnography

The science which deals with systematic recording of cultural, physical and linguistic traits of a community is known as ethnography.

In ethnographic studies, a researcher goes to stay with the people whom he wants to study. On the basis of his different kinds of observations, interviews, case studies, life histories and his daily experiences as participant observer, he records different cultural, physical and linguistic traits of the community under study.

It was British anthropologist B.K. Malinowski who introduced the ethnographic study of the community through the technique of participant observation. Since then this tradition is observed by all anthropologists in their study of a community.

Chief Features of Ethnography: Chief features of ethnography are as follows:

- It is a science of systematic recording of cultural, physical and linguistic traits of a community.
- It is based on personal experiences of the researcher.

- It utilizes contextual approach.
- It uses synchronic approach.
- It also applies comparative methods and cross-cultural analysis.
- It studies material cultural traits like house, dress, ornaments, basketry, utensils, furnitures, musical instruments, war weapons, arts, crafts and language of the community.
- It studies the non-material cultural traits, beliefs, behaviour, knowledge, science, magic, religion, economic organization, political organization, religious organizations, games, plays, sports, language and art.
- It studies physical traits like skin colour, stature, nose form, head form, liptypes, hair types, hair styles, eye colour, blood groups of members of the community. It also studies nutritional and health status of members of the community.
- It also reconstruct micro history of the community under study.
- It may apply inductive approach.
- It is based on participant observation and empirical findings.
- It also studies various developmental aspects of a community

Difference between Ethnology and Ethnography: The main points of differences between ethnology and ethnography are as follows:

- Ethnology is concerned with historical reconstruction of races and cultures of mankind, where ethnography is concerned with the recording of cultural, physical and linguistic traits of a community.
- Evolutionists and diffusionists were founder of ethnology in Anthropology, whereas Franz Boas in America and Malinowski in Britain were founder of ethnography in Anthropology.
- Ethnology generally uses deductive approach, whereas ethnography uses inductive approach.
- Ethnology applies only textual approach, ethnography utilises textual and contextual both approaches.
- Ethnology is based on deduction and speculation, ethnography is based on facts observed and experienced.

- Ethnology is speculative in nature, ethnography is empirical in nature.
- Ethnology uses diachronic approach, ethnography uses synchronic approach.
- Ethnology uses comparative methods to establish stages of historical development, ethnography uses comparative methods to find similarities and differences within and between communities.

Culture

The term culture is very popular among the people. They use this term a number of times in their day-to-day mutual talk and discussion. Even a layman knows to use this term frequently. People use this term for their food items, cloth, ornament, customs, traditions, manners, habits and a number of other traits practiced by them. They treat such traits as identity of their culture. There is no doubt that such traits are not cultural traits. But these traits do not provide a scientific definition to the term culture.

In medical science also, the term culture is used. For example, urine culture, hair culture, skin culture etc. The term culture is also used by people engaged in different occupations. For example, lac culture, fish culture, work culture, sericulture etc.

But in anthropology, the term culture is used in specific sense. That is why anthropological meaning of culture is different. Anthropologists have used scientific approach to define the term culture. Now, it will be the fitness of the thing to present some definitions of culture provided by anthropologists.

The credit to provide a first scientific definition to the term culture goes to the founder of British Anthropology E.B. Tylor who in his book, "Primitive Culture" (1871) gave a first scientific definition to the term culture. He in this book, defined culture as that complex whole which includes knowledge, art, belief, value, moral, attitude, habits and all other capabilities acquired by man as a member of society. From this definition of Tylor, two important characteristics of culture emerged—

- Culture is complex whole because it includes a number of traits.
- Culture is a social heritage because it is acquired and learnt.

An another British Anthropologist and functionalist B.K. Malinowski in his book, "Scientific Theory of Culture" (1944) provided a functional and humanistic definition of culture. He opined that Tylor gave a scientific definition of culture, but he could not provide functional and humanistic definition of culture. His definition could not solve the answer as to why culture came into existence, why it is existing and why it will continue to exist in future. Malinowski attempted to answer these questions on the basis of function. That is why he is known as functionalist.

Malinowski defined culture as an instrument or means for the satisfaction of human needs such as primary, secondary and tertiary needs. From the definition of Malinowski, three important characteristics came into existence. These are as follows:

- Culture is man-made.
- Culture satisfics human needs.
- Culture has two forms—material and non-material.

American neo-evolutionist anthropologist Leslie A. White in his book "The Science of Culture" (1949) attempted to define culture from the point of view of language. Man is a linguistic being. He has invented a number of verbal and non-verbal symbols for the communication of messages. Therefore, culture should be defined from the point of view of language, which has provided speech power, expression power and work power to man.

From the point of view of language, he defined culture as a symboling things and events. According to him culture has provided symbols to all things and events which occur in and around the community. From his definition, linguistic symbols are characteristics of culture.

An American anthropologist A.L. Kroeber in his book "Nature of Culture" (1952) has defined culture as super individual and super organic. According to him, the most significant feature of culture is that it is super individual and super organic. It is true that each individual gets cultural training from old generation and imparts training to new generation. Each individual, thus, plays important role in transmission of culture from one generation to the next. But it is also true that culture is a social heritage and it is not an individual property. Thus, culture is super individual. As individual bodies are made up of organic substances and culture is super individual, therefore, culture is super organic, too.

Characteristics of Culture: The following are chief characteristics of culture:

- Culture is man-made.
- Culture is a complex whole.
- Culture is learnt, acquired and transmitted.
- Culture is social heritage.
- Culture is a means for satisfaction of human needs.
- Culture is material and non-material.
- Culture shapes human personality.
- Culture is super individual and super organic.
- Culture provides symbols to things and events.
- Culture has artistic and aesthetic behaviour.

Elements or Components of Culture: In each culture one finds structure and organization. The structure of culture comes into existence when different elements, traits or parts of culture are organized into an inter-dependent and interrelated whole. Thus, we can say that culture is an integrated whole of elements, traits, parts or components. The main components of culture are as follows:

Culture Trait: Culture trait is the smallest and indivisible unit of culture. They cannot be divided further into parts. If a culture trait is subjected to further division, it becomes meaningless. As culture is material and non-material both, therefore culture traits are material and non-material both. A culture includes thousands of such material and non-material traits. For example, touching feet, shaking hands, meeting shoulder to shoulder, tipping hats, kiss on cheeks, touching cheeks, giving seats to ladies first, lying flat before idols, bowing heads before idols, wearing white dress at mourning, not wearing black dresses in marriage rituals, saluting flags, eat vegetarian or non-vegetarian food, sprinkling water on idols, offering *Agarbati*, *Dhoop*, *ghee*, coconut to deities, walking bare footed, carrying *Kripans*, sharing breakfast after bath and worship, putting *tilak* on forehead, wearing sacred thread, having beard or clean shave are examples of some culture traits. Culture traits differ from one culture to another. Culture traits distinguish one culture from other culture. A trait of one culture is not significant for another culture. Offering water to sun is significant for Hindu culture, but not for western culture.

Culture-Complex: When several cultural traits are assembled they give rise to culture complex. For example, performing bath, wearing clean dress, entering bare footed in temple, sprinkling water and *chandan* on idols, offering flowers, fruits and *prasad*, bowing before idol, sacrificing *ghee*, coconut and *dhoop* before idol, taking help of priest, enchanting *mantra*, *Bhajan* and *Kirtan*, distributing *prasad* to all present people, giving *Dan* and *Dakshina* to priest form a culture complex of Hindu worship.

Culture Pattern: When culture complexes become related to each other in functional roles, a culture pattern comes into existence. A culture pattern consists of several culture complexes. For example, Indian culture pattern consists of Gandhism, spiritualism, Joint Family System, Caste System, *Jajmani* System and ruralism. Each of this is a culture complex consisting of numerous culture traits.

Culture Area: Culture area concept is based on practice of particular culture traits, complexes or culture patterns in a particular geographical area. The culture patterns of hilly, forested, plateau, coastal, desert and island area are quite different. Thus, different geographical regions have contributed the concept of culture area.

Edos and Ethos: The concepts of ethos and edos were developed by an American anthropologist in order to find out universal characteristics of culture. According to Kroeber, there are two universal characteristics of culture. They are edos and ethos. Edos are social and formal appearance of culture derived from its elements. Ethos are those aggregate of elements which determine quality interests and patterns of culture. Edos are *Lokachar* conduct of people practiced by the people or community. It is formality for all members to follow the cultural norms and values of the community. Ethos are spiritual charateristics of culture. They are world-view, the views of people regarding their community, gods, goddesses, kins, friends, souls, ghosts, natural and super natural words.

Implicit and Explicit: The concepts of implicit and explicit were propounded by Clyde Kluckhohn while he was attempting to classify cultural elements. He divided cultural elements into two items—implicit and explicit. We cannot know everything about life of people merely through sense organs. Those traits of culture which are known through sense organs are known as explicit elements of culture. But those elements of culture which cannot be known through sense organs but are perceived only by the people who are to trained and skilled to look for them. These elements of culture are known as implicit items of culture.

Cultural Integration: The concept of cultural integration was propounded by British anthropologist and functionalist B.K. Malinowski in his book, "Scientific Theory of Culture" (1944). In this book he defined culture as an instrument for the satisfaction of human needs. He classified human needs into three categories—Primary needs, secondary needs and tertiary needs. Primary need is also known as basic need or biological need such as sex, feeding, nutrition, growth, health etc. Secondary need is also known as derived need or instrumental needs. They are those needs which are derived from primary needs or which are instrumental in the satisfaction of primary needs. For example, education, economy, social organization and social control. Tertiary needs are also called as integrative needs because they provide integration in the society. For example, magic, religion, science, knowledge and art. Culture satisfies all three levels of human needs but the main function of culture is to keep human individuals in existence. Thus, integration of cultural traits, complexes and patterns have taken place to maintain the existence of human beings. It is because of this reason that the functional theory of Malinowski is known as biological functionalism.

Paradoxes of Culture: American anthropologist Herskovits in his book, "Man and His Work" (1956: 18-21) has discussed some paradoxes of culture which clarify more the nature and characteristics of culture. These paradoxes are as follows:

- Culture is universal as well as local.
- Culture is stable as well as changing.
- Culture is material as well as non-material.
- Man is creator of culture, but culture is super individual and super organic.
- Culture is our ways of lives, but it rarely intrudes into conscious thought.

Difference between Society and Culture: It is very difficult to distinguish culture and society. It is because without society one cannot think of culture and without culture a society cannot get its identity. Thus, both are interdependent, interrelated for maintaining their co-existence. Thinking to isolate culture from the society is similar to taking fish out of water. Both are two faces of the same coin of human life. But in spite of all such interdependency and co-existence some scholars have attempted to distinguish the concept of culture and society. The main points of differences between culture and society are as follows:

- Society is found even among animals but culture is creation of mankind.
- Society has come into existence earlier than culture.
- Society is an abstract concept, but culture is abstract as well as concrete concept. Culture exists in material and non-material both forms.
- Society is abstract system of social relationship, which has no boundary, but culture has geographical boundaries.
- Society may be small or big but culture is neither big nor small.
- Society may be developed and undeveloped or poor and rich, but culture is neither developed nor undeveloped or neither rich nor poor.
- Society consists of group of human beings, but culture consists of material and non-material traits.
- Society has some objectives and culture is means to fulfil those needs of the society.
- Individuals occupy significant place in society, but culture is super individual.
- In society, one finds hierarchy and stratification, but stratification and hierarchy are not features of a culture.

Civilization

Like the terms society and culture, general people also use the term civilization in their day-to-day discussions and talks on anti-social and anti-human behaviour. When youngers obey the olders in well manner, people say that they are civilized. When some body behaves in bad or ill manners, people say that they are uncivilized or barbarous. Similarly, people involved in theft, dacoity, loot, human traffic-king, murder, rape, gang rape, etc., people call them uncivilized. In the same way, for anti-social and anti-human behaviour, the laymen use the term uncivilized or barbarous. For behaviour supporting the systems and established norms laymen use the term civilized. For them civilization is related to good manner and well behaviour.

But for scholars, the concept of civilization is quite different from the concept of civilization of a layman. Now, let us discuss some of the definitions provided by anthropologists, sociologists, historians, economists and other scholars.

A scientific definition of civilization along with culture was provided by the founder of British Anthropology and evolutionist E.B. Tylor. Tylor in his book, "Primitive Culture" (1871) defined culture or civilization as a complex whole which includes knowledge, art, beliefs, customs, moral, habits and all other capabilities acquired by man as a member of society. From this definition of civilization provided by Tylor two characteristics of civilization have come into light. These are as follows:

- Like culture civilization is also a complex whole.
- Like culture civilization is also a social heritage acquired or learnt by the people as a member of society.

E.B. Tylor in his another book, "Researches into Early History of Mankind and Development of Civilization" (1865) provided an evolutionist view of culture. As a cultural evolutionist he defined civilization as the most evolved form of culture. He opined that researches into early history of mankind reveal that the culture of mankind has passed through three successive stages of development—savagery, barbarism and civilization. In the beginning mankind was in savagery and he survived through gathering and hunting. He was not a producer of food, rather he was consumer of food provided by nature, particularly, forest. With acquiring basic knowledge of domestication of plants and animals, mankind entered in the stage of barbarism. By inventing phonetic alphabets, writing, iron implements, systems in every walk of life and state, mankind entered into the stage of civilization. Thus, civilization is most evolved form of culture.

An American evolutionist L.H. Morgan in his book, "Ancient Society" (1877) has also expressed his views on civilization similar to E.B. Tylor. Like Tylor he also defined civilization as most evolved form of culture. According to him, with the invention of phonetic alphabets and writing mankind reached into the stage of civilization.

British diffusionist anthropologist Elliot Smith in his book, "Origin of Civilization" (1928) has defined civilization as series of inventions like canal for irrigation, agriculture through canal as assured means of irrigation, specialization of labour, labour payment, metals weapons, towns and civil organization. All such civilization related inventions were made for the first time by the people of Egypt. So, Egypt was the originator of civilization and rest parts of the world were imitators. It is because of this view, he is known as Pan Egyptologist.

Pre-historians have regarded the emergence of pre-historic urban centres and primitive state as the beginning of civilization.

Historians have accepted the origin of writing as the beginning of civilization.

MacIver and Page in their book, "Society:" 1950 has opined that civilization is social organization, where technology and material apparatus were established by the society in order to regulate social life.

Political scientists have regarded the state organization as civilization.

Some sociologists consider the development of material traits as civilization. For example, bicycle, scooter, motorcycle, car, truck, tractor, bus, railway, ship, aeroplane, radio, cinema, T.V., Computer, internet.

For economists, civilization is specialization of labour and payment of wages.

For literaturists, civilization is social charm and intellectual achievements.

According to A.W. Green, culture has entered into the stage of civilization through written languages, philosophy, complex technology, division and specialization of labour and political system.

American anthropologist Golden Weiser in his book, "Anthropology: An Introduction to Primitive Culture" (1937) has treated culture and civilization synonymously. According to him, civilization is found even in pre-literate society.

American Anthropologist Robert Redfield in his book, "Thinking about Civilization" (1955) has attempted to know civilization on the basis of lifestyle approach and religious approach.

According to lifestyle approach, civilization is a complex structure of specialists in relation to folk and peasant society. From the point of view of lifestyle folk, peasant and urban are different dimensions of civilization.

From religious point of view, civilization is a complex whole of great and little traditions. Little traditions are heritage of folk and peasant society characterised by illiteracy, magic and religion. Great traditions are heritage of primary urban centres characterised by the patronage of the then *Rajas* and *Maharajas* with *Pandas* and *Pujaries* as literate class. These two kinds of religious traditions developed in two distinct societies—Folk and Peasant and Primary urban centres with principal deities. But they were not in isolation. Rather they were in interaction, they were interdependent and interrelated.

An another American anthropologist A.L. Kroeber in his book, "Style and Civilization" (1967) has attempted to describe civilization on the basis of style of life. According to him each civilization has its own style by which one civilization is distinguished from the other. Each civilization has birth, growth and death. After death of one civilization, another civilization is born.

Characteristics of Civilization: On the basis of opinions expressed by different scholars as given above, the following characteristics of civilization came into existence:

- Civilization is man-made.
- Civilization is social heritage.
- Civilization is material and non-material both.
- Civilization is the most evolved form of culture.
- Civilization is style of life.
- Folk, peasant and urban are different dimensions of civilization.
- Civilization is complex structure of specialists in relation to folk and peasant societies.
- From religious point of view civilization is complex whole of great traditions and little traditions.
- Civilization has birth, maturity and death.
- Civilization is related to invention of writing, invention of towns and emergence of primitive state.
- Civilization is establishment of social organization.
- Civil organization, technology and philosophy in civilization control social life.

Difference between Culture and Civilization. The main points of differences between culture and civilization are as follows:

- Culture is earlier in origin than civilization.
- Culture is learnt, civilization is built.
- Culture is way of life, civilization is style of life.

- There is continuity and change in culture, but civilization has birth, maturity and death.
- Culture has prehistoric dimensions, but civilization has proto-historic and historic dimensions.
- Hunters, gatherers and barbarous, too had culture, but civilization came into existence by settled village life, urban life and industrial life.
- Civilization is always advancing but not culture.
- Civilization has a precise standard of measurement, but not culture.
- Civilization passed on without efforts, but not culture.
- Civilization can be improved by any body, but not culture.
- Civilization is body and culture is soul. Civilization is means for the expression and manifestation of the culture.
- Civilization is borrowed without loss, but not culture.
- In political sense, civilization is establishment of State, Government and civil life, but in culture political organizations are part of social organization.
- In economic sense, civilization is related to surplus production, exchange, trade and market, but in culture economic organization is part of social-cultural organization.
- In social sense civilization is concerned with systematic social organizations like marriage, family, kinship, clan organization and territorial organization, but culture is concerned with rules governing those organizations.

Caste System

You might have heard the terms like Brahmins, Kshatriya, Rajput, Yadava, Koeri, Gareri, *Barahi* (Carpenter), *Lohar* (Blacksmith), *Kumhar* (Potter) and so on. What these terms indicate. These terms indicate the caste status of an individual or a group. It is peculiar feature of Indian society.

We may define caste as a social endogamous group whose membership is obtained on the basis of birth and whose members observe a number of taboos related to marriage, food, occupation and social interaction. If class is a basis of social stratification in western societies, caste is the basis of social stratification in Indian society. The caste has been a centre of social, cultural, economic, political, religious and other activities in Indian Society.

The system by which different castes are interrelated socially and economically is known as caste system. It is true that each caste maintains its own identity, but different castes are not in isolation, they are functionally related to each other to maintain the existence of society as a whole. They are interdependent, interrelated and maintaining their co-existence by performing different activities for the society. On the basis of caste system, the Hindu organize their society. But elements of caste are seen in non-Hindu communities, too. Those religions and sects that emerged as a reaction to caste inequalities have ended up to force their followers for following caste system. The caste system is also found in non-Hindu communities such as Muslims, Christians, Sikhs, Jains, Buddhist, Jews and Zoroastrians. Many tribal communities have also been absorbed into caste system. This process is known as Tribe-Caste continuum. The meaning of Tribe-caste continuum is that some tribes have become castes over time.

Caste system derives its basis from Hinduism. The Hindu Text, *Rig Veda*, pronounces that different castes have emerged from the different parts of body of Lord Brahma, the God of creation. Brahmins have emerged from the head and mouth, Kshatriyas from arms, Vaishyas from thigh and Shudras from the feet of Lord Brahma. The Hindu society is divided into four social categories known as *Varna*. With each *Varna*, a particular kind of occupation was performed. But *Varna* was not hereditary and endogamous. In course of time, each *Varna* was divided into a number of categories identifying their separate identity as castes. To maintain caste identity, caste endogamy came into existence followed by clan exogamy.

Characteristics of Caste System

The chief characteristics of caste system are as follows:

- Social group
- Segmented division
- Membership on the basis of birth
- Social hierarchy
- Food taboos
- Sitting arrangement
- Endogamous rule
- Traditional occupation

- Social and religious disabilities
- Existence of Caste Panchayat
- Caste-based festivals
- Concept of purity and pollution
- Each caste has a dialect
- Interdependence of caste

Social Group—Caste is a social group. It is divided further into moieties, moiety into Phratries, Phratry into clans, and clan into lineages, a lineage in to families. Thus, moiety, phratry, clan and lineage all are social groups.

Segmented Division of Society: Caste system reveals segmented division of Hindu societies. It is because each caste has its own traditional Caste Panchayats to solve the problems of only caste concerned.

Membership on the Basis of Birth: One gets the membership of a caste on the basis of birth. He or she gets the membership of a caste from his/her parents. Sons or daughters get membership of their father's caste. If father is Brahmin, his sons or daughters are also Brahmins, if father is Rajput, sons and daughters are also Rajput. If father is Vaishya, sons and daughters are also Vaishya and if father is Shudra, sons and daughters are also Shudra. In this way, birth determines the caste status of an individual.

Social Hierarchy: In caste system one finds hierarchy. The position of all castes is not same. Rather they are placed in hierarchical order. Brahmins occupy the topmost position in caste hierarchy and Shudras occupy the lowermost position. The remaining castes are placed in between the two castes. A poor Brahmin priest commands far larger respect than a politically powerful person and a rich merchant. Both the king and the merchant touch the feet of Brahmin priest and seek his blessings.

Food-Water Taboo: Different castes follow a number of taboos related to food-water relation with other castes. People accept uncooked food materials from any castes. But they do not accept cooked food from all castes. The members of same caste follow food-water relation through *Kachcha* food such as rice, pulse and vegetables. But they maintain food-water relation with other castes through *Pucca* food materials such as bread, *puri*, *Halwa*, *Pua*, Sweets and so on. Shudras accept food and water of all other castes, but all other castes do not accept food-water of Shudras castes.

Sitting Arrangement: The own caste members and caste of higher status can sit on cot, but other castes do not sit on cot. They sit on wooden tools, bench, chairs and even on ground.

Endogamous group: Each caste is an endogamous group. Each caste performs marriage of sons and daughters in other families of the same caste. They do not follow inter-caste marriage. Inter-caste marriage is tabooed.

Traditional Occupation: Each caste has its traditional occupation. The traditional occupation does not make any member of the caste unemployed. It provides occupational base to all members. The members of different castes are interrelated functionally.

Social and Religious Disability: In caste system all castes do not avail equal rights in the society and performance of rituals. The members of lower castes are made disabled socially and religiously. They have separate hamlets, wells and tanks.

Existence of Caste Panchayat: The caste system exhibits hierarchy but at the same time it also exhibits segmentation of castes. Each caste has its own Caste Panchayat where members of other castes are not allowed. In Caste Panchayat only problems of concerned caste are discussed and solved. Now-a-days, the Caste Panchayat has become a regional political force to press various kinds of demands before the Government.

Caste Based Festivals: The caste system also reveals caste based festivals. For example Yadavas perform Gobardhan Puja, Dusadh perform Goraiya Puja, Chamar perform Devas Puja, Bhokta perform Fire Puja and Kayasthas perform Davat Puja.

Concept of Pollution and Purity: The concept of pollution and purity was also attached to caste system. Certain functions were not treated as pure. Rather they were treated as relating to pollution. For example, carrying dead animals and taking out their skins, carrying night soils, cleaning laterrine, cow shed and so on. As they were performing unclean occupation, concept of pollution and purity was attached. They were treated as impure and hence as untouchables. As untouchables, they were made disables. Even Shudras were divided into clean Shudra such as Dhobi and Dusadh. While other Shudras were treated as unclean Shudra.

Caste Dialect: Caste system is also characterised by the existence of caste dialect. Each caste has their own dialect in which they have communication with fellows of own caste and with members of other castes.

Interdependence of Caste: Each caste has its own ethnic identity which they maintain on the basis of caste endogamy and clan exogamy. But a caste does not exist in isolation. A caste is interdependent on other castes. Each caste performs a special function for the other castes. Thus, caste system shows interdependence of castes in functional relation.

Theory of Origin of Caste System

A number of theories have been propounded by different scholars regarding the origin of caste and caste system. In order to have a thorough knowledge of caste system, it is fitness of the thing to understand about those theories. Different theories of origin of caste system are as follows:

- Divinal Theory
- Racial Theory
- Political Theory
- Religious Theory
- Occupational Theory
- Union Theory
- Evolutionary Theory

Divinal Theory: According to sacred textual traditions of Hindu, the credit for the establishment of caste system goes to Lord Brahma, the God of creation. When Lord Brahma created mankind, he established the caste system to maintain social and reciprocal relation in the society. He imagined the society like an organism having different parts, performing different functions but mutually maintaining a co-existence. He created Brahmins to perform the work of teaching religions and traditions in the society. Brahmins are supposed to have emerged from the mouth or head of Lord Brahma. Lord Brahma created Kshatriyas for ruling and providing protection in the society. Kshatriyas have originated from the hands of Lord Brahma. Lord Brahma created Vaishyas to meet different types of economic necessities of people in the society. They have emerged from the thigh of the Lord Brahma. The lord created Shudras to perform manual work in the society. They were originated from the feet of the Lord Brahma. Thus, all castes occupied different positions in caste system, but they are not in isolation, they are interdependent and interrelated.

Racial Theory: The racial theory of origin of caste system has been propounded by Western scholar Herbert Risley and Indian Scholar D.N. Majumdar. They attempted to provide a racial description of caste system in India. According to them, caste system was established in India after the arrival of Aryans. In order to distinguish their own social system from the local original inhabitants, they established caste system in India. This system was established in the region between Ganges and Yamuna. Then it spread in entire north India and finally it reached south India.

Religious Theory: According to this theory, the caste system has come into existence to observe religious traditions. Brahmins occupied the position of priest and began to get the rituals performed for various castes. Different castes emerged to contribute in the performance of religious rituals.

Political Theory: The political theory of origin of caste system has been propounded by Indian sociologist G.S. Ghurye in his book "Caste, Class and Occupation" (1961). In the beginning being religious priest, the ruling of the society was in the hands of Brahmins. In order to rule the Hindu society, Brahamins established the caste system.

Occupational Theory: According to this theory, caste system emerged to perform different kinds of occupations in the society. Later on, their sons began to carry over the same occupation. The occupation became the base of caste system. The people of same occupation started caste endogamy and clan exogamy. Thus, it was occupation which gave rise to caste system.

Union Theory: According to this theory, caste system emerged on the basis of concept of union. Castes are transformed form of union. When unions were formed on the basis of occupations, caste system was originated.

Evolutionary Theory: According to this theory, caste system is a result of evolution. In the evolution of caste system, belief, tradition, occupation, political system, economy and social structure have played significant roles.

Functions of Caste System

- We may discuss the functions of caste system under three broad headings:
- Function of caste in Individual life

- Function of caste in Community life
- Function of caste for Nation (Entire society)

Functions of Caste in Individual Life

In individual life caste performs the following functions:

- Determination of Social Status
- Mental safety
- Determination of occupation
- Determination of marriage
- Social security

Functions of Caste for the Community

The caste performs the following functions for the community:

- Protection of religious sentiment
- Purity of blood
- Social status determination
- Protection of culture
- Maintenance of caste unity

Functions of Caste for the Nation

The caste performs the following functions for the Nation:

- Helpful in development of society
- Social security
- Political stability
- Division of labour
- Religious Tolerance
- Discharge of Responsibility

Changes in Caste System

The caste system has witnessed a number of changes due to democratization, secularization, modernization, education and globalization. The following changes in caste system can be observed:

- Change in status of Brahmins
- Change in caste hierarchy
- Change in caste occupation
- Change in food-water relation
- Change in concept of pollution and purity
- Change in birth based status
- Inter-caste marriage
- Inter-religious marriages
- Change in status of Dalit
- Change in caste interdependence
- Formation of caste committees.

Factors Responsible for Change in Caste System

The following factors are responsible for changes in caste system:

- Western education
- Urbanization
- Industrialization
- Secularization
- Democratization
- Modernization
- Globalization
- Untouchability (Prohibition Act)
- Hindu Marriage Act
- Importance of wealth
- Freedom movement
- Religious movement
- Reformist movement
- Feminist movement
- Disorganization of joint family
- Decrease in Caste Panchayat
- Decrease in traditional Village Panchayat
- Modern Gram Panchayat
- Decrease in *Jajmani* system
- Recent Act
- Judiciary

Demerits of Caste System

The following are the demerits of caste system:

- Hindrance in caste mobility
- Hindrance in economic mobility
- Hindrance in labour skill
- Hindrance in National Unity
- Anti-democracy
- Exploitation of lower castes
- Responsible for religious conversion
- Disturbance in social unity
- Against progress
- Catalyst of social problems
- Low condition of women
- Originator of untouchability

Casteism

Casteism is a process of organizing and integrating the members of own caste. It is different from caste system. The caste system is weakening day-by-day but casteism is increasing. In the context of national integration, the term casteism is negatively defined. It is because in casteism an individual favours the members of own castes at the cost of other castes. In doing so he forgets his national identity and began to behave with his own caste identity. Casteism leads to caste riots. Now-a-days, the help of casteism is taken to put pressure on the Government. Caste factor is also taken into account at the time of distribution of tickets in M.P. and MLA elections. Caste sentiments and feelings are arisen at the time of elections. The poor and innocent people cast their votes in favour of their caste candidates.

Jajmani System

Closely related to the caste system, there is an another system known as *Jajmani* system. It is a system in which different castes are related socially and functionally for the fulfilment of needs of the society. In the beginning, the system included Brahmin priests and kings. The Brahmin priest used to call kings as *Jajman*. The Brahmin priest was known as *Raj Purohit*. Thus, *Raj Purohit* and the king as *Jajman* were related socially and economically in the system in the beginning. The *Raj Purohit* used to perform rituals in the house of his *Jajman*, the king. The king used to make payment in cash and kind.

Later on, this system incorporated the village priest, artisans and the peasants. The peasants were termed as *Jajmans*, the village Priest as *Purohit* and Artisans or serving castes as *Pawania*. The *Purohit*, artisans or serving castes (*Pawania*) used to render their services to peasants and in turn get annual payment in kind. This system is still found in rural areas where village purohit, artisans and serving castes serve the peasants on annual payment basis in kind. On the occasions of birth, marriage and death *Pawanias* and *Purohits* were rewarded by gifts in cash and kind other than their annual payment in kind. Thus, Brahmin, Nai (barber), potters, blacksmith, carpenter, washer man, gardener, sweet maker, goldsmith etc. were brought under *Jajmani* system. This system has provided jobs in our society since Vedic times. Modernization and modern education have brought some changes in this system. As a result occupational mobility has taken place. But, the system is still a truth for rural India where peasants and serving castes have been functionally and socially interrelated even to-day. Now-a-days, payment in cash is preferred in place of kind. A peasant is not free to give up his *Purohit* and *Pawania*. But they can express inability to serve to their *Jajmans*. The *Purohit* and *Pawania* can sell or mortgage his *Jajmanika* village in the hands of their own caste brothers.

Characteristics of Jajmani System

The *Jajmani* system has the following characteristics:

- Social relation between peasant castes, Brahmin and artisan castes
- Economic interdependence between different castes
- Existence of *Jajmanika* village
- Annual payment
- Payment in kinds
- Provision for reward
- Sale of *Jajmanika* village
- Mortgage of *Jajmanika* village
- Division of *Jajmanika* village among sons
- Intergenerational relationship among castes

- Inclusion of Muslim castes in *Jajmani* system

Merits of **Jajmani** *System*

The *Jajmani* system has following merits:

- Supporter of caste system
- Arrangement of occupations for all castes
- Social interdependence between castes
- Economic interdependence between castes
- Functional importance of all castes
- No class conflict

Demerits of **Jajmani** *System*

The *Jajmani* system has following demerits:

- Supporter of casteism
- Against occupational mobility
- Supporter of exploiter class
- Supporter of untouchability
- Lack of competition among castes
- Against progress

Changes in **Jajmani** *System*

The following changes have taken place in *Jajmani* system:

- Increase in caste mobility
- Increase in occupational mobility
- Conflict in social relation
- Origin of class struggle

Class System

The class is an economic concept. It refers to a social group whose members share the same relationship to the means of production. Class is changing. An individual is born in a class, but he can change his class such as lower class to middle class, middle class to high class, high class to middle class and middle class to low class. Thus, the membership of class is not fixed rather it is changing.

The class does not derive its origin from religion. The class is not related to the concept of pollution and purity. It is also not related to the practice of untouchability.

Characteristics of Class

The class has following characteristics:

- Class is an economic concept.
- Membership is not based on birth but on income.
- Membership of class is not static, rather it is changing with the change in income.
- The class has no restriction on mobility.
- The class has mobility of individuals not group.
- The class has no concept of purity and pollution.
- The class has no concept of untouchability.
- The class is an open system because of individual mobility.
- The class does not derive its legitimacy from religion.

Social Stratification

The concept of social stratification came into existence in 1940s. The term stratification was borrowed from the earth science, i.e. the Geology. According to geologists the earth is composed of a number of layers. One layer is placed upon the other. Each layer has its own composition and can be distinguished from the other. Each layer is known as stratum and the plural term is strata. This system of composition of earth is called stratification.

Taking clue from the layered structure of earth, social anthropologists have made attempts to think layered structure of human society. Therefore, we may define social stratification as division of society into strata. But there is a difference between strata of earth and strata of society. In geological strata equal value is attached to each stratum. But in the concept of social stratification, one stratum is more privileged than the other. In human society one finds an unequal distribution of privileges across the strata. In other words, we can say that the strata of human society are ranked. Those who occupy higher position are more privileged than those who occupy lower position.

We can illustrate the phenomenon of privileged and non-priviledged people with some examples. We see that rich live in costly houses in clean colony, they wear costly clothes and ornaments, they have costly cars, refrigerators, furnitures, have varieties of food, avail air travel, A.C. train travel and 5 stars hotels. Why?, It is because they are privileged. On the other hand, we see the poor struggling hard for their survival and bread, cloth and house, why so? It is because they are non-privileged people. Similarly, we see our MLAs and MPs availing every type of facility and leading a luxurious life because they are privileged. But the voters who cast their votes to get them elected are found leading a very struggling life because they are not privileged. We find Brahmin Priests enjoying privileges even in the house of king, leader and the rich. But a Shudra does not enjoy any status even in his village community. These examples show clearly that privileged people are outcome of unequal distribution of power, wealth and prestige.

Difference and Inequality

Difference between individuals and groups is universal characteristic. It does not imply that one individual is superior to other or one group is inferior to other. Thus, we can say that difference does not imply ranking. It only shows that diversity exists.

It is necessary to distinguish the concept of difference from the concept of inequality. By difference we mean the existence of dissimilarity between objects under consideration. But these dissimilarities are complementary. Men and women are different in biological compositions, but they are complementary to each other. Similarly, potters are different from blacksmiths, but they are dependent upon each other. Similarly, weavers and carpenters are different, but they are dependent upon each other.

Inequality is concerned with distribution of privileges and resources. It shows that some are more privileged than the others. Some have more resources than the others.

Power, Wealth and Prestige

As social stratification deals with the inequalities of power, wealth and prestige, therefore, it is necessary to distinguish the concept of power, wealth and prestige. Power refers to degree to which individuals or groups can impose their will on others and seek obedience from them even in absence of their consent. When the exercise of power is legitimate, it is called authority. Wealth refers to material possessions such as house, building, cattle, tree, land, gold and livestocks. It includes all forms of properties which are valuable. Privilege refers to honour and respect associated with social position of individuals for the society. It is also related to the quality of individuals and their lifestyles. Certain qualities and lifestyles are regarded as more prestigious than the others.

In society inequality is not only between groups in terms of amount of power, wealth and prestige possessed by members. It is also between members of different age and sex groups. The inequalities based on age groups such as infants, children, adolescents, youth, adults and aged and male and female are not examples of social stratification. Therefore, social stratification deals with inequality, but all inequalities are not social stratification.

Undoubtedly, social stratification is a type of social inequality. It refers to the presence of social groups which are ranked in hierarchical order, i.e. one above the other usually with respect to power, wealth and prestige. Those who belong to a particular stratum share common sentiments and interests. They also share a common style of life which distinguishes them from members of other strata of the society.

Universality of Social Stratification

Now, question arises whether stratification exists universally? The anthropologists are of the opinion that simple societies, i.e., societies of hunters and gatherers did not possess groups ranked one above the other so far as amount of power, wealth and prestige of members in the group is concerned. All clans were equally placed. There was no ranking. All members of the community had equal access to the resources. There was no concept of rich and poor. But inequality existed among them on the basis of age and sex groups. For example, children, youth and aged and men and women. Women had to observe a number of taboos in comparison to men because of physical composition, pregnancy and lactation. Children were loved and aged were respected. Some kinds of conflicts were prevalent there. But they were not related to stratification. We may say that egalitarian society or stateless society had social inequality and conflict, but not social stratification. On this basis, we can say that social stratification is not universal.

According to anthropologists, there was a stage primitive communism in the beginning. In this stage society possessed a state of complete equality. These societies lacked social stratification but had age and gender based inequality. They had concept of best hunter, best magician and best craftman. These persons commanded more respects than other members of the community. It means that even in simple society, some persons excelled the others and possessed more prestige than the others. But such power, prestige and wealth was not associated with a group. It was associated with an individual.

Thus, from above discussion, it is quite clear that social stratification was not a universal phenomenon.

Chapter 3
Marriage

Definition

It is very difficult to provide a universal definition of marriage because marriage customs and laws differ from society to society. Due to the existence of pluralities in marriage rules and customs, a universal definition of marriage is not possible. But we can attempt to provide such a definition of marriage which is applicable in majority of cases.

We may define marriage as an association of two or more individuals of opposite sexes bound as couple through custom or court. The couple, thus formed, has to share the responsibility of reproducing, rearing and caring children born out of this union. This definition of marriage has following characteristics:

- Marriage leads to the formation of couple.
- The couple may be monogamous, polygamous and polyandrous.
- Marriage gives rise to the family of procreation.
- In marriage, individuals of opposite sexes become couple through customs or court.
- The couple has to share the responsibility of reproducing children, rearing and caring them.
- The reproduction of children is must to continue the family name and inheritance of paternal property.
- The children born through such union are legal.
- The marriage provides life-long sexual satisfaction.

Problems of Universal Definition

It is not possible to provide a universal definition of marriage because aim of marriage is not same all-over the globe. In some societies, marriage is related to sex satisfaction and reproduction of children, in another society the main function of marriage is economic cooperation. Still in some other society the aim of marriage is to provide security to woman and children. The forms of marriage are also not same all-over the world. Some societies practice monogamy, some practice polygeny and still some other practice polyandry. No one custom or law is found all-over the globe related to the marriage. That is why it is very difficult to provide such a definition of marriage which is universally applicable. We may discuss this problem with following examples.

Majority of scholars are of opinion that satisfaction of sex, reproduction of children and their rearing and caring are objectives of the marriage. But empirical researches do not support this objective of marriage. In some simple societies, marriages are performed only for social-cultural purposes; For example, in Sema Naga tribe, there is a custom by which a son is allowed to marry his step mothers after the death of father, but not with own mother. This marriage is held not for sexual satisfaction and reproduction of children, but to provide security to step mothers and their children after becoming widow and to inherit the property of widow.

In some tribal societies, the custom of ghost marriage has been reported. In this custom, a man marries with a woman in the name of his dead brother or a male relative. Children born from this union get the name of the deceased as father. This custom of marriage is also known as proxy marriage. This exotic custom of ghost marriage or proxy marriage was reported for the first time from the Nuer, an African tribe. E.E. Evancepritcherd has described this exotic custom in his book, "Nuer" (1940). This custom allows even a deceased male member of the community to continue his progeny. From this custom a difference between biological father and social father has come into existence.

In some societies of the world, there is a custom to allow a widow to arrange her remarriage with the younger brother of the husband if she is young. This rule of marriage is also known as levirate. But when the widow is aged and the younger brother is married, then widow's remarriage with husband's younger brother takes place only for social security of the widow and her children.

In Garo tribe of Assam, there is a custom by which a son-in-law marries his mother-in-law when she becomes widow to inherit her property. The main objective of this kind of marriage is not sexual satisfaction and reproduction of children, but to provide social security and inherit property.

In Hindu society, marriage is regarded as a religious sacrament. The couple is bound together as *Ardhanga* and *Ardhangani* to hold Dharma, to reproduce children and to continue the progeny. In high caste Hindus widow remarriage is not allowed because couple is bound together for seven births.

Different kinds of marriage rules prevalent in different communities also create problems in universal definition of marriage. For example, group marriage, polyandry, polygeny and monogamy. Tribes of Brazil, Cyberia and Australia follow a custom of group marriage in which all brothers of a family are married to all sisters of another family and *vice-versa.* This is one example of polygeny and polyandry both. Here several husbands of a women and several wives of a man reside together in a group.

In some tribal societies, custom of polyandry is found in which a woman marries with more than one man. This is of two types—fraternal and non-fraternal. When all husbands married to a woman are brothers, it is known as fraternal polyandry. But if all husbands married to a woman are not brothers, it is known as non-fraternal polyandry. Khasa of Dehradun are fraternal polyandrous. But Kota of Nilgiri are non-fraternal polyandrous.

Polygeny is also practiced by different societies particularly when first wife becomes barren. Monogamy is a custom of marriage between one man and one woman.

Incest taboo also creates problem in universal definition of marriage because extension of incest taboo is not same everywhere. Some societies prefer cousin marriages, while others treat cousins as blood relative. In South Indian Brahmins cross-cousins are preferred for marriage. Marriage between maternal uncle (*Mama*) and sister's daughter (*Bhanji*) is also preferred in South Indian Brahmins. Cross-cousin marriage is prevalent in tribals, Hindus and Muslims. Parallel cousin marriages are also preferred in Muslims.

Now-a-days, the practice of live in relationship has come into existence which has got legal acceptance in different countries of the globe. In this practice, a young man and a young woman who are not married live together and have physical contact too. They enjoy sex but do not like to reproduce children. If by chance, a child is delivered, the man has to share responsibility of rearing, caring and other expenses. Man has to share the responsibility of biological and legal father.

Now-a-days, the practice of marriage between individuals of same sex has also come into existence in which two or more individuals of same sex can establish marriage and live like husband and wife or life partner. This practice has also got legal status in different countries. Due to this practice gays and lesbians have emerged as homo-sexual life partners. This practice is against the practice of heterosexual life partner.

Now-a-days, the practice of surrogacy has emerged which is helpful for those couples who are barren or who do not want to deliver a child, but to rear the child born from surrogate mother.

The above cited examples from different societies of the globe reveal clearly that there are plural customs, practices and laws prevalent among different societies of the world. The purpose of marriages are also different in different societies. Differences in customs, practices, purposes and laws of marriage create a great problem in providing a universal definition of marriage. Hence, a universal definition of marriage is not possible.

Is Marriage only a Biological Concept?

In order to solve this problem let us deal with the various kinds of functions performed by the marriage. Only then we can assess that marriage is only a biological concept or not. Now let us discuss various functions of marriage one by one. The various functions of marriage are as follows:

- Biological function
- Social function
- Cultural function
- Religious function
- Economic function
- Political function
- Entertainment function
- Educational function
- Psychological function

Functions of Marriage

Biological Function: Marriage performs the following types of biological functions:

- Satisfaction of sex
- Reproduction of children
- Rearing and caring children
- Maintaining health and hygiene

Satisfaction of Sex: Although customs related to marriage are various and its purposes also vary, but in majority the satisfaction of sex is important function. Although sex can be satisfied even without marriage, but marriage provides legal status to sex relation. Without marriage sex relation is not taken well by the society and guilty persons are punished. Pre-marital and extra-marital relations are also taken as a crime and those involved are punished. Without marriage sex can be satisfied temporarily. But marriage provides permanency to sex relation because it is a life-long association of husband and wife.

Now-a-days, homosexual partners have also emerged and they also satisfy their sexes with unnatural means.

Reproduction of Children: Reproduction is a biological process. Reproduction of children is one of biological functions of the marriage. Barren couples do not receive good treatment in the society. They are abused frequently. The reproduction of children is an important function of marriage. After reproduction, the husband and wife receive status as father and mother.

Breastfeeding and Rearing: Breastfeeding and rearing is a biological function of marriage. Reproduction of children requires continuous breastfeeding for a long period of time. When the child gives up breastfeeding, then the mother provides him raw and cooked food items and takes every care for the proper nourishment and growth of the child.

Maintenance of Health and Hygiene: After marriage husband and wife have to follow the rule of division of labour to run the family properly. It is the duty of a married woman to cook food properly and serve food items to her husband, children and other family members. While cooking and serving food, she takes every care of nutritional value of the food and serving them to family members. She also takes care of members who are ill and what kind of food and nutrition they want. Thus, maintenance of health and hygiene is also a biological function of the marriage.

Besides these biological functions, marriage also performs a number of other functions, a description about which are being given below:

Social Function: Marriage performs social functions. It provides the couple of social status as husband, wife, son-in-law, daughter-in-law. After reproduction of children the couple attains status as father and mother. Before marriage they are socially termed as Bride and Bride-groom. Bride and groom are tied to other kins of both families. It is because marriage is not only a union of two individuals, but of two families too.

Socialisation Work: Marriage plays significant role in socialization of children born from the union. At the time of birth a child is just a mass of bone and flesh. But parents gradually make him a social being. They develop good habit, toilet training, and social qualities. Thus, they make a child social being from a biological being.

Cultural function: Marriage performs a number of customs and rituals according to values of the society. Observing different kinds of rituals is a must. Besides, marriage includes special dress, assemblance of relatives on invitation, special ornaments, special food and feast, special dance and songs, special drawing and painting of house, reciprocal exchange of gift and hospitality, special vehicles etc. In this way a number of cultural activities are related to rituals of marriage.

Religious Function: According to Hindu Dharma Shastra, marriage is not just a union of two individuals of opposite sexes, rather it is a religious sacrament. Before marriage a boy is *Ardhanga* and girl is *Ardhangani*. But after marriage they become complete for leading a life as couple and family in the society. They have to obey the rules of *Grihastha Ashram* and earn money observing the *dharma*. Marriage is a tie of not only one birth, but for seven births. Husband and wife maintain *dharma* of family life. They observe fast and worship deities for welfare of the family and all-round development of family members.

Economic Function: The married couple struggle hard to earn money for the maintenance of family. They cooperate each other in raising family income. All members perform works in family as per rule of division of labour. Husband and wife also earn wages to raise the family income and provide food, cloth, shelter, education and treatment of diseases from their hard earned money. After father, sons inherit his property left at the time of death.

Political Function: Marriage gives rise to family of procreation. Each family has a head. The family head takes all family level decision and represents his family in the Village Panchayat and other kinds of village level functions.

Entertainment Function: Marriage also performs entertainment function. Husband, wife and children have discussion, make funs and entertain each other.

Educational Function: Marriage performs educational function by providing toilet training and inculcating good habits in children. It also teaches about traditions, customs, practices, and cultural behaviours to the children.

Psychological Function: Marriage provides stability and security to husband, wife and their children. They feel secured psychologically. They have always in mind that there are some one to take care of them on illness and in the period of trouble. From above discussions on functions of marriage, it is quite clear that marriage is not only a biological concept, but, it is, social-cultural concept, too.

Evolution of Marriage

According to cultural evolution, the marriage has passed through the following stages of development:

- Promiscuity
- Group marriage
- Polyandry
- Polygeny
- Monogamy

Promiscuity: According to classical cultural evolutionists in the beginning there was no marriage, no family and no kinship. Mating was random. Men and women were free to have sex relations with any member of the group or outside the group. This was stage of promiscuity or sex communism. At the time of study by evolutionists, and anthropologists, the practice of promiscuity was not reported from any society of the Globe. But practices like wife hospitality, offering wives to guests were reported from African tribes. Similarily, temple prostitution in the name of *Devadasi* was also reported from India.

These customs were indicative of the stage of promiscuity in the marriage history of mankind.

Group Marriage: This was the first stage of marriage in the history of mankind. In this custom two groups exchanged their girls with each other for the purpose of marriage. In this custom all men were husbands of all girls brought in marriage from the other group. All married women in the group were wives of all men of the group and all men of the groups were husbands of all married women in the group. Such practices were reported from Canada, Cyberia, Australia and American Indians. This form of marriage would have emerged due to incest taboo with girls reproduced in the group. The practice would have started to avoid conflict in the group and to establish relationship with other group. But this was also a kind of promiscuity.

Polyandry: In this stage, the custom of marrying one woman by several men started. All men married to a woman were either brothers (fraternal) or not brothers (non-fraternal). The same women had to satisfy sexual urges of all men married to her. All husbands of a wife had to adapt themselves with this practice. Khasa of Deharadun and Tharu of Tharuhat area are fraternal polyandrous. Fraternal polyandry is also known as Tibbetan polyandry because it was reported for the first time from Tibbet by McLenann, a British evolutionist. The Kota of Nilgiri hills practice non-fraternal polyandry. Non-fraternal polyandry is also known as Nayar polyandry because it was reported by McLenann from Nayar of Kerala. This is also a kind of promiscuity but in limited sense. The practice of polyandry would have started due to shortage of women caused by female infanticide. Female infanticide was reported from African and American tribes. McLenann did not explain this practice of female infanticide as cruelty. Rather, he explained this practice as a functional necessity. In early days, the only means of survival for mankind was hunting and gathering. The human groups had to struggle hard to maintain their existence. When no food was available they used to kill female child to satisfy their hunger and maintain their existence. Solution of starvation by this practice gave rise to an another problem. Now, the male-female ratio was badly disturbed. Now, all men did not have equal opportunity for sex. They solved this problem by the practice of polyandry.

Polygeny: Polygeny is a social-cultural practice in which a man marries with more than one woman. This practice would have been started in neolithic period when mankind became food producer and now there was enough food so that practice of female infanticide would have been stopped. Agriculture and domestication of animals would have demanded more and more manpower. This was possible by more and more reproduction of child through the practice of polygeny.

Monogamy: This is most evolved form of marriage. When man entered in the stage of civilization, the practice of monogamy was started. It became the form of marriage for all civilized society.

Types of Marriage

The main types of marriage can be shown by the diagram given below:

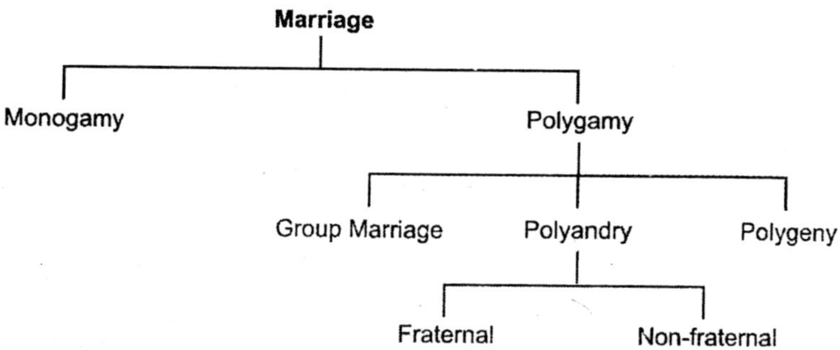

Monogamy: It is a form of marriage which allows a male to marry with a female or *vice-versa*. This is the most evolved form of marriage. Now majority of societies are following this from of marriage.

Polygamy: It is a form of marriage in which more than one man establish marriage with a woman or, more than one woman with a man or, both. Polygamy may be classified into three groups as follows:

Group Marriage: A form of marriage in which all boys of a group are married to all girls of an another group and all boys of another group are married to all girls of the first group. In this form of marriage two groups establish marital relation through exchange of girls among themselves. All boys of a group are husbands of all girls got from other group in marriage. Similarly, all girls are wives of all boys married to them. In fact, this custom was a mixture of polygeny-polyandry. Group marriages were reported from Canadian, Cyberian Australian and American tribes.

Polyandry: A form of marriage in which a woman marries with more than one man who maybe brothers or not. When husbands married to a woman are brothers, it is termed as fraternal polyandry, but when husbands married to a woman are not brothers, it is called as non-fraternal polyandry. Khasa and Tharu are examples of fraternal polyandry, whereas Kota of Nilgiri area and Nayar of Kerala are examples of non-fraternal polyandry. Polyandry is also reported in *Mahabharata*. For example Draupadi was married to five Pandavas.

Polygeny: A form of marriage in which a man marries with more than one woman. In this form several women have a common husband. Polygeny has also been reported in *Ramayana*. The King Dasarath of Ayodhya had three wives namely, Kaushalya, Kaikeyi and Sumitra. When first wife becomes barren a man marries with another woman to continue his race and progeny.

Rules of Marriage

Marriage takes place by observing rules established by the community. The rules of marriage may be classified into two categories:

- Prohibitive rules
- Preferential rules

Prohibitive rules: Prohibitive rules are those rules of marriage which put restriction on the selection of the mates. These rules does not allow men and women to enter into marital alliance with certain category of people. Prohibition is done as per religious norms and customary values. Prohibitive rules are as follows:

- Incest taboo
- Exogamy
- Endogamy
- Hypergamy (*Anuloma*)
- Hypogamy (*Pratiloma*)

Incest taboo: Sexually tabooed persons are known as incest. In every known society, incest taboo is a universal feature of nuclear family which consists of husband, wife and their unmarried children. In every society marital relation is prohibited between father-daughter, mother-son and brother-sister. This prohibition is known as incest taboo.

Extension of incest taboo is not same in every society. For example in High caste Hindus of North India extension of incest taboo is up to cousins, daughter-in-law, son-in-law, elder brother' wife and younger brother's wife. But in South Indian Brahmins cross-cousin marriages do not come under incest taboo. Marriage between sister's daughter and mother's younger brother also does not come under incest prohibition. In some society brother's younger brother and elder brother's wife are incest, while in some other societies they are under prescribed marriage rule. Similarly, in some societies parallel cousins are incest, but in some other societies they are prescribed marriage partner. This is also true with father-in-law and daughter-in-law and mother-in-law and son-in-law.

Exogamy: A prohibitive rule of marriage which does not allow a boy and girl of the same family, lineage, clan, kin group and village to enter into marital relation. According to this rule a boy or a girl is expected not to enter into marital relation with a girl or a boy of same family, lineage, clan, kin groups and the village in which he or she lives.

Endogamy: A prohibitive rule which does not allow a boy or a girl to select marriage partner outside his/her caste, tribe and religion. Tribes are endogamous. Hindu castes are also endogamous. Among Muslims, there are two endogamous units—Shia and Shuni. Among Christians, the endogamous groups are Roman Catholics and Protestants.

Traditionally, Indian castes are endogamous groups, but inter-*varna* or inter-caste marriages were permitted in ancient India under the rule of hypergamy (*anuloma*) and hypogamy (*pratiloma*).

Hypergamy: A custom by which a lower caste girl is married to a higher caste boy. According to this custom, a Brahmin boy can marry a lower caste girl.

Hypogamy: A custom by which a higher caste girl marries a lower caste boy. According to this custom, Brahmin girl can marry a lower caste boy.

But such rules were not encouraged in traditional Indian society.

Preferential Rule: Preferential rule of marriage allows a boy or a girl to select marriage partners from kin groups. As this rule allows to select marriage mates from one's own kin groups over the other groups, that is why this rule is known as preferential rule. The examples of marriages on the basis of preferential rules are as follows:

Parallel Cousin: The children of two siblings of same sexes are known as parallel cousins. For example children of two brothers or children of two sisters. Such types of marriages strengthen the bond between two brothers or two sisters. Such rules are exception to lineage and clan exogamy rule. Parallel cousin marriages are preferred among Muslims.

Cross-cousin marriage: The children of two siblings of opposite sexes are known as cross-cousin. For example children of brother and sister. This form of marriage strengthens the bond or alliance between brother and sister. Cross-cousin marriages are preferred among tribals of our country and Brahmins of South India.

Mother's younger brother and Mother's daughter marriages: This is also known *Mama* (maternal uncle) and *Bhanji* (Niece) marriage. In this custom, a maternal uncle prefers to marry his sister's daughter. This kind of marriage is preferred among some Brahmins of South India.

Levirate Marriage: This is also known as *Bhabhi* (elder brother's wife) and *Devar* (younger brother of husband) marriage. In this custom widow of elder brother is preferred for marriage by the younger brother. This kind of preferential marriages are found among tribes and lower caste Hindus.

Sororate: This is also known as *Sali* (wife's sister) marriage. According to this preferential rule a man selects his wife's sister as marriage partner. This kind of preferential marriage is prevalent among some tribes and castes of India.

Ways of Acquiring Marriage mates in tribals

Tribals of our nation has their own ways of acquiring marriage mates. Various ways of acquiring marriage mates in tribal societies are as follows:

- Marriage by probation
- Marriage by capture
- Marriage by trial
- Marriage by bride price
- Marriage by service
- Marriage by exchange
- Marriage by elopement
- Marriage by intrusion

Marriage by Probation: In some tribal communities, there is a custom to allow an unmarried boy and an unmarried girl to stay together before the occurrence of marriage. In this period of living together they try to know each other's nature and behaviour so that they could live peacefully and happily after the performance of their marriage. This period is known as probation period. If a boy does not accept the girl for marriage in probation period, he has to pay compensation to the girl's family. If a girl gets pregnant during the period of probation, then the boy cannot refuse marriage with her.

Marriage by Capture: In this type of marriage mate (the bride) is acquired by capture. This was the earliest form of acquiring mate. Now, this way of acquiring mate is vanishing. But its relics can be seen in some tribal societies of India and abroad. For example in Bushman, Kalmuk, Eskimo, Naga, Gond, Bhil, Ho, mock capture is practice at the time of marriage. Ho call it Upertipi and Gond call it Polether. Capture marriage has been reported in *Mahabharata*. For example Gandhari and Subhadra.

Marriage by trial: In order to get a mate, a tribal has to go through trial in some tribal society. If he succeeds the test, he is entitled to select any girl from the group as his mate. The Bhil of Gujarat call it as *God Gadhadi* festival. In this festival unmarried boys and girls perform dance together. The boys have to appear in test during the dance period. In this marriage mate test loaf sugar and coconut are tied on the top of a pole with the help of cloth. The girls encircle the pole. Boys attempt to break the circle and climb upon the pole to eat loaf sugar and coconut. The boy who succeeds is entitled to select anyone girl of the circle as his marriage mate.

Marriage by Bride-price: This is the most prevalent form of acquiring marriage mate in tribal societies of India. The bride price is very nominal. Previously it included Rs. 5/- in cash, clothes of bride and her parents. But now it has gone in thousand in cash and also costly clothes and gift in kind. The prevalence of bride price has social, cultural and economic importance. Well to do families pay more bride price than poor families. In the payment of bride price all relatives of bride groom make some contribution. This custom shows reciprocal cooperation. When divorce takes place, bride price is returned.

Bride price is also reported from the Nuer, Thonga and Bantu tribe of Africa. Nuer have to pay 40 cattle as bride price. In the payment of 40 cattle as a bride price all maternal and paternal kins of bride groom contribute according to their status. The father of girl distributes 40 cattle among all paternal and maternal kins of the bride according to their status. This contribution is based on reciprocity.

Thonga and Bantu call bride price as Lokala. Sheep and blankets prepared from the furs of sheeps are given as bride price. Lokala is distributed among maternal and paternal kins of bride or given as Lokala in the marriage of bride's brother.

In some low caste Hindus, the bride price is also prevalent. This is not considered as good by the society.

Marriage by Service: In some tribal societies marriage mates are obtained by offering service. In this practice, a boy has to go and stay in the house of his 'would be' father-in-law and perform domestic and outside work. He stays there as a family member and tries to please his 'would be' father-in-law and mother-in-law. When they become pleased with the services of the boy they accept him as their son-in-law and get their daughter married to the boy. Thus, by performing satisfactory and excellent services, he acquires a marriage mate. Those boys who are not able to give bride price, they take help of their services in order to get a marriage mate. If the couple has only a daughter he is also adopted by father-in-law to look after during old age. In the tribes of Chota Nagpur Dhangar system is also related to marriage by service.

Marriage by Exchange: In this way of acquiring mates two male individuals of two families acquire marriage mate by exchanging their sisters. Since two families exchange women for the purpose of marriage, this way of acquiring mate is known as marriage by exchange. In Hindu this way of getting marriage mate is known as *Golat Vivah*. In this way of acquiring marriage mate bride price is not required.

Marriage by Elopement: In some cases, some boys and girls do not get permission of their father for the marriage. In this situation, the boy and the girl elope from their houses secretly. They go to an unknown place and reside their as husband and wife. During their stay at a strange place they also procreate children. After a long gap, they come back to their original place of stay. As they become father and mother, the society considers their case sympathetically and accept them as husband wife after purification rituals and feast.

Marriage by Intrusion: In this way of acquiring marriage mate a girl decides to go and stay in the house of a boy whom she selects as her marriage partner. In this attempt she is abused, scolded, beaten and thrown out of the house. But she bear all such insult without any reactions. Family members get tired of abusing and beating her. Finally they accept her as bride for the boy with whom she wants to enter into marital relation.

Divorce Rule in Tribals: Tribals of India have their own rule regarding the divorce. Divorce is allowed theoretically in all tribal societies. It is allowed in case either husband or wife is found guilty of adultery or extra-marital relation, apathy towards rearing and caring children and is not of compromising nature. For the purpose of divorce husband or wife goes to village Panchayat. The members of the Panchayat attempt to make a compromise and give the couple ample time to reconsider their opinion regarding divorce. But when they are not ready to compromise, a final decision regarding the divorce is taken in the Panchayat meeting with consensual decision. The decision of divorce is publically announced. All bride price given at the time of marriage are returned. Now the couple is free and treated separated. Both are free to establish remarriage and lead a fresh marital life with other partners.

When the woman is pregnant divorce is not allowed till she not delivers her child. After delivery the case of divorce is heard and if they are not ready to compromise, divorce is allowed but the child is kept in the custody of mother and the husband has to pay a compensation till the child is minor. When the child becomes major, the child goes in the custody of father.

Hindu Marriage

In Hindu society marriage is regarded as an important *Sanskar*. It is religious duty of parents to get their son or daughter married as soon as they attain marriageable age. The ritual of marriage purifies a boy and girl to hold *dharma* of *Grihastha Ashrama*. In traditional Hindu society, only married man enjoyed the right to participate fully in social and religious activities along with his wife. A widow was not allowed to participate in social and religious performances. A widower was allowed to participate in social and religious performances by putting a symbol of his wife. The main objectives of a Hindu marriage were as follows:

- Performance of religious duty, i.e. *Dharma*.
- Giving birth to children, i.e. *Praja*.
- Sex satisfaction, i.e. *Rati*.

Among all three objectives, observance of *Dharma* was given the greatest importance. It implied that one must marry to fulfil social and religious duties. A married couple is expected to procreate children to carry lineage and family name forward from one generation to next generation. A couple was expected to earn money according to *dharma* to maintain family and hospitality to the guests.

Hindu Marriage—A Sacrament: According to Hindu sacred texts, marriage is a sacrament which purifies a person to hold *Dharma* in *Grihastha Ashram*. It is considered so sacred that there is no scope for divorce in Hindu texts. In fact, marriage is considered a union of two souls which remain faithful to each other for ever or atleast for seven births. Marital rites are performed before the fire God Agni by moving seven times around the fire tank reciting sacred *mantras* by the specialist Brahmin priest. The bride and the bridegroom exchange promises to remain dutiful and faithful to each other. Wellwishers bless the couple for a happy married life. The couple seeks blessing by touching their feet.

Traditional forms of Hindu Marriage: In the traditional Hindu society, the eight forms of marriage have been reported. They were as follows:

- Brahma Vivah
- Daiva Vivah
- Arsha Vivah
- Gandharva Vivah
- Prajapatya Vivah
- Asura Vivah
- Rakshasa Vivah
- Paishach Vivah

Brahma Vivah: In this type of marriage, a father gifted his daughter to a Brahmin, i.e. learned man of good character.

Daiva Vivah: In this form of marriage, a father gifted his daughter to a Brahmin Priest, mediator of God on this earth.

Arsha Vivah: In this form of marriage, a father gifted his daughter in marriage to an *Arsha* (noble man).

Gandharva Vivah: In this form of marriage, a father gifted his daughter to a *Gandharva*, semi God through *swayamvara* ritual.

Prajapatya Vivah: In this form of marriage, a father gifted his daughter to a man through proper negotiation between parents of both sides. Most of marriages in the Hindu are of this nature.

Asura Vivah: In this form of marriage, a father gifted his daughter to an Asur on receiving bride price.

Rakshasa Vivah: In this form of marriage, a man kidnapped and married the girl without her or her parents' consent.

Paishach Vivah: In this form of marriage, the girl was intoxicated and forced to surrender her chastity before a man. The girl was given the status of wife later on.

Muslim Marriage

Muslim marriage, known as *Nikah,* is a civil contract between a man and a woman for the purpose of legalizing sexual relation and procreation of children. In this sense, it is different from Hindu marriage. Muslim marriage contract or agreement can be broken at the will of husband and wife. It can also be broken if either husband or wife fails to fulfil promises made at the time of marriage.

Muslim marriage is solemnized in presence of witness including the Priest-Maulavi. The Maulavi recites holy hymns from *Quran* and asks the bride and the bride groom to give their consent called *Kabula.* The husband has to agree to pay the dowry or the Maher to the wife in case of a divorce.

***Forms of Muslim Marriage*:** The important forms of Muslim marriage are as follows:

- Nikah or Shahi Nikah
- Fasid
- Muta
- Batil

Nikah or Shahi Nikah: The marriage which takes place as per marriage rule of the community is known as regular marriage or *Nikah* or Shahi Nikah.

Fasid: The marriage which fails in fulfilling few conditions initially is known as irregular marriage or Fasid. The irregularity can be removed later on and it can be converted in Shahi Nikah.

Muta: The Muslim call temporary marriages Muta. In this type of marriage contract is valid for a fixed period of time. After the expiry of contract period, marital relation is automatically dissolved. However, children born out of this temporary union get a share in father's property.

Batil: Batil is that form of mating which cannot be regularized because it violates certain basic principles of Muslim marriage.

***Divorce or Dissolution of Muslim Marriage*:** The Muslims have a very simple procedure of divorce. A husband can divorce his wife by paying the dower (*Maher*) promised at the time of marriage as a compensation for the loss of financial stability. This is known as *Talaq*. A wife can also seek divorce from her husband but the husband must agree to her proposal of divorce. Such a divorce is called *Khula* (release).

If husband and wife separate each other by mutual consent, it is called *Mubarak*.

Marriage can also be dissolved by legal means through Muslim Divorce Act, 1939.

Changes in Marriage

Over the years, the institution of marriage has undergone many changes due to various processes of social-cultural change such as urbanization, industrialization, westernization, modernization, secularization and globalization. Important changes in the institution of marriage are as follows:

Change in Form of Marriage: Modern education and Government institutions are encouraging monogamous marriage. As a result—monogamy is the most preferred form of marriage of present day society. It has affected the institution of polygeny and polyandry. The educated boys and girls of polygenous and polyandrous societies are preferring monogamy. After education, they become independent economically and select their monogamous life partner from own choice.

Change in Role of Marriage Negotiator: In traditional society, relatives and friends used to play the role of marriage negotiator. They are locally termed as Aagua or Bertehor. But now-a-days in global society print-media and space media are playing significant role in marriage negotiation.

Change in Preference of Marriage: Previously caste, family, lineage, dowry, beauty were preferred in selection of mate. Now-a-days, status, merit, education, service, business etc. are being taken into consideration for selection of marriage partner.

Change in Endogamy and Exogamy Rule: The Special Marriage Act, 1954 has allowed inter-religious marriages. Now, modern and educated boys are not preferring caste endogamous and clan exogamous partners. They are selecting mates from other caste and religious groups. They are also selecting mates from own clan.

Change in Parent's Role: Previous parents of boys and girls used to play significant role in selection of mate. But now-a-days, their role has decreased. Boys and girls are selecting their mates from their own choice, mutual attraction, same type and same class jobs, similarity of nature. Now caste, class, religion and region are not a hindrance in selection of marriage partners. Thus, role of parents in selection of marriages is decreasing.

Impact on Marriage Rituals: In traditional society, marriage require performance of a series of rituals in the houses of both bride and bride groom. It took much time and more money. Now-a-days, court marriage is preferred form of marriage of present day youth. In Court, marriage is held before marriage officer by signing a legal document. After court marriage a reception party is organized and all wellwisher assemble to bless the couple.

Change in Marriage Age: Now-a-days child marriage has been banned. Girls are attending schools, colleges, technical and management institutes. They are involved in making their career and are occupying several dignified posts. As a result marriage age has gone up. Educated and working girls prefer to get married in late age, i.e. between 25 to 35 years of age.

Change in Value of Divorce: Previously marriage in Hindu was regarded as a religious sacrament and a tie of couple for birth after birth. But Hindu Marriage Act 1955, has permitted divorce among Hindus. Husband and wife can seek divorce legally when they find it difficult to stay together. Legal divorce allows payment of compensation and share in husband's property or salary. As a result, divorce in Hindus is a common phenomenon now-a-days.

Change in Value of Widow Remarriage: Widow Remarriage Act 1865, has permitted widow for remarriage. As a result now-a-days, widowhood is not taken as a life-long curse and sacrifice of life for deceased husband. Rather widows are leading a happy life after remarriage.

Change in Dowry: In traditional society dowry used to play a significant role in marriage. But now-a-days, in place of dowry status, education, merit, business and service are playing significant role.

Change in Arranged Marriage: The present day youth are preferring choice marriage in place of arranged marriage.

Impact of Marriage Dress and Ornaments: In place of traditional dress and ornaments, branded dresses and ornaments are preferred which are too costly.

Impact on Marriage Gift: Now-a-days items of gift has changed. It is now two wheeler, four wheeler, dresses, ornaments and cash. Dowry has touched new heights. Anti-dowry Act is not effective.

Impact on Marriage Entertainment: Now-a-days staging music and modern dances with the permission of administration have come into existence to provide entertainment to guests.

Emergence of Live in Relationship: Now-a-days, in place of marriage, live in relationship has emerged in which adult man and woman can live in relationship with mutual consent. This relationship has sexual contact but avoids pregnancy and procreation of children. Unknowingly when a child is delivered the man has to become the father of the child and to give share in his property to the woman and child.

Emergence of Same Sex Marriage: Now-a-days gay marriages and lesbian marriages have emerged. Such types of marriages were regarded as unnatural, but now they have got legal base.

Change in Couple: Now-a-days inter-caste, inter-religious and inter-regional and interlingual marriages are very common leading to formation of couple of plural caste, religion, language and region.

Chapter 4
Family

Family is the smallest and the basic unit of society. It is an important social group. It is very important for an individual. It is because every individual is born and brought up in a family. An individual can live unmarried, but he cannot survive without a family. With birth of children, the size of family is increased. The family may consist of husband, wife and their children, but sometimes family may consist of a number of relatives of different generations.

Family is the focal point. It is centre around which our whole life revolves. It is centre of our social, cultural, economic, political, religious and health activities. We begin our day with family members. We go out to perform our duty. We come back after completing our duties to be with our family members. When we go to a distant place for some days, we share talks with our family members. We are there physically, but emotionally and mentally we remain in touch of our family members. The desire to be with family reflects the strong emotional bond we share with our family.

Meaning and Definition

Family is the basic social unit. It is a primary social group. In its smaller form family consists of husband, wife and their unmarried children. But in its larger form it consists of relatives of several generations connected to each other through marriage, blood and adoption.

A couple is different from a family. A couple gets status of a family as soon the couple is blessed with children. Thus, a family as a unit gets birth from a couple. The birth of children gives completeness of the family.

A family is an institution and an association both. It is a kin group based on the institution of marriage. It can be defined as a durable association of persons united by marriage, blood or adoption to provide legal status to children and safety of all members.

A family is different from a household. A household need not include only family members. Sometimes, it may include all such persons who may or may not be related to each other, but share the same dwelling unit. The dwelling unit may be a house, apartment or a room. A person living alone in a room or a house or an apartment may be considered as household but not family. Similarly, different friends of same sexes sharing same building or room may be considered as household but not family.

Significance of Family

Family is the most important institution and association. It is found everywhere in every society of the globe. A person can decide to live an unmarried life, but he cannot survive without the support of family.

At the time of birth of a child, a family is there to welcome the child. Family breast feeds the child and takes every care of his health and nutrition. It binds husband, wife and their children in a stable relationship. At the time of birth, a child is just a biological being of bone and meat. But family transforms him into social-cultural being. The family is also known as nursery of human nature. It is because the manners which a family teaches to the child play significant role in the way he reacts to different situations. In other words, we can say that family lays the foundation of human personality.

Family is also known as transmitter of culture from one generation to the next. Culture is man-made and social heritage, it is learnt and acquired. A child acquires culture from his parents and transmit it to his children. In this way, culture goes from generation to the next.

The family satisfies various kinds of needs of family members such as social, cultural, economic, religious, political, psychological, emotional, health and hygiene.

Family is a universal institution. It is found in every part and in every society of the globe. It was in past, it is in present and will continue to exist in future because of its significance. Now-a-days, some institutions have emerged which are trying to perform the functions of a family. Such as nursery school, play schools, hospitals, old age house. But they cannot take the place of a family.

Characteristics of Family

The characteristics of family can be discussed under two headings.

- General characteristics or common characteristics
- Specific characteisitics

Common Characteristics: Common characteristics of family are as follows:

Mating Relation: A family is born when a man and a woman get married according to prescribed social norms. Marriage allows a husband and a wife to enter into socially approved sexual union to satisfy their sex-instinct. Satisfaction of this basic instinct is imperative for a healthy living.

Common Habitation: A common characteristic of family is common habitation. A family provides common residence to all members—husband, wife, children and other relatives.

A Form of Marriage: A family acquires its form according to types of marriage. For example monogamous family, polygenous family, polyandrous family, group marriage family.

Reckoning of Descent: Family is basically a bilateral group made up of husband, wife and relative of both sides. But children inherit family name, title and property of either father or mother depending on the local tradition.

Economic System: Every family has its own economic system to provide shelter, cloth, food, medical treatment and other requirements of all members.

Specific Characteristics of Family: Specific characteristics of family are as follows:

Universality: Family as a social unit is universal. There is not a single society where there is no family. Thereon, behind the universality of family is that it performs many functions for individual and society both. The biological, social, cultural, occupational, political, religious, health, psychological and entertainment functions are performed universally by the family so efficiently and simultaneously that it has become indispensable for everyone. In fact society has not been able to find out an alternative association of family which can perform so many functions at the same time with selfless devotion.

Emotional Basis: Family members are emotionally bound to each other. They provide love, care and protection to each other. They are ready to make any kind of sacrifice for the welfare of family members. Thus, family has emotional basis.

Limited Size: A family is basically made up of a husband, a wife and their unmarried children. It is a small group and its membership is continued to those who are related either by marriage or by blood. Large families are becoming rare day-by-day.

Nuclear Position in Social Structure: Family is regarded as basic or fundamental to all social groupings. In simple as well as advanced societies, the whole social structure is built largely on the basis of family.

Social Regulations: Each family has its own customs, traditions, norms and values. Its members get training to follow them through the process of socialization. Interrelationship and interaction of family members are guided by social and legal regulations.

Permanent and Temporary Nature: The nature of family is permanent as well as temporary both. The family is universal institution. It is found in every society. But an individual family lasts till husband and wife are alive. After their death or divorce, new families of their sons and daughters perpetuate the family name and tradition and the cycle goes on. Thus, the nature of family is both permanent and temporary.

Functions of Family

Family performs a number of functions in the society. An individual and society at large are highly dependent upon the family for the fulfilment of basic requirement. If needs of individual and society are not fulfilled properly, the survival of both will be at risk. The functions performed by family are of great significance. The important functions of family are as follows:

Biological Functions: The family performs following biological functions:

Sexual Gratification: The first and the foremost function of family is sexual gratification of husband and wife in an orderly and socially approved manner.

Procreation of Children: The next biological function of family is procreation of children to continue family, lineage, clan and his ethnic group.

Breastfeeding and Caring: After procreation of children, the next biological function of family is rearing the child on breastfeeding and then with supplementary food. Supplementary feeding goes even after the period of breastfeeding till a child becomes young. The family looks after the child and make him to enter from one stage of life to another stage.

Maintenance of Health and Hygiene: Family maintains health and hygiene of family members right from new borns to old ones. Physical care and protection is a very important biological function of family. It is said that the mother is first doctor who scientifically recognizes the diseases of children and attempts to cure them by folk medicine. When folk medicine is not effective she visits doctors for the treatment of the diseases of children. The family nourishes all members and provides food materials according to requirement of different age and sex groups and ill persons.

Social Function: The family performs a number of social functions. It socializes the child and makes him a social being. It develops in him social qualities so that he could lead a social life with prestige. The family controls the anti-social behaviour of its members. The family provides a name, lineage, descent, clan and title to the member. The family makes member aware about their status in the society.

Cultural Function: The family inculcates beliefs, attitudes, traditions, customs, habits, manner, knowledge, art, moral values etc. These cultural traits are transmitted from one generation to the next.

Economic Function: The family performs economic functions by meeting the requirements of food, cloth, residence, division of labour, paternal occupation, treatment of diseases and other requirements which are related to day-to-day expenditure. The family is unit of production and unit of consumption in simple society. Family provides assets and liabilities to dependants.

Religious Function: The family performs religious functions. It makes members aware about *Kul Devi* (Lineage Goddess) and *Kul Devata* (Lineage God), the manner of worship to them, other deities of its religion, festivals, religious fairs and pilgrimage. Father and mother observe fasts for welfare of children and their alround development.

Psychological Function: The family provides emotional support, security and stability to its members. It takes care of members in both good time and bad time.

Entertainment Function: The family also performs entertainment function. When a husband comes back from work, his wife appears before him laughing and offers food and water. Both husband and wife plays with their children with various types of games. They tell stories of various types, sing songs, tell proverbs, riddles and a number of verbal and action jokes. Such a pleasant environment provides entertainment to family members.

Educative Function: It is generally said that the education of children starts from the family. The family is primary school and mother is its first teacher. A child learns about names of different relatives, plants, animals, natural objects, man-made objects from family. They acquire social virtues, good habits, manners and behaviour in family.

Political Function: The family also performs political functions. Each family has a head who may be generally husband. He represents his family in Village Panchayat and other ceremonies, social and religious occasions. He takes family level decision with the consent of his wife. He also involves his children in family level decision if they are young.

Types of Family

The form of family is not same all-over the globe. Different societies of the world have different types of family. Difference in forms of family is due to geographical, social, cultural, economic and political situation of different societies. On the basis of number, authority, residence, inheritance, descent, marriage and status of an individual during birth and marriage; forms of families are as follows:

Forms of Family on the Basis of Number of Family Members

On the basis of number of family members, the different forms of family are as follows:

Nuclear Family: This is a smallest form of a family which consists of husband, wife and their unmarried children.

Compound Family: This is a polygamous form of family. It can be classified into three categories:

Polyandrous Compound Family: This form of family consists of a wife, her all husbands and all unmarried children.

Polygenous Compound Family: This type of family consists a husband, his all wives and his all unmarried children.

Compound Family of Widow-Widower Remarriage: In this form of compound family remarried widow and widower live along with their own children as well as unmarried children born from previous marriages.

Joint Family: A form of family which consists of father's family, father's brother's family, married son's families or married daughter's families. In fact it is a family of several nuclear families. Common residence, common hearth and common head are its chief characteristics. Joint family may be of following types:

Patrilineal Joint Family: In this type of joint family, families of several married sons descended from the same father or a male reside together.

Matrilineal Joint Family: In this type of joint family, families of several married daughters descended from the same mother or a female reside together.

Avunculocal Joint Family: In this type of joint family, families of mother's brothers and sister's married sons or daughters reside together.

Amitatal Joint Family: In this type of joint family, father's sister's family and brother's married sons or daughters family reside together.

Extended Family: Extended family consists of several joint and nuclear families whose residences are located nearby each other and who corporate each other during joys and sorrows. For example lineage and clan.

Form of Family on the Basis of Residence: The rule of residence decides the stay of bride and bridegroom after marriage. On the basis of practices of residence of bride and bride groom, the family may be classified into following forms:

Matrilocal Family: In this form of family, a bridegroom has to leave his father's village and stay in the house of mother-in-law with bride. For example Nayar of Malabar, Garo and Khasi of Assam.

Patrilocal Family: In this type of family, a bride has to leave the house of her father and stay in the house of father-in-law. This is a very common practice among Hindus and majority of tribals.

Neolocal Family: When bride and bridegroom stay in a new house erected by either father of bridegroom or mother of bride or by a husband himself or a wife herself, this form of family is known as Neolocal family.

This type of residence is very common in Baiga tribe of Madhya Pradesh and Chhattisgarh, Korwa of Jharkhand, Sauria Paharia of

Santhal Pargana and a number of tribes of country. It is because marriage requires at least a room for the stay of couple. Therefore, it is duty of parents to erect a new room with the help of their kin for the stay of newly married couple. This type of residence is also being practiced in urban and metropolitans.

Bilocal: In this type of residence, husband and wife stay at two places. In this residence practice husband stays in his own father's house and wife stays in her own parents house. But this type of residence is practical when marriage is held in the same village or nearby village. During night husband visits to stay with wife but during day time he comes back in his own house. Sometimes, wife come to stay in the house of husband during night and goes to her own house during day time. Such type of practice is very common among Ashanti tribe of Africa.

Verilocal: When a bride goes to stay with the bridegroom in his own house, it is known as verilocal residence.

Uxorilocal: When a bridegroom goes to stay with the bridegroom in her own erected house, it is known as Uxorilocal residence.

In these both types of residences, father-in-law and mother-in-law are absent or no more.

Ambhilocal: Sometimes, the residence of bride and bridegroom is not clear. This happens particularly in those cases when bride and groom do not have parents alive and they have been brought up by their maternal uncle or paternal uncle. In this case, the residence of bride and the bridegroom is not prefixed. They have to live sometimes with maternal uncle and sometimes with paternal uncle.

Changing Residence: When the residence of bride and the bridegroom is changing, it is called changing residence. In this case, the couple live for a fixed period at one place, i.e. six months in the house of husband and other six months in the house of wife.

On the basis of Authority: On the basis of authority, family can be divided into following types:

Matriarchal Family: In this type of family authority lies in the hand of mother or a woman. For example Garo and Khasi.

Patriarchal Family: In this type of family authority lies in the hand of father or a man. For example majority of Hindu, tribal and Muslim families.

On the Basis of Inheritance: On the basis of inheritance family is divided into following types:

Matrilineal Family: In this form of family inheritance of property goes from mother to daughter or daughters. For example Garo and Khasi of Assam. This is a special feature of matriarchal family.

Patrilineal Family: In this form of family inheritance of property goes from father to son or sons. This is special feature of patriarchal society.

On the basis of Descent: On the basis of descent, forms of family are as follows:

Matrilineal or Matrilateral Family: In this type of family descent is traced through mother or a woman. Male members are not included in descent-group. This is feature of matriarchal society.

Patrilineal or Patrilateral Family: In this type of family, descent is traced through father or a man. Female members are not included in this descent group. This is feature of patriarchal family.

Double descent family: When descent is traced through both father and mother side, such type of family is known as double descent family. For example: Adistan islanders.

On the basis of Marriage: On the basis of forms of marriage, family may be divided into following forms:

Monogamous Family: This form of family appears due to the practice of monogamous marriage.

Polygenous Family: This form of family is formed due to the practice of polygenous marriage.

Polyandrous Family: This form of family is formed due to the practice of polyandrous marriage.

Group Marriage Family: This form of family is formed due to the practice of group marriage.

On the basis of Childhood status and Marital Status: On the basis of childhood status and marital status, an individual belongs to two types of family:

Family of Orientation: A family in which an individual is born as a son or a daughter.

Family of Procreation: A family in which an individual is husband or wife and procreate children.

***Processual forms of Family*:** The family has following processual forms:

Premarital Stage: In this stage; attraction of individuals towards individuals of opposite sexes takes place.

Marital Stage: In this stage, two individuals of opposite sexes are tied together as husband and wife (couple) through marriage.

Child Rearing Stage: In this stage, husband and wife procreate children and share the duties of rearing and caring them.

Maturity Stage: In this stage, the biological function of a couple is completed. They hand down the responsibility of family on their married sons or married daughters.

Evolution of Family

American anthropologist L.H. Morgan in his book, "System of Consanguinity and Affinity in Human Family" (1870) has discussed that the family has passed through five evolutionary stages. They are as follows:

Consanguine Family: The form of family in the beginning was consanguineal. The concept of taboo on sex relation between blood relatives or incest taboo was not developed. No rule regarding sex relation was established. As a result consanguine family came into existence.

Group marriage Family: This was the next stage in the development of family. This form of family had emerged due to the emergence of practice of group marriage.

Syndasmian Family: In this stage of family, a man was married to a woman but he was free to have sexual relation with other woman married to his brothers.

Patriarchal Family: In this stage of family, a man had authority over the family. He was free to have more than one wife.

Monogamous Family: This is the most evolved form of family. This family emerged due to the initiation of the practice of monogamy.

Characteristics of Joint Family

A family is a small but essential community of human society which includes father, mother and their children and justifiable division of love and responsibility.

A joint-family is a family of families bound together through blood and marriage. Its members live under one roof, eat food cooked at one hearth by one hand, hold property in common, participate in common worship and share joys and sorrows together. Thus, a joint family has following characteristics:

Common house to live: In this type of family, several families live together under one roof. They have common house. There is no need of erecting a separate house for all families sharing a common residence in joint family.

Cooking of Food at One Hearth: The members of joint family share food cooked at one hearth by one hand. As soon as cooking of food starts at several hearths in the same building dissolution of joint family takes place.

Common Property: All families under joint family system have property in common. They have common house, homestead land and agricultural land. They have common cattle wealth, tree wealth, pond wealth, wells, hand pumps and latrine.

Common Head: The joint family is characterized by a common head. The head of joint family is generally senior male member of the family in case of patriarchal family. He controls the behaviour of all members and fulfils the requirement of all members.

Common Worship: As all families of a joint family have same religion, therefore, they have common worship of deities and celebration of festival.

Related by Blood and Marriage: Joint family has all members either related through blood or marriage.

Merits of Joint Family

A joint family has following merits:

Economic Stability: This is first merit of a joint family. There is economic stability in joint family during troublesome periods. Even after death of a member, his widow and children have economic stability. If a member becomes disable due to accident or other reason, he or she is cared properly in joint family.

Useful for Agricultural Country: Joint family system is useful for agricultural country like India. It is because agriculture requires more manpower to do and look after works related to agriculture. As joint family has more members, so agricultural work is performed properly at low expenditure.

Helpful in development of merits of an Ideal citizen: Joint family is helpful in development of merits of an ideal citizen. Love, Sympathy, Service, Selfless, Sacrifice are merits of an ideal citizen. The joint family develops such merits in their members under the discipline of a common head. Members of individual family lack this merit. An individual has to work for the good of the joint family. Thus, joint family plays significant role in ideal citizenship building.

Comparatively Less Expensive: The joint family is less expensive than the individual family. As a number of families live together under one roof, and share the same house, same food, and same servant. But in individual family, each family has to erect house, cook food and have servant separately. Thus, joint family is comparatively less expensive.

Facility of Division of Labour: The joint family has facility of division of labour. Some members do agriculture, some members look after cattle, some members are engaged in purchase and sale of commodities, some are engaged in looking after kids, women are engaged in cooking and serving food. The joint family is organized on the principle of division of labour. All works are performed properly and in time.

Social Insurance for Family Members: Joint family provides social security to its family members. The family has property in common. Therefore, aged, widow and her children and other disabled members of the family are taken care of properly from the same and common source of income. Thus, joint family system works as a social insurance for the members.

Protection of land from division and sub-division: Joint family system does not allow further division and sub-divisions of homestead land and agricultural land. Division of lands into small plots create a number of problems in doing agriculture.

Prestige of Family: Joint family has special prestige in the society. Joint family has experienced, able and skillful members. Its family size is big. Therefore, it enjoys special prestige and respect in the society. No other family tries to enter into conflict and quarrel with joint family.

Discipline and Control Over Member: The head of the joint family imposes strict discipline over family members and puts strict control over behaviour of all family members.

Occasion to Serve Nation: As joint family has a number of members, some members get opportunity to serve the nation.

Demerits of Joint Family

There is no doubt that Joint Family System has a number of merits, but it has some demerits, too. Demerits of joint family are as follows:

Hindrance in the Development of Personality: As joint family imposes strict and over discipline and control over its members, therefore, it creates hindrance in proper development of personality of members. Members do not have freedom to speak, express and work. This is most important demerits of a joint family.

Idleness and Lack of Responsibility: Majority of members of a joint family become idle. Only some members go on working, while other members spend their time in gossip and indoor games. They do not like to share their responsibility of any kind. They claim their rights only but not share responsibility. They create hindrance in proper functioning of a joint family.

Centre of Quarrel: In joint family there is more prevalence of jealousy and conflicts. It is seen that different members have different nature, interest, clash of nature and interest takes place which gives rise to various types of quarrels. Thus, joint family system becomes centre of quarrels. Every individual claims his/her rights but not share any kind of responsibility.

Anti-progress: The joint family is anti-progress because it does not fulfil the requirement of all members due to its limited resources and income and dictatorship of head.

Not Favourable for Higher Education: Joint family is not favourable for higher education of children. Till school education children get education free of cost, but after secondary education children require more and more money for college and technical education. As head of the family has to run family in limited resources and income, he does not provide expenses of higher education. He is also not able to provide school education in private or public schools.

Shelter of Court Cases: At the time of division of property, members of the family have to file cases in court when it becomes impossible to solve the problem through Panch or Village Panchayat. Thus, joint family becomes shelter of court cases. Sometimes, murder and physical assault also takes place for division of property.

Bad Condition of Woman: In joint family system, the condition of women is very bad. They are treated only as a machine of child production and household chors including cooking breakfast and food. They do not find sufficient time to share with their husbands. They are not given any facility and freedom.

Lack of Family Planning: In joint family system members do not have control over procreation of children. As they get sufficient food to eat and space to live, they go on procreating. As a result the size of family becomes very big and head becomes unable to fulfil all requirements of all members.

Due to above demerits decline in joint family is taking place rapidly. Previously, sons used to wait for the division of joint family so long as their parents were alive. Now-a-days, separation of joint family is taking place even in the life time of parents. Joint family is disintegrating and individual family is increasing.

Conditions Essential for a Good Family Life

For leading a good family life, the following conditions are essential:

Education: For a good family life, it is essential to become its all members educated. Education is mother of all merits. Education makes our views humanistic and our feeling very liberal. Uneducated parents do not understand the feeling and attitude of their children. As a result development of children does not take place properly. The educated parents are capable of knowing the attitude and feeling of their children. They provide full affection and love to their children and guide them properly. As a result proper development of children takes place. It is truly said that educationless men are like animals.

Reciprocal Love, Cooperation and Tolerance: For a good and ideal family life, sense of reciprocal love, cooperation and tolerance among members is a must. Ideal and good family life is based on these merits. The love between husband and wife, between brother and sister and affection between parents and children are essential for family life. Cooperation between different members of the family is also essential. Family life becomes hell in absence of family cooperation and unity. Tolerance among family members is also a must. In family-members of different nature and opinions reside together, therefore, a coordination is essential to run the family smoothly. Through coordination and tolerance clash of nature and opinion can be removed. In this way, for an ideal family life reciprocal love, cooperation and tolerance is a must.

Economic Stability: For a good and ideal family life economic stability is also a must. The economic condition of family must be such that proper rearing and caring of members could take place. The family income should be such as to provide food, shelter, clothes, education and treatment expenses of all family members. Without fulfilling these needs of all members, a good and ideal family life can not be expected. It is useless to expect civilization, culture and morality from an individual who suffers from starvation. Poverty leads towards the pit of fall to individual and society both. Thus, for an ideal family life, the family income must be such as to provide the basic minimum needs of all members.

Good Residence: For an ideal family life good residence is must. Good residence means healthy and airy house. Airy house provides good health to its members. To be healthy is a must for spiritual, mental and physical development of man.

Willing to Work: Willing to work is essential for a good family life. Every member must be dutiful. Every member must be ready to do his duty according to power and ability.

Small Family Size: For an ideal family life, family size should be small, not big. Big family has many children which create problem in rearing and caring due to limited income. Proper education of children also does not take place in big family. As a result proper development of children does not take place. Thus, for an ideal family life, family size should be small.

Proper Respect of Women: For ideal family life proper respect of women should be given. The real success of family lies in the hand of women. Women are builder of family, society and nation. They are first teacher, first doctor, birth giver, life builder and fate builder. Therefore, for an ideal family life proper respect should be given to women. It has been truly said that where women are worshipped, gods reside there.

Familial Coordination: For proper family life coordination among members of the family is a must. There should not be clash of ego, nature and opinion.

Change in Family

Like other institutions, the institution of family is also not static, rather it is changing. The institution of family has undergone change. Change in family can be discussed under the following heading as below. A number of processes have contributed towards change in family such as urbanization, industrialization, westernization, modernization, globalization and feminist movement.

Change in Family size: Now-a-days, family size has undergone change. Involvement of couple in various modern occupations, long time period required for conception, delivery, rearing and caring children, heavy expenditure at the time of delivery and rearing and expensive education have forced to make a change in family size. Now-a-days, majority of couples want only one baby. To-day the slogan like *Ham Do Hamare Do* (We are two and one must procreate two) has changed. It has changed to *Ham Do, Hamare Ek* (we are two but we should procreate one baby). As a result the size of family has been reduced. Youth of to-day believe in eat, drink and be merry. It is possible either live in relation or by procreation of only one child.

Change in Form of Family: Individual family is choice of the present-day people. Even in villages where main mean of livelihood is agriculture and joint family is most suitable for agriculture, preference is being given to individual family. It is because joint family is not catering the educational need of children at least of higher stage due to heavy expenditure. But individual family is encouraging their children to achieve higher educational degree for present-day global job markets. For this, head of individual family is taking loan from the banks and other agencies. Thus, joint family is rapidly disintegrating and individual family is the need of the present-day because the youth wants to establish marriage after completing career and achieving suitable jobs. Number of single parents family is increasing.

Change in Educational Status: The educational status of members has undergone change. Now education is being provided to all members including girl children. Education is being preferred at the time of marriage in family. Educated couples are increasing in family. Education has been able to eradicate a number of taboos imposed particulary on girls and women of the family.

Change in Occupational Status of Family: Due to modern education and urbanization and industrialization, the occupational status of family has changed. An occupational mobility has taken place. Now it is not necessary to carry on traditional occupation in family. Now each family is free to go in service, business and other types of modern jobs. Now-a-days, a number of family has husbands and wife both employed. Educated women are now not confined to work as house wife. They are also doing their jobs on prestigious posts. Instead of cooking food, they are preferring to visit restaurants. Engagement of women in jobs has raised the family income and standard of living. Such family has big modern home, modern furniture and all accessories in different rooms of the house. They travel on costly car, A.C. ticket in train and on plane tickets. They are wearing costly dresses and ornaments. They have a number of servants for performing different kinds of work. They are being empowered socio-economically and independently by NGOs.

Change in Status of Women: Now-a-days, women are enjoying equal status. A number of taboos imposed on them regarding education, age of marriage and marriage rituals have become non-functional due to several laws protecting the interest of women. Now girls are going to school, colleges and technical institutions independently. They are doing jobs at several places and living in hostels or rented houses or in shared houses with a group of girls-friends. Women are being empowered in the family socially, economically, politically and independently. They are being treated as asset not as a liability. All such developments have brought a change in the status of women in the family.

Existence of Inter-caste and Inter-religious Marriage Family: In urban, industrial and metropolitans families having husbands and wives from different castes and religions are increasing. Now, kins are not limited to own caste and religion. They rather belong to different castes and religions. This is playing a very positive role in establishing peace and harmony in different communities. This, kind of practice is also developing secularism in family and society.

Change in Residence of Family: Now the residence is not only patri-local and matri-local in family. A number of families are neo-local and practicing changing residence because they have to migrate from one place to another for jobs.

Change in Religious Practices: Traditional families are religion bound but modern families are preferring secularism. They are believing in court marriage in place of customary marriage. Couples are of different caste and religious background and they observe customs and festivals of each other. Remaining on fast, observing worship of different Gods and Goddesses, visiting to pilgrim-centres, visiting to temples daily and other religious place do not form daily routine of present-day couples. They prefer to visit to sacred places as tourist not as devotees. Religious observances in present-day family are decreasing.

Change in Political Status of Family: Now-a-days, Panchayati Raj Institutions have emerged. This has created political awareness among rural families. Women are also now emerging as Panchayat leaders, Ward members, Mukhiya, Sarpanch, Panchayat Samiti members, and Zila Parishad Chairman. Election of women on these posts have changed the political status of those families who acquired very low status in society. With these developments, concepts of Mukhiya Pati and Mukhiya Putra have emerged in the family and society. In traditional tribal societies, women were not followed to participate in village Panchayat. They were represented by their father, son or brother. But now-a-days, they are being elected as leader on different posts in Gram Panchayat election.

Lack of Discipline and Control in Family: Emergence of more and more individual families have resulted in lack of discipline and control over family members, particularly children. Husbands and wives have their own jobs or business. Children become free either to play or study. They are given pocket money. They fall in bad companion and become victim of drug addiction, juvenile delinquency and sexual abuse. They do not obey their parents.

Lack of Emotion and Affection in Family: Now-a-days, emotion and affection are lacking. It is because parents do not have time to sit, to talk, to gossip, to share views and emotions, share breakfast and dinner together and to understand the problems of each other. As a result children are lacking emotional and affectional attachment.

Family not as Unit of Production and Consumption: Now-a-days, due to emergence of urban and industrial occupation, the unit of production and consumption has changed from family to individual. Individuals are now unit of production and consumption.

Emergence of Some Institutions to Perform the Function of Family: Now-a-days, some institutions have come into existence which are trying to perform the functions of family. For example play schools, nursery schools, crèche, day care centre, oldage home, nursing homes, hotels, hostels, restaurant, bank, club and so on. These agencies are reducing the functions of family. However, it is very difficult to find emotional support and selfless devotion elsewhere as in family.

Increase in Physical and Mental Distance between Family Members: With the arrival of industrial system of production, family is now no more unit of production in most of societies. Family members have to look for jobs outside home. Husbands and wives are performing jobs at different places and they do not find sufficient time to share feelings and emotions with each other. In case of house wives, they have to share responsibility of looking after of children and their education because their husbands do jobs far away from house. This change in family has increased physical and mental distance between family members.

Instability Problem: Present day family is also facing the problem of instability. Now-a-days, separation and divorce is very common in every society. This has increased in the single family, children are worst victim of this practice.

Artificial Behaviour in Family: Now-a-days, artificial behaviours are very common. Hello, hay, ya, dad, mom, mam terms are used frequently. Speaking these terms are taken as pride. Natural behaviour are not found among family members.

Existence of DINK Family: DINK means double income no kids family. Now-a-days, a number of married and employed couples are preferring not to have children despite sufficient financial stability. They consider children as liability on them. That is why they do not want to reproduce any kids.

Change in Means of Entertainment: The present-day families have modern means of entertainment like T.V., Computer, Cell phones and indoor games. Its members visit parks, tourist spots, restaurants, clubs etc. for entertainment on holidays.

But in spite of all such changes in family, the family will continue in future because of its universal functions. No institution claiming to perform the functions of a family can provide emotional support and selfless devotion to family members. They have emerged to fill-up their own pockets in the name of function of family. Therefore, future of family is bright and no institution can fill-up the gap left by a family in the life of an individual.

Domestic Group: The concept of domestic group is a western concept. This concept involves a group of such families who do not share the same house, do not share the food cooked by the same hand on same hearth, do not have common property and common head. Rather this group includes such a group of families whose houses are situated close to each other. Each family has its own house, own number of family, own land, own property and own head. But each family cooperates with other families in fulfilment of certain purposes of production and consumption. Domestic group is an economic unit because its formation is closely related to cooperation in production and consumption. The concept of domestic group should not be confused with the concept of joint and extended family.

Kibbutz: A unique family system found in Israel where 50 to 2000 people reside as community. It exists as a community of families and individuals which cooperates in raising children. Children reside in children's home away from parents. Each Kibbutz operates as a house where children are treated as responsibility of whole community. Parents and children live in separate residences. Parents and children meet with each other at weekend.

Chapter 5
Kinship System

Man is a social animal. As a social animal we start our living in family. In family we find family members whom we call by different names like father, mother, brother, sister, Grandfather, Grandmother and so on. Who are they? They are our kins related through blood or they have genetic relations. Again after marriage of a member in family, names like father-in-law, mother-in-law, brother-in-law, sister-in-law, i.e. *Devar-bhabhi*, *Jija-Sala*, *Jija-Sali* and so on come into existence. Who are they? They are also our kins related through marriage. Thus, we find that kins are those persons who are related to each other through blood or marriage. Kins related through blood are known as consanguineal kins and kins related through marriage are known as affinal kins.

In society we have relationship with a number of persons. But the most of these relationships is known as kinship. Thus, kinship is relationship based on parentage and marriage. Bride and bridegroom come from two families through the relation of marriage. But after becoming couple they are treated as *blood relation*. Adopted sons and daughters are also included under the category of *blood relation*. In some societies, cross-cousins and parallel cousins are treated as *blood relations*, while in some other societies they are regarded as potential marriage partner and not treated as blood relative.

Kinship system is a system of relationships based on parentage (blood) and marriage.

Explanations of Kinship Terms

Before discussing the various aspects of kinship system in detail, it will be the fitness of the thing here to present explanations of some terms used in kinship system:

Kin: A person related to other persons or *vice-versa* through blood or marriage is called a kin. The kins are of two types: consanguineal kins and affinal kins.

Consanguineal Kins: The kins related genetically or through blood are known as consanguineal kins.

Affinal Kins: Kins related through marriage are known as affinal kins.

Couple: Two or more individuals of opposite sexes tied as couple either through customary rituals or through legal procedure of court for the purpose of cohabitation and procreation of children are termed as couple. Based upon the forms of marriage, a couple may be classified as Monogamous, Polygenous, Polyandrous and group marriage couple.

Siblings: The children or offsprings of a couple are called siblings. The siblings may be divided into two category: Full siblings and half siblings.

Full Siblings: Full siblings are children of same husband and same wife or same father and same mother.

Half Siblings: Half siblings are children of same father and different mothers or same mother and different fathers. Half siblings may be divided into two: maternal half siblings and paternal half siblings.

Maternal half siblings: The children of same mother and different fathers.

Paternal half siblings: Children of same father and different mothers.

Cousins: Children of two siblings are called cousins. Cousins are of two types: Cross cousins and Parallel cousins.

Cross cousins: Children of two siblings of opposite sexes are known as cross-cousin. For example children of a brother and a sister.

Parallel cousins: Parallel cousins are children of two siblings of same sex. For example children of two sisters and children of two brothers.

Kindered: All paternal and maternal kins of a person are termed as kindered.

Stock: All descendants of a couple tracing descent from both father and mother's sides are called stock. The stock has both patrilineal and matrilineal descent.

Collateral kins: The kins related in horizontal lines are called collateral kins. For example brother-brother, sister-sister and brother-sister.

Kinship Rule

The rule by which kinship is established is known as kinship rule: Rules related to kinship are as follows:

Consanguineal Rule: According to this rule, kinship is established on the basis of blood relation. This rule is based on genetic or biological relation. It is held that blood of parents is transferred to offspring through the process of copulation and procreation. This relation continues from generation to generation. Formation of couple is starting point of this relationship. Husband and wife come from two families and are of different blood, but after marriage they become blood relative. Their offsprings are also related to their blood. Blood relationship includes both ascendants and descendants. Thus, couple sibling, family, lineage and clan are kin groups based on blood relation.

Exception to Consanguineal Rule: There are some customs prevalent in different societies of the world by which some persons are included as blood relative, though he or she is not related through blood. For example adopted son, adopted daughter, children born from proxy or ghost marriages and polyandrous marriages.

Adopted son or daughter is not related to parents through real blood relation, but he or she is accepted socially as blood relative of parents who inherit them.

Among Khas of Deharadun area polyandrous marriage is practiced. All brothers who are descendants of a couple marry with the same women, but as per custom of Khasa society the eldest brother is father of all children born to the common wife, though he may not be the biological father of all children.

Similarly, Tharu of Tharuhat region of Tarai area, the eldest brother is recognized as father of all children born to a common wife of all brothers.

As per the custom of Kota of Nilgiri, a woman has more than one husband at a time and all husbands of a woman are not brothers. The children born to her may have different biological father, but a husband who performs last armorial presentation of bow and arrow to the common wife is regarded as father of all children born to her, though he may not be biological father of all children.

Among Nuer of Africa, there is a practice of Ghost marriage in which a male member of the community marries with a woman in the name of a deceased male to continue his progeny. He remains as couple and procreates children. But the deceased male member is regarded as father of all children born to a woman who marries with a male member in the name of Ghost. This is also known as Proxy marriage.

Extension of Consanguineal Rule: Couple, sibling, individual family, lineage and clan show definitely an extension of blood relation in different societies. But the extension of blood relation in joint family and cousins is not similar in all societies of the globe. There are societies where cousins are treated as blood relative and they cannot be marriage partners. But there are some societies where cousins are not treated as blood relatives, rather they are treated as potential marriage partners. In these societies extension of blood relation is not found up to cousins. For example, South Indian Brahmins and Muslims.

Affinal Rule: According to this rule, kinship is established through marriage following marriage rules of the society concerned. Now-a-days, in place of custom, court is preferred for the marriage purpose. Following types of marriage rules are practiced:

- Endogamy
- Exogamy
- Monogamy
- Polygeny
- Polyandry
- Preferred rule

The marriage establishes not only kinship between bride and bridegroom, but all members of bride family and bridegroom family are related to each other and are designated by kinship terms. For example husband, wife, father-in-law, mother-in-law, brother-in-law, son-in-law, sister-in-law, daughter-in-law, i.e. *Jija-Sala*, *Jija-Sali* etc. are kins related through the marriage.

Category of Kin

On the basis of nearness and distance kins may be categorized into following types:

- Primary kin
- Secondary kin
- Tertiary kin

Primary Kins: The kins who are directly related to each other are termed as primary kins. In this type an ego is directly related to his/her kins. According to Murdock, there are eight types of primary kins: Husband-wife, father-son, father-daughter, mother-son, mother-daughter, brother-brother, sister-sister and brother-sister. These kins are directly related to each other without any medium. That is why they are known as primary kins. They are regarded as very near to each other.

Secondary Kins: Primary kins of an ego's primary kins are termed as secondary kins. There is no direct relation between secondary kins because they are related directly to our primary kins. There one finds a distance between secondary kins. Secondary kins do not show nearness as Primary Kins have. According to Murdock, there are 33 Secondary Kins. For example Grandfather, Grandson, Graddaughter, Grandmother, brother's wife, sister's husband, wife's brother, wife's sister, husband's brother, husband's sister etc.

Tertiary Kins: The primary kins of our secondary kins or secondary kins of our primary kins are termed as tertiary kins. Here distance between tertiary kins are more than secondary kins. According to Murdock, there are 151 types of tertiary kins of an ego or an individual. For example our brother-in-law's wife or his children are our tertiary kins because brother-in-law's wife or children are his primary kins and brother-in-law is our secondary kins. Similarly, father's, brother's wife, father's sister's husband, father's mother's brother, father's mother's sister are also examples of tertiary kins.

In this way, the degree of kinship may be extended to 4th, 5th, 6th and..... nth degree.

Function of Kinship

Kinship is significant in a number of ways for an individual and society. It is most researched topics in anthropology right from beginning of anthropological researches. It is because it has played significant role in social organization and formulating rules regarding formation of kin groups and establishing control over them. The functions of kinship can be discussed under the following headings:

- Biological function
- Social function
- Economic function

- Religious function
- Political function
- Cultural function
- Psychological function
- Security function
- Control function
- Entertainment function
- Legal function

Biological function: The biological functions of kinship are satisfaction of sex, procreation of children and rearing them. Kinship establishes marital relation between two or more individuals of opposite sexes. Kinship binds them as couple and provide sanction for satisfaction of sex and reproduction of children. It bestows responsibility on couple of rearing and caring of children born out of their sexual union.

Social function: Kinship provides social status and role of individuals. An individual attains status as son or daughter, bride or bridegroom, husband or wife, father-in-law or mother-in-law, brother-in-law or sister-in-law, grand-father or grand-mother etc. Each individual has to perform role according to his/her status in different age cycle. This is very important social function.

Another important social function of kinship is that it provides a family name, lineage name and clan name to individuals born.

The third important social function of kinship is that it has brought the concept of social organization for the fulfilment of various kins of needs of individual and society.

Kinship is cradle to graveyard social arrangement where kins participate in joys and sorrows together. Kinship plays significant role in socialization of children. It inculcates social qualities in children.

Economic function: The kinship has given birth to rules of inheritance of property which vary from society to society. In majority of societies, it is patrilineal, but some socieiteis also practice matrilineal inheritance. In simple society kin group family, lineage and clan participate in production, consumption, exchange, trade and market. Kinship has also brought to the light the concept of reciprocity, gift and hospitality. Well placed kins make an attempt to pull and push their kins in matter of education, job and business. They help each other by paying cash or kind.

Religious function: Kinship has religious function, too. The family, lineage and clan have common family-deity whom they call *Kuldevata* and *Kuldevi*. They offer worship to their deity together. They celebrate their festival together. They follow the common religious taboo.

Political function: Kinship has given birth to political control over kins. Traditional society is kinship based where several families of same lineage and clan reside together. In order to control the behaviour of kins, kinship has brought in to light the concepts of family head, lineage head, clan head and village head. Through these institutions, the kinship governs and controls the behaviour of kin groups. It has also brought the concept of reward, compensation and punishment to its members when they work according to social sanction or against social sanction.

Cultural function: Kinship is centre of cultural activities. Life cycle rituals, social functions and religious festivals are full of cultural activities where different kins sing and dance together, gossip together and term each other by different names and terms of address and terms of reference. On different occasions, kins exchange reciprocal visits, gift and hospitality.

Psychological function: Kinship fulfils psychological functions for kins. A number of emotional needs are satisfied through kinship. It is because kinship provides emotional support to kins during miseries and trouble. They call each other by kinship terms and are always ready to extend support to each other through services, money, material and kind.

Security function: Man is a social animal and in his kinship based society he feels secure. It is because in kins group he feels extra strength and support. Other groups cannot cause harm to him.

Control function: Kinship provides control function. Kin group head controls the behaviour of all its members. For right work it extends rewards and for wrong work it imposes compensation, compromise and punishment.

Entertainment function: Kinship also performs entertainment function. Joking relatives cut jokes with each other through verbal and action behaviour. Parents and grant-parents tell stories, proverbs, riddles etc. to children which provide entertainment to them.

Legal function: The kinship provides sexual union and children born out of this union get a legal status in the society. It also provides legal status to inheritance and succession.

Kinship Terminology

An American anthropologist L.H. Morgan in his book, "League of Iroquis" (1851) has divided kinship terminology into two types:

- Classificatory Kinship Terminology
- Descriptive Kinship Terminology

Classificatory Kinship Terminology: In this type of terminology, a class of relatives are termed by the same name. For example father-in-law, mother-in-law, brother-in-law, sister-in-law, son-in-law, daughter-in-law, cousin, *Samadhi*, *Samadhin*, uncle-aunt, grandfather, grand mother, grand son, grand daughter etc. These are classificatory terms because the same term is used for a class of relatives.

Descriptive Kinship Terminology: In this type of terminology, the particular term describes a particular relation. Thus, each relative has a separate name. For example Father, mother, brother, sister, son, daughter. In Hindi we have majority of descriptive terms.

According to Morgan, classificatory and descriptive terminologies reveal the evolutionary status of kinship terminology. In the beginning there was classificatory kinship terminology by which a group of relatives were called by the same term. Descriptive kinship terminologies are evolved form of kinship terminology.

Terms of Reference: The terms of reference are those terms by which kins are referred to in day-to-day talk by their relatives. In this system real term of kins are used while they are referred to. For example Father, mother, brother, sister, son, daughter etc. These terms refer to the exact relation of a kin who is referring to. For example my father has done this. Her mother has come here. His brother is going. His sister is eating apple. His wife is educated. His daughters are very beautiful. My son-in-law is well placed. Her daughter-in-law is doing job. His sister is very clever. My daughters are my strength. My son has saved my life. Thus, in our day-to-day life we refer to our kins for conveying messages of various kins.

Terms of Address: The terms which are used frequently by kins to address their different kins are known as terms of address. We frequently use kinship terms while addressing our relatives in our day-to-day discussion, letter writing and address a meeting. For example Papa is coming, Mammy is going, Uncle has given this book, Aunty has told me this story, Grand Pa has given me this money,

Grand Ma knows a number of stories, My Bahana is a doctor, My Beta is a lawyer, My Beti is engineer, My Bhaiya and Bhabhi both are doctors. His *damad babu* is businessman. His Bahu is a doctor.

Cognitive Aspects of Kinship Terms

Kinship terms can also be explained on the basis of linguistic approach and cognition of kinship terms. Kinship terms reveal the following cognitive aspects:

Age distinction: The cognition of kinship terms reveal age distinction. For example Ist brother, 2nd brother, 3rd brother, 4th brother, eldest brother, youngest sister etc.

Generation distinction: The cognition of kinship terms indicate generation distinction. For example Great grandfather, Grandfather, son, grandson and Great grandson.

Sex distinction: The kinship terms reveal sex distinction. For example. father-mother, husband-wife, brother-sister, uncle-aunt, grand-father, grand-mother, Grand-son, Grand daughter, etc.

Lineality and Colaterality: The kinship terms also provide us cognition about lineality and colaterality. For example Grand father, father, son and Grandson and brother-brother, sister-sister, brother-sister.

Sex of speaker: Speakers of both sexes use the same term for their kins. For example, son and daughter both call their father as father, mother as mother, brother as brother, sister as sister. Father and mother both call their son as son and daughter as daughter.

Consanguineal and Affinal Relation: The kinship terms reveal the cognition of blood and marital relatives. For example father-son, Mother-son, Father-daughter, Mother-daughter, brother-brother, sister-sister, and brother-sister are consanguineal kins. But bride, bride-groom, father-in-law, mother-in-law, brother-in-law, sister-in-law, son-in-law, daughter-in-law, *Samadhi-Samadhin* etc. are affinal relatives.

Sex of person who establishes relationship: The kinship terms also indicate sex of a person who establishes relationship. For example, father's father, father's mother, mother's brother, father's brother, father's sister, mother's sister etc.

Evidence of death: The kinship terms also show evidence of death of a relative. Late father, Late mother, widow of son, widow of brother.

The above types of kin distinctions have been discussed in detail by an American evolutionist L.H. Morgan in his paper, "Classificatory System of Relationships".

Kinship Behaviour or Kinship Usages

In a society a kin behaves with another kins according to the rules of behaviour. The rules by which a kin behave with another kin are known as kinship behaviour or kinship usages. The following types of kinship usages have been reported:

Avoidance: According to this kinship usage two kins avoid each other in their behaviour. Such type of kinship behaviour is found due to taboo imposed by the society on close interaction of some kins. Such kins do not behave directly. They avoid talking, calling names and physical contact with each other. For communication of news and views, they take help of another kin who is not their avoidance relative. In Hindu society following types of avoidance kins have been reported.

- Father-in-law-Daughter-in-law
- Mother-in-law-Daughter-in-law
- Father-in-law-Son-in-law
- Mother-in-law-Son-in-law
- Husband's elder brother (*Jeth* or *Bainsur* both terms are used)–Younger brother's wife (*Bhawoh*)
- Wife's elder sister–Younger sister's husband

Significance of Avoidance Behaviour

- To pay respect to elders in family
- To introduce social traditions
- To maintain incest taboo
- To avoid conflict
- Inculcation of discipline

Joking: This kinship usage is opposite to avoidance usage. In avoidance usage two kins avoid each other observing the taboo imposed on them, but in joking usage two kins have been allowed to appear face to face, to exchange news and views, to cut verbal and action jokes and have physical contacts. Joking usage permits the following relatives to behave in funny way:

- Sister's husband (*Jija*)—Wife's younger sister (*Sali*)
- Husband's younger brother (*Devar*)—Elder brother's wife (*Bhabhi*)

- Husband's younger sister (*Nanad*)—Elder brother's wife (*Bhabi*)
- Younger sister's husband (*Jija*)—Wife's younger brother (*Sala*)
- Husband's sister's husband (*Nandoi*) —Wife's brother's wife (*Sarhaj*)

Significance of Joking usage: The joking kinship usage occupies the significant place in society due to its following functions:

- Creation of pleasant environment
- To make social relation permanent
- Use as a means of entertainment
- To provide sex education
- To act as means of communication
- Socialization of bride and bridegroom.

Takenonymy: This kinship usage allows two avoidance kins to behave through a third kin or a symbol. For example in Hindu society father-in-law and daughter-in-law are avoidance kins. But daughter-in-law take help of her son, daughter or husband's younger brother or husband's sister for the purpose of exchange of news and views. Similarly, father-in-law takes help of his grandson, grand daughter, own daughter, for the purpose of communication. Sometimes, a symbol is used for the purpose of communication. For example in Hindu society, the symbol for addressing father-in-law is Babu Saheb and for mother-in-law is Sarkar Ji. Now-a-days, they are addressed as Papa Ji and Mammy Ji.

Significance of Takenonymy: Takenonymy has following social significance:

- Communication between avoiding kins
- To maintain social value and tradition
- To use respectful words for elders and affectionate terms for youngers.
- To avoid magical performance through real names.

Avunculate: In this kinship usage a maternal uncle plays a significant role in the life of his sister's son (*Bhanja*) or daughter (*Bhanji*). He adopts his *Bhanja* or *Bhanji* and takes every care of him or her. He or she inherits the property of maternal uncle. After marriage, the *Bhanja* practices avunculocal residence. During oldhood the *Bhanja* takes every care of his maternal uncle and maternal aunt. The *Bhanji* leaves the house of maternal uncle after marriage to live with her husband, but she maintains every relation with the family of maternal uncle by frequent visits.

This kinship usage was reported by Malinowski in his study on Trobriand Islandars. Among Trobriand islanders maternal uncle has to play special role in the life of his sister's son or daughter (*Bhanja* and *Bhanji*). After death of sister, her brother adopts her children and plays a special role in shaping their life.

This kinship usage is a feature of matrilineal society, but the usage also occurs in patrilineal society when maternal uncle is barren or childless.

Amitate: This kinship usage is related to a special role played by father's sister in the life of her nephew or niece. The father's sister (*Bua* or *Phua*) adopts her nephew or niece with the mutual consent of her husband. She takes every care in rearing and caring her nephew or niece. Nephew or niece inherits her husband's property. This kinship usage is practiced particularly when father's sister is childless.

Couvade: In this kinship usage, the father of new born child has to play the role of mother at the time of delivery of the child. When would be mother enters in delivery room, the would be father also accompanies her. He also sleeps on delivery bed with her and cries with her as if he is also suffering from delivery pain. After delivery he also observes all taboos related to food, bath, visit, cloth etc. which a mother of new born child has to observe. He spends pollution period with his wife.

This kinship usage has been reported by E.B. Tylor, the founder of British anthropology in his book "Mexico Mexican". According to him, society in the beginning was matriarchal. The male would have established his authority in family and society through the practice of this usage of couvade. Through the practice of couvade usage patriarchal society would have emerged.

Kin Groups

The smallest form of kin group is family. Lineage is bigger than family. Clan is bigger than lineage, phratry is bigger than clan and moiety is bigger than phratry. Thus important kin groups are as follows:

- Family
- Lineage
- Clan
- Phratry
- Moiety

About family, a detailed description has been given under Chapter 4. Therefore, here we are going to deal with lineage, clan, phratry and moiety one by one.

Lineage

Lineage is a unilateral descent group. It consists of all consanguineal kins who trace their descent from a real ancestor or ancestress of four or five generations above. It includes real ancestor or ancestress from whom present descent group trace genetic relation. It is a corporeal kin group. It is exogamous. Lineage member may or may not share a common residence. Joint family is also an example of lineage. Lineage is always unilateral and exogamous.

Type of Lineage: Lineage can be divided into two types:

- Matrilineage
- Patrilineage

Matrilineage: In this type of lineage, the descent group trace their genetic relation from a common real ancestress. It includes only female descendants of an ancestress.

Patrilineage: In this type of lineage, the descent group trace their genetic relation from a common real ancestor. It includes only male descendants of an ancestor.

Characteristics of Lineage: The lineage has following characteristics:

- It is a descent group.
- This descent group is unilateral
- It is a consanguineal kin group.
- It is exogamous kin group.
- It is a corporeal kin group.
- It is of two types—matrilineage and patrilineage

- In matrilineage descent is traced through mother or an ancestress, but in patrilineage descent is traced through father or an ancestor.
- The lineage has real ancestor or ancestress.
- Joint family is also a lineage
- Members of lineage may or may not share a common residence.

Difference between family and lineage: The family and lineage both are consanguineal and corporeal kin group but family is bilateral, whereas lineage is unilateral.

Clan

A clan is also a unilateral descent group, but it has a common mythical ancestor or ancestress who may be of supernatural character or a totemic object. It is also a consanguineal kin and corporeal kin group. Its member may or may not reside at the same places. It is exogamous descent group.

Type of clan: The clan is of two types: Matriclan and patriclan.

Matriclan: This type of clan includes members tracing their descent in the line of mother. This descent group includes only female descentants tracing descent from a common ancestress. For example Garo and Khasi of Shillong. Boys after marriage become member of their clan.

Patriclan: This type of clan includes members tracing descent from a common ancestor. This descent of group includes only male descendants because girls after marriage become the member of their husband's clan.

Hindu Clan (*Gotra*): In Hindu, clan names have been derived from seven mythical great sages called *Saptarshi* (Seven sages). They are: Marichi, Atri, Angira, Pulah, Kratu, Pulastya and Vashishtha.

Tribal Clan: The tribals have derived their clan names from totemic objects such as flora, fauna, river, mountain, hill, and other natural object with whom they have mystic relation.

Characteristics of Clan: A clan has following characteristics:

- It is a unilateral descent group.
- It is a corporeal kin group.

- It is a consanguineal kin group.
- It has a mythical or totemic ancestor.
- It is of two types: matriclan and patriclan.
- In matriclan, the members get clan name of mother, but in patriclan, the members get clan name of father.
- In matriclan boys after marriage become the member of their wive's clan, but in patriclan girls after marriage become member of their husband's clan.
- Hindus have derived their clan names from seven great mythical sages, but tribals have derived clan names from their totemic object.
- Clan is exogamous descent group.

Difference between Lineage and Clan: Lineage and clan both are consanguineal kin group. Both are unilateral descent group, both are corporeal kin group and both follow the practice of exogamy at the time of marriage. But in spite of all such similarity, there are some differences between lineage and clan. The chief points of differences between lineage and clan are as follows:

- Clan is bigger in organization than lineage.
- A clan has several lineages, but a lineage has only one clan.
- Clan has mythical or totemic ancestor, but lineage has real ancestor.
- The members of a clan may or may not reside at same place, whereas members of a lineage may or may not reside in the same residence at a place.
- The same clan is found in several castes or tribes, but the same lineage is not found in several castes and tribes.

Descent and Descent group

Descent: A genetic relation between an ancestor/ancestress and his/her descendants is known as descent.

Descent group: When a group is formed on the basis of genetic relation between an ancestor/ancestress and his/her descendants is known as descent group. For example lineage and clan.

Filiation: The relation of an individual from his father is called filiation. It is concerned only with father and son, but the descent has more generational depth.

Types of Descent: Descent may be classified into following types:

- Unilateral descent
- Double unilateral descent
- Bilateral descent
- Ambhilateral descent.

Unilateral Descent: When descent is traced either through father or through mother, it is called a unilateral descent. Unilateral descent is of two types:

- Patrilateral or Patrilineal
- Matrilateral or Matrilineal

Patrilateral Descent: When an individual traces his descent from father side, it is known as patrilineal descent. All kins related through patrilineal descent are termed as Agnate.

Matrilateral Descent: When the descent of an individual is traced through mother side, it is known as matrilateral descent. All kins related through matrilateral descent are known as Uterine.

Matrilateral descent is characteristic of matrilineal societies. For example Garo and Khasi of Shillong and Meghalaya.Patrilateral descent is characteristic of Patrilineal society.

Double Unilineal Descent: In some societies descent is traced through father side for some purposes and through mother side for some other purposes. Such type of descent is known as double unilineal descent.

Bilateral Descent: When descent is traced through both father and mother sides, it is known as bilateral descent. All kins related through bilateral descent are termed as cognate. It includes agnates, uterines and other relatives.

Ambhilateral Descent: When the tracing of descent of an individual is doubtful, it is called ambhilateral descent. For example Hapumaoris of New Guinea.

Inheritance Rule

The rule which govern the inheritance of property among kins is called inheritance rule. Inheritance rule is not same for all societies. It differs from society to society. The following types of inheritance have been reported:

- Patrilineal Inheritance
- Matrilineal Inheritance
- Avunolateral Inheritance
- Amitatal Inheritance
- Ambhilateral Inheritance
- Equal Inheritance

Patrilineal Inheritance: According to this rule, the properties of a father are inherited by his all sons. Daughters are not allowed to inherit paternal property. This is characteristic feature of a patriarchal society.

In this type of inheritance generally all paternal properties such as house, agricultural land, cattle, furniture, agricultural tools, utensils and trees are inherited equally by all sons after the death of parents or even their life time. But two types of behaviours are also related to the inheritance of paternal property. These are:

- Primogeniture
- Ultimogeniture

Primogeniture: According to this rule of inheritance, the eldest brother gets a special share in paternal property for looking after and enhancing it after death of father. In Hindi, it is called *Jayesthansh*.

Ultimogeniture: According to this rule of inheritance, the youngest brother gets a special share for being young and discharging family liability.

Matrilineal Inheritance: According to this inheritance rule, the property of mother is inherited equally by all daughters. Brothers do not get share in maternal property. This inheritance rule is characteristic feature of matriarchal society like Garo and Khasi of Meghalaya and Shillong.

Generally maternal properties are divided equally among all daughters after the death of mother. But when mother dies leaving children small and the eldest sister looks after the property and other economic activities, she is given a special share which is termed as Primogeniture. But when division of family takes place and the youngest sister gets special share which is known as ultimogeniture

Avunolateral Inheritance: When a nephew inherits the property of a maternal uncle, it is known as avunolateral inheritance. It is characteristic feature of matrilineal societies.

Amitatal Inheritance: When the property of a father's sister is inherited by her brother's son or daughter, it is termed as amitatal inheritance.

Ambhilateral Inheritance: When the inheritance of property is not clear, rather it is doubtful, it is known as ambhilateral inheritance. Such cases appear in case of childless couple when they do not dispose of the inheritance right during life time.

Equal Inheritance: Now-a-days, court has given equal inheritance right to both sex siblings of a couple in their earned property. The earned property of a couple is shared equally by all sons and daughters.

Succession Rule

The rule which deals with transfer of title and post among kins is known as succession rule. The succession rule is of two types:

- Patrilineal Succession
- Matrilineal Succession

Patrilineal Succession: According to this rule, the title and post of a father is transferred to his all sons. This is characteristic feature of a patrilineal family.

Matrilineal Succession: When title and post of a mother is transferred to her daughters, it is known as matrilineal inheritance. It is characteristic feature of matrilineal society.

Phratry

A phratry is a group of some clans of the same tribe for the purpose of social activities. In other words, we can say that when some of clans of the same tribe forms an alliance group for the fulfilment of some specific purposes, we call the alliance group as phratry. It is a unilateral descent group made up of two or more clans for social activities. It may be endogamous or exogamous. Phratry is an example of Dual organization or Double organization.

Characteristics of Phratry: A phratry has following characteristics:

- It is group of two or more clans.
- It is a unilateral descent group.
- The clans united as phratry show unity in their activities.
- It may be endogamous or exogamous.
- The clans united under phratry maintain their own clan identity but for social activities they are organized and maintain unity.
- It is an example of dual organization or double organization.

Function of Phratry: The main function of phratry is to maintain reciprocal amity among clans who make an alliance under phratry.

Moiety

It is a division of a tribe into two equal halves. Each equal half is termed as moiety. This kind of social organization is known as *Dual organization*. A moiety may be exogamous, asexual or endogamous. The moiety shows stratification. It is because all moieties of a tribe do not occupy equal place in their society. The position of some moieties are high and of some moieties are low. Each moiety is unilineal descent group.

Among Ao Naga, Rengama Naga and Angami Naga of North-eastern Himalayan region, the existence of moiety can be observed. The Ao Nagas have two moieties namely Mangsel and Changeli. Rengama Nagas have two moieties named Eastern Rengama and Western Rengama. The Angami Nagas have two moieties namely Persoma and Peptuma. The Tharus have two moiety namely High Tharu and Low Tharu. The Munda tribe of Jharkhand have two moiety Patar Munda or Mahali Munda and Kampat Munda. The Savara Tribe of Orissa have two moieties namely Malik Savara and Ryot Savara. The Bhokta of Orissa have two moieties namely Bado and Son. Bhuiya of Orissa have two moieties namely Netam and Makram. The Korku have two moieties namely Rajkorku and Pathari Korku.

Totem and Totemism

A totem is a name of a natural object or plant, an animal or a bird with which tribals have mythical relation. Tribals regard totem as their ancestor or ancestress. They derive their names of clan from totems and thus they have totemic clan.

Beiiefs and practices related to totem is known as totemism.

Totemism is found among all tribes of our country. Killing and eating of a totem is a taboo which is observed by each tribal families. As a totem is their ancestor or ancestress from where they trace their origin. But on some specific occasion the meat of totem is shared by the clan members as grace of the ancestor.

Changes in Kinship System

Kinship system is a system of building kins through parentage and marriage. As parentage is related to blood relation or genetic relation, it is continuing through procreation of children by a couple. But kin formation through marriage has undergone changes, as a result a change in kinship system has also come into existence. Due to enactment of Marriage Acts, modern education, urbanization, industrialization and globalization, a number of changes in kinship system have also come into existence. Some important changes in kinship system are as follows:

Marital kins of different castes, tribes and religion: Now-a-days, inter-caste marriage and inter-religious marriages are occurring and increasing in each marriage seasons. Inter-caste and enter-religious marriages have brought couples and affinal kins of different castes and religions.

Increase in Cousin Marriages: As Hindu Marriage Act has allowed marriage between cousin, cousin marriages have found place even in those societies where cousin marriages were not allowed.

This has resulted in formation of couple among cousins of opposite sexes.

Increase in DINK Couple: In present day DINK couples have come into existence. DINK couples are those couples who have double income but no kids.

Adopted Son and Daughter: In present day kinship system number of adopted sons and daughters are increasing.

Number of Surrogate mother increasing: Today number of such children has increased who are born from surrogacy.

Increase in Intra-clan Couples: Now-a-days, a clan is not necessary an exogamous group and intra-clan marital and affinal relations have come into existence.

Marriage between same Sex: Marriage between same sexes have come into existence.

Clan as an Scattered Kin Group: Now-a-days, clan is no more a corporeal kin group. Its members are scattered in different parts of the country and globe right from villages to towns, cities, metropolitans and foreign country. They are not living together. On social-ceremonial occasions they assemble for some hours and then return to their respective places.

Family as an Scattered Primary King Group: Now-a-days, family members are also not staying at a common residence and sharing joys and sorrow together. Husband is working at one place, wife is doing service on another place, children are staying in hostels for education. They spend day and night together on some holidays.

Decrease in Role of Kins: Now-a-days, court marriages are held. Court marriages have reduced the ritualistic cultural and social roles of a number of kins like father's sister, father's brother, wife's brother, son-in-law, daughter-in-law and other relatives. These relatives play significant cultural roles in marriage rituals.

Decrease in Economic Function: Now-a-days, kin group is not a unit of production and consumption. Individual has become unit of production and consumption. Reduction in reciprocity, gift and hospitability of relatives has also come into existence.

Decrease in Psychological Function: As family members and clan members are scattered, this has reduced the emotional attachment of kins.

Decrease in Control Function: Now-a-days, control function of kinship has been reduced due to friendship based society in place of kinship based society.

Reduction in Entertainment Function: The entertainment function of kinship has gone under change due to T.V. Cinema, Internet etc.

Thus, from the above account, it is clear that biological, social, cultural, economic, political, religious, psychological, control and entertainment functions of kinship have undergone change to a considerable extent in modern and post-modern society.

Chapter 6
Magic, Religion and Science

You would have seen an earthen pot hanged on a stick with black and white spots, you would have seen new born babies with black thread tied in their hands, legs and neck and a *Tilak* of black ointment (*Kajal*) on their forehead. Have you thought what are these? These are magical practices. You would have seen men and women wearing *Tabij* (amulets). This is also magical practice. You would have seen somebody going for *Jhar-Phunk* treatment. This is also a kind of magical practice. Like above examples, there are a number of magical practices prevalent in societies. Some of them are related to the welfare of people, while others are related to cause harm to other people.

You would have seen people going to temple, mosque, Gurudwara, Church, *Matha* and so on. You would have also visited these places along with your parents to offer worship. You would have seen people offering worship before idols and other religious symbols. You would have also seen people celebrating festival of their belief system. What are these? These are religious practices. They are related to the welfare of family and society.

Again you would have seen farmers ploughing their lands with oxen and plough or tractor. You would have seen farmers manuring fields and using chemical and bio-fertilizers. You would have seen farmers storing and processing seeds and using H.Y.V. Seeds. You would have seen them using pesticides, weedicides and germicides. You would have seen bullock cart, bicycle, scooter, rickshaw, motor cycle, auto rickshaw, thela, Tam-tam, Car, truck, railway, ship, aeroplane, electric bulb, fans, hand pumps, boring, Gas stove, Radio, phone, mobile, internet etc. What are these. These are products of our knowledge tradition and science.

Thus, magical, religious and scientific practices are prevalent in our society.

Renowned British Anthropologist Frazer in his book, "Golden Bough" has attempted to present magic, religion and science in evolutionary sequence. According to him, the society of mankind has progressed through three successive stages—magic, religion and science. According to him, in the beginning society was in the stage of magic in which the behaviour of mankind was controlled by magic. Magicians occupied significant place and they were supposed to have super human power by which they used to control the members of the group and food gathering and hunting. In the early time man lived in band and each band had a leader who was powerful and knowledgeable individual of the group. He was probably the first magician of mankind. He used to draw figures of animals to be hunted on the walls of cave and attacked with bow and arrow on them. This practice used to bring him success in hunting animals. Gradually, members of the group began to believe that he is possessed by super human power by which he controls the hunting game. In this way magic came into existence. The leader-*cum*-magician of the band was offered horns, feet, head, skin, nail, hairs, bones etc. of the animal hunted as gift and presentation. He used to perform magic for welfare of the group particularly hunting game which was related to the survival of the group.

But gradually mankind witnessed that all kinds of natural events were beyond the control of a magician. For example flood, fire, starvation, birth, death and movements of natural object. Such observations of mankind made him to think that there was a super human power which controls every event related to the life of human beings and all other natural objects. The belief in super human power gave rise to belief in Gods, Goddesses and their worship. This was second stage of society of mankind which was governed by religion.

The society of mankind reached in the final stage of development when he began to establish cause and effect relationship on the basis of his observations and experiences. On the basis of cause effect relationship, he began to challenge the authority of super human power or Gods and Goddesses. On the basis of knowledge acquired by observation, experiences and cause-effect relationship, he began to put logic that flood is an effect of heavy rains, starvation is effect of draught, illness is effect of change in environment. On the basis of his knowledge gained through logic, experience, observation and cause-effect relationship, mankind entered into the stage of science.

Co-existence of Magic, Science and Religion

There is no doubt that mankind is leading his life in scientific stage today. He is not sitting like an idle keeping his hands on hands in the name of Gods and Goddesses. But on the basis of his scientific knowledge acquired through observation, experience and experimentation, he is able to develop technology to get production by exploitation of natural resources. He is doing animal husbandry, fishery, piggery, goatery, dockery and poultry on the basis of scientific knowledge. He is carrying out agriculture through HYV seeds, manuring, bio-fertilizer and chemical fertilizer. He is using weedicides, pesticides and germicides to protect crops from the attack of germs. He has invented varieties of technology and machines for the production of goods, cloths, tools, furniture, utensils, artifacts, bulb, Radio, T.V., Phone, Cell Phone, computer, internet, varieties of vehicles, medicines and medical instruments. The benefit of science is so deep rooted in our mind, heart and society that we are dependent upon science from our cradle to cremation. For every kind of our needs we are looking towards scientific products and their use in day to day life. With the help of science man is flying in sky, travelling in ship and train. With the advent of computers, Cell phones and Internet, we have all to redefine the distance and time. We are sending our fellow in space to make a journey of different planets and to come back safely.

We are curing our diseases with modern doctor, technology and medicine. We have invented atom and nuclear bombs to destroy the enemy country. But in spite of all such scientific achievements, we have not been able to get victory over death. Death is still a mystery even for the scientists. Not only this, but a number of our scientific experiments become unsuccessful. For getting victory and success, we still seek blessing of our almighty God. Before starting a scientific experiment, worship is performed and a coconut, *dhoop*, *ghee*, *Agarbati*, flower, *Prasad* are offered in the name of deities to seek blessing for success. Doctors also say patient that God bless you. They extend thanks to God for successful operations and treatment. Similarly, before starting the erection work of a multistorey building or an industry, the *Bhumi Pujan* (worship of land) is performed. When the building or industry is completed, worship of deity of the building is performed. Such religious practices are going on not only in folk and peasant society, but also in urban, industrial and global society.

Not only religious practices are mixed with scientific practices in present-day modern society but magical practices are also going on along with religious and scientific practices. Even in modern urban, industrial and global society, the practice of magic is going on. Even well to do and well educated people are offering sacrifice of goat, sheep, coconut to please super human power under the supervision of a magician. They are wearing amulets given by magician, *shaman* or sorcer. People are taking help of *Jhar-Phunk* method of treatment for cure.

In this way we find that the form of society is simple or complex, sacred or secular, primitive or advanced, folk, peasant or urban, industrial, local or global but in all forms of societies the co-existence of magic, religion and science is found. Modern states are also promoting these institutions.

Magic

Magic may be defined as an act by which an individual makes super human or super natural power under his/her control for the fulfilment of desired work. The individual who makes magic is known as magician. In order to be a magician the first task is to bring a super human power under his/her control. It is because of this very fact magician is believed to have a spirit and magical acts are related to spirit possession. The magician gives an order to the possessed spirit to get the desired work performed and his/her possessed spirit do needful. Magic differs from the religion on this very point. In magic, the magician controls the spirit which he or she controls for the performance of desired goal. But in religion an individual surrenders his/her existence before the super human power or supreme almighty deity.

In his book, "Magic, Religion and Science" (1929) Malinowski has attempted to define magic. According to him, magic is a combination of pure applied actions by which human beings satisfy their various kinds of need. Thus, according to him, magic is a means for the satisfaction of human needs.

In his posthumous published book, "Scientific Theory of Culture and other Essays" (1944), Malinowski divided human needs into three categories—Primary, Secondary and Tertiary. For the fulfillment of all these three categories of needs, human beings have given birth to three types of cultural systems. The first need is biological need such as satisfaction of sex and hunger. Biological need is also known as Primary or basic need. In order to satisfy biological needs, human beings have developed kinship system. The second category of need is known as derived or instrumental needs. They are helpful in satisfaction of primary needs. Such as economy, education and social control. In order to satisfy these derived needs, human beings have developed traditions, economic organizations and political organizations.

The third category of need is integrative need which provides integration in the society. In order to satisfy the tertiary need or integrative need, human beings have developed cultural systems like magic, science, religion, knowledge, art, etc. Thus, according to Malinowski, Magic brings integration in the society and inculcate the feeling of safety in the group.

British evolutionist anthropologist Frazer in his book "Golden Bough" has attempted to define magic. According to him magic is that collection or accumulation of human action and behaviour which should not be criticized or re-examined. He has seen magic as Pseudo science and Pseudo art. He accepted theoretical aspects of magic as Pseudo science and applied aspect of magic as Pseudo art.

Frazer has treated magic in both positive and negative senses. He has placed sorcery under *positive magic*. It is because in sorcery a specific kind of action is performed to achieve specific result. He has placed taboo under *negative magic* because in taboo certain restrictions are imposed on actions, otherwise they can bring negative result. Negative magic prevents inauspicious events.

Characteristics of Magic

On the basis of above description about the magic, the following characteristics of magic appear:

- Magic is a means for the satisfaction of human needs.
- All individuals cannot perform magic.
- Only those individuals can perform magic who are possessed by a spirit or super human power.
- The individuals who perform magic are known as magicians.
- The magician has full control over the spirit which he/she possesses.

- The magician utilizes the possessed spirit to get desired result.
- The magic is performed either for the welfare or for the destruction both.
- Magician do not occupy good position in the society.
- Magic is a part of our belief system.

Types of Magic

Different anthropologists have classified magic into different categories. We are going to present a detailed description about those categories of magic.

British evolutionist anthropologist Frazer has divided the magic into following two catgegories:

- Imitative Magic
- Contagious Magic

Imitative Magic: This magic is based on the principle that like produces like. For example if any body desires to cause harm to his enemy, he makes figure of his enemy with soil, sand or ash and inserts a *keel* in his eye, chest, stomach and forehead. It is believed that this brings desired result by causing harm to the enemy. In order to get rain, people throw boulders down from the mountain or hill. The sound produced by boulders cause the clouds to shower rain. Some societies burn wood leaves and straw to cause smoke. The smoke goes to the clouds in sky and cause them to shower rains. In African societies, tears are flown from the eyes to get rain. In order to cause harm to the enemy, effigy of enemy is burnt. Such magical practices are examples of imitative magic.

Contagious Magic: This magic is based on the principle that once in contact is always in contact. For example dresses worn, slippers, pen, spectacles, hairs of an individual have always contact with the individual who uses them. With the help of such goods used by a person, contagious magic can be performed by getting them anyhow by a magician. It is because the contact of these goods always remains with the person who has used them even after separation, thrown or rejection. The dresses, nail, hairs, and other goods used by a child are either thrown in deep water or placed deep in earth so that magician could not get them to perform contagious magic.

British functionalist anthropologist B.K. Malinowski has divided magic into following two categories:

- White Magic
- Black Magic

White Magic: White magic are those magic which are performed for the welfare of an individual or the community as a whole. Magic performed to prevent diseases in the community, to cure an ill person, to enhance production, to cause rain to fall, to prevent startvation and to bring good harvest are examples of white magic.

Black Magic: Black magic are those magic which are performed to cause harm to an individual or his property. Witchcraft is an example of black magic.

S.C. Dube in his book, "Manav Aur Sanskriti" has divided magic into following three categories:

- Productive Magic
- Protective Magic
- Destructive Magic

Productive Magic: When a magic is performed for the success in hunting, gathering, animal husbandry, agriculture, business and service, it is known as productive magic.

Protective Magic: When magic is performed for the purpose of protection from enemies, illness, inauspicious events, evil spirits, witchcrafts etc., it is known as protective magic.

Destructive Magic: When magic is performed to cause harm to enemies and their properties, it is known as destructive magic.

Elements of Magical Act

The following are the chief elements of magic:

Spell: Spells are essential elements of magical act. In absence of spells, magical acts cannot be performed. Through spells super human powers are attracted and brought under the control. Thus, spell is very important element of a magical act.

Materials: In order to perform a magical act, the magician requires some materials such as ash and bones of cremation place, bones of a graveyard, human skull, black cloth, needle, nail, seven colour flower, scent, sunfried rice, black *urad*, green cloth, bear or wine, meat, etc. Through these materials super human power are attracted and made under control. Once the super human power comes under control, they begin to work as per the direction of the magician.

Method: In order to perform a magic, the magician applies a definite method. This method is quite established. The method of magical performance is systematic. One step is followed by another steps systematically. If steps are not followed systematically, the desired goal of a magic cannot be achieved and the magician may face negative impact.

Pronunciation and Expression: In magical performance *mantras* or spells and words must be pronounced correctly and followed in expression to get desired result. For example in performing magic to cause harm to enemies, the expression of anger should appear on face. Similarly, to peace and prosperity related magic, the facial expression must be peaceful.

Fetishism: Magic is also deeply related to fetishism. The magician captures the power of super human in fetishes. When fetishes are worn, the super human power captured in them help the individual in many ways. It also helps in wishfulfilment.

Function of Magic

The following are main functions of magic:

Productive Function: Magic is performed to enhance productivity, properties, and wealth. People engaged in various types of economic activities, perform magic to achieve good success in their occupation and their wealth and properties could grow more and more.

Protective Function: Magic is performed to protect an individual and society from the evil effect of witchcraft, evil eye, evil mouth, and evil tongue. It is also performed to save an individual from *Bhut Pret* (evil spirits), illness and accidental death. It is also performed to save a community from starvation, fire, flood and epidemic. In this way, magic performs protective function.

Preventive Function: Magic performs a number of preventive functions. It imposes taboo on individual to avoid inauspicious events in the life of individual and community. Taboos are imposed on infants, pregnant women, lactating women, travel, dresses, food etc. The main function of these taboos are to avoid any accidents or inauspicious events.

Destructive Function: Magic is also performed to cause harm to enemies and their properties. Such magic is known as black magic. For example witchcraft. Through witchcraft damage is caused to the health and property of enemies.

Welfare Function: Magic is also performed for the welfare of the community. For example magic for showering rains and prevent epidemic, are example of welfare activities for the community.

Integrative Function: Magic integrates the members of the community in the name of welfare and well-being.

Psychological Function: Magic is performed for the psychological needs of the individual. Attempts are made to create love, affection, attraction etc. among those individuals who are at the verge of separation.

Enhancement of Tradition: Magic enhances the tradition and puts us in mystical world.

Control Function: Magic controls the behaviour of individuals and prohibits them from doing a number of works.

Religion

The word religion has been derived from the Greek word Religare, the meaning of which is binding. From this point of view religion is a binding force between man and super human or super natural powers.

In anthropology, the credit of providing the smallest definition of the term religion goes to the founder of British anthropology and cultural evolutionist anthropologist E.B. Tylor. He in his book, "Primitive Culture" (1871) gave the smallest definition of religion as *belief in soul*. Belief in soul was a definition of religion in minimum words.

E.B. Tylor provided not only the definition of religion, but he also presented an evolutionary sequence of religion. According to him primitive religion has passed through three successive stages of development in unilineal sequence.

In its early form religion originated as a belief in soul. This stage is termed as animism. Man would have witnessed man dying. He would have experienced that there is a super human power in the body of all living beings. So long as this super human power resides inside the body of an individual he or she eats, walks, speaks, works and does a number of activities. But as soon as this power goes out of the body, an individual dies due to departure of the super human power, i.e. soul or anima. This was the earliest form of religion.

Man would have seen that each individual possesses a soul. There were as many souls and individuals. This experience of man compelled him to think that there were many souls. All souls make departure leaving the individuals dead. This belief gave rise to polytheism, belief in many souls or deities. This was the second stage of development of religion.

In final stage of development of religion man would have developed a philosophy that all souls are parts of the great soul and they join the great soul after departure from the body. Thus, the theory of monotheism would have emerged.

In this way, Tylor reconstructed the evolutionary sequence of religion as Animism, polytheism and monotheism.

British evolutionist anthropologist Frazer in his book, "Golden Bough" has defined religion as satisfaction of those super human powers through worship and rituals which show path to man and nature and control them. According to him in the beginning there was a magical stage in mankind in which super human powers were controlled by some individuals termed as magicians. Religious stage developed later on when mankind began to think that super human powers cannot be brought under control. Rather they can be pleased with rituals and worship. As a result of this, man entered into religious stage. On the basis of his observations and experiences mankind began to develop cause-effect relationship. With this development he began to challenge the authority of Supreme power. This gave rise to scientific stage. Now we are living in scientific stage.

A functionalist British anthropologist B.K. Malinowski in his book "Scientific Theory of Culture and Other Essays" has defined religion as cultural response of tertiary or integrative needs. Religion brings integration in the society.

French anthropologist and sociologist Emile Durkheim in his book, "Elementary Forms of Religious Life" (1912) has defined religion as a social facts characterized by the concepts of *beliefs* and *ritual* or *thought* and *Action* and *Sacred* and *Profane*.

Characteristics of Religion

On the basis of above explanations related to religion the following characteristics of religion come into existence:

- *Belief in Super Human Power*: Every religion of the globe has a deep faith in super human or super natural power. It is believed that there is a super human power or super natural power whom we call God, Deity, Almighty, Allah, or by different local terms in local religions. The Almighty God is omnipresent. He is responsible for all kinds of events in the world including birth and death. The Super human power may be in shape or shapeless. But he controls all living beings and natural events in the world. The religion is based fully on belief in this Super human power. Man has provided a shape to super human power in sacred centres and offers worship before their idols.

- *Rituals*: Rituals are human actions to carryout religious activities according to belief. For example worship, sacrifice, offerings, *Prasad*, *hawan* (sacrificing *dhoop*, ghee, dry coconut and *prasad* to fire), *Yagya,* fasting etc. These human actions are made in order to please Super human power or deities. These actions are known as rituals. They are performed according to belief system of the community.
- *Prayer or Bhajan*: In all communities people sing religious songs in order to please the deities. The religious songs are known as prayer, *Bhajan* and *Kirtan*. They are sung according to religious traditions of the communities.
- *Religious Specialist*: There are some rituals which are performed even by individuals or head of the family or any member of the family. But there are some rituals which require a specialist to get them peformed. Each community has its own specialist or priest. For example Hindus have *Panda*, *Pujari* and *Pandit*. Muslims have *Maulavi* and Christians have *father* and Sikh have *guru*. These sacred specialists act as a mediator between deities and the devotes of the communities concerned. The specialists enjoy high status in their communities.
- *Religious Centre*: Each religion has its own religious centres. For example, Hindus have temples, Muslims have mosques, Christians have churches, tribals have Sarmna, Sikhs have Gurudwaras, Buddhists and Jains have *mathas* and temples. Religious performances take place in these religious centres of different communities.
- *Concept of Purity*: All religious institutions and objects are treated as sacred, pious and pure. They are separated from profane or impure objects.

- *Lack of criticism*: There is no scope for criticism in a religion. It is because religion is based on belief system. It cannot be criticized scientifically.

Elements of Religion

The main elements which form a religion are as follows:

- Beliefs
- Rituals
- Specialists
- Sentiments and Feelings
- Organization
- Symbols
- Myths and legends
- Taboo
- Religious Stratification

Function of Religion

Religion is an integral part of our culture. It is a means through which we achieve our various kinds of needs. It brings integration in the community. With the help of religion we travel in strange world or golden world. Due to its such universal functions, religion is accepted as universal institution. The main functions of religion are as follows:

Psychological Function: Human beings have to struggle hard in his life time. He has to face several situations and to make struggle for his existence. He has to face the situations like of anger, hate, conflict, tension, quarrel, exploitation, oppression and deprivation. If such psychological stress continues for a long time, a man can become mad, can commit suicide or may become antisocial elements. In the situations of utter stress and distress, people visit before the deities and seek their blessings. They feel that almighty God is always behind them to extend all kinds of help during the period of need. By offering worships, singing prayers and performing rituals, people get mental peace and they face all kinds of eventuality with the grace of deities.

- *Social Functions*: The religion protects our social values. All communities have their own customs and traditions established by ancestral deities. To disobey them is taken as a crime. For this criminal act people are punished by the almighty God who is omnipresent. In this way religions protect our social values.

- *Moral Function*: The religion performs moral functions. Incest relation, premarital relation, extramarital relation, theft, dacoity, rape etc. are related to immorality. The breaking of these customs and tradition are treated as immoral. For immoral acts people are punished by almighty God because he is everywhere observing our good and bad deeds. The individuals involved in immoral acts get punishment from God in different ways.
- *Integrative Function*: The religion integrates its followers on the occasion of rituals, worship and festivals. The followers of a religion feel integrated. Integration removes fear of different kind and people feel secured.
- *Control Function*: The religion also performs the control function. The religion teaches us that almighty God is always with the people observing their good and bad behaviour. For good behaviour they are blessed and for bad behaviour they are punished. The crime doers become poor and poor day-by-day, they loose their health, property and meet death soon. Such feelings related to religion control our behaviour and help us in character building.
- *Purity Function*: The religion performs purity functions. It distinguishes sacred from profane. Man of pure character are blessed by God, but man with impure character are punished. The religion also purifies the people if they accept their bad deeds and surrender themselves under the feet of Almighty.
- *Safety Function*: The religion builds the feeling of safety and security in the people. The devotees get every kind of protection from the God. It is God who gets every work properly done of his devotees.
- *Welfare Function*: The religion is also related to the welfare of the community. The worship of deities brings pleasure, happiness, peace and prosperity in the community. It inculcates the value of social welfare works such as helping of the disabled, needy, poor and aged. For the welfare services people are rewarded by the deities.

Universality of Religion

The existence of religion is universal fact. There is no society in the world where religion does not exist. The forms of society may be folk or peasant, urban or industrial, global or local and simple or complex, but religion is found in every type of society.

With the advent of science, the process of modernization was started. The modernization was a value-based concept. This process gave rise to democracy, capitalism, industrialization and secularization processes. But industrial and secular societies also could not ignore the importance of religion. Rather they advocated the existence of all religions at equal status. They gave equal opportunities and value to all religions so that they all could maintain their existence. Different states of the globe promoted the pluralities of religion. As a result, a number of missionaries and organizations have emerged to protect the interest of their respective religions and to increase its followers through conversions. Thus, from simple tribal society to complex metropolis society religion is existing universally and performing its universal functions for individuals and societies.

Similarities and Differences between Magic and Religion

Magic and religion show similarity as well as differences. The chief points of similarities and differences between magic and religion are as follows:

Similarities: Magic and religion show certain similarities such as:

- Both believe in super human or supernatural power.
- In both rituals are performed.
- Both have specialists.
- Both perform integrative functions.
- Both have psychological functions.
- Both observe taboo.
- Both believe in strange world and strange action.

Differences: The main points of differences between magic and religion are as follows:

- In religion people bow their heads and existence before super human power, but in magic super human powers are kept under control.
- In religion people offer worship, rituals, prayers to please super human power for seeking his blessings to get success of various kinds. In magic individual performs worship, ritual and pronunciation of spells to bring the super human power under control to get the desired goal fulfilled by exerting pressure on super human power under control.

- In religion people fear from super human power and surrenders their existence, but in magic an individual keeps a super human power under his full power and he does not fear from the super human power.
- In religion people see super human power with great respect, but in magic people do not regard super human power.
- The specialists of religion are termed as Priest, *Pujari* and *Pandit* and *Panda*, but in magic the specialist is known as magician.
- In religion priest is regarded by all members, but in magic magician particularly black magicians are not regarded in the society.
- Religion is always related to welfare of an individual or a community, but black magic is concerned with destruction of individual or community.
- For performing worship any place can be selected, but magic is always performed at a lonely place.
- In religion worship offered does not bring negative impact, but in magic, if magical acts are not performed properly, negative impact is expected.
- Religion is always related to sacred and welfare, but magic is also related to profane and causing harm.
- Religion is a social fact, but magic is individual concerned.
- Sacrifice of any body or objects is not necessary in religion, but sacrifice of any individual of family or any animal is a must for learning black magic.

Theories Related to the Origin of Religion

A number of theories have been propounded by different scholars related to the origin of religion. They are as follows:

- Animism Theory
- Animatism or Manaism Theory
- Naturalism Theory
- Functional Theory
- Frazer's Theory
- Structural-Functional Theory
- Sociological Theory
- Structural Theory

Animism Theory: The theory of animism for the origin of religion was propounded by E.B.Tylor in his book, "Primitive Culture" (1871). In this book Tylor opined that religion originated as belief in soul. The meaning of anima is soul that is why this theory is known as animism. The belief in soul provided the definition of religion in minimum terms. He has treated animism as a base of religion in simple to complex societies. In order to know the origin of religion Tylor studied myths and belief of primitives. He came to the conclusion that belief in soul would have been the reason behind the origin of religion. Savage would have seen some super human power in the body of individuals. This super human power keeps body alive. But as soon as this power goes out of the body, the individual becomes dead. The savage called this super human power as anima or soul.

The savage world have experienced two kinds of souls—Body soul and Ghost soul. The body soul makes permanent departure leaving the body after death. But Ghost soul continues to exist. But these both types of souls were related to the life of mankind.

In the next stage of development, all living and non-living objects would have appeared as manifestation of soul. All natural objects such as plants, crops, birds, animals, rivers, mountain, lake, sea etc. would have appeared as souls in dreams. Appearance of these types of souls would have given a belief in existence of souls in all movable or immovable or living and non-living objects. Souls would have appeared travelling in sky, through water of river, lake and sea, climbing on mountain, residing in caves and trees. The body soul would have reached in heaven but the Ghost soul would have remained on earth. The body soul leads the same kind of life in heaven, but the Ghost soul has to lead its life on earth according to his good and bad deeds. Tylor has termed first one as *continuance theory* and second one as *resultant theory*.

Due to belief in Soul-Ghost, a high stage belief would have emerged which was termed as ancestor. Ancestor would have emerged from the soul. But due to special qualities, they have been placed under the category of God and demon. This belief would have given birth to ancestral worship. The concept of pleasant and destructive souls would have emerged.

Later on, the concept of incarnation of soul would have find a place. A belief would have emerged that the soul could incarnate as God or Goddesses. The concept of soul control would have also emerged which is termed as fetishism. Temples and fetishism were all manifestation of animism. In temples souls are incarnated through worship and rituals. In fetishism, souls are captured in amulets for getting the desired goal.

Later on, a particular type of soul would have been made responsible for a particular type of natural event. For example, a particular soul for air, a particular soul for storm, a particular soul for flood, a particular soul for fire, a particular soul for starvation, rain, snow etc. Due to such type of belief system, the concept of polytheism would have emerged.

In the last stage of development, all souls were believed as part of a great soul. Thus, the concept of monotheism would have developed.

Criticism of Animism

- Tylor used the term savage which is not acceptable.
- He extended his theory up to animatism and naturalism.
- His theory lacks empirical experience.

Animatism or Manaism: The theory of animatism or manaism was propounded by R.R. Marret, a pupil of E.B. Tylor, in his book, "Threshhold of Religions" (1906). The theory of animatism is also known as Manaism. Because the inhabitants of Malaynesia call super human power as Mana. According to this theory each movable or immovable object possess invisible super human power because of which the object performs a special function. Thus belief in super human power is responsible for the origin of religion. Super human power or Mana is responsible for all kinds of success and failure. Thus, pen, sword, chair, pencil, horse, elephant etc. all possess mana. That is why they perform a special function.

Indian anthropologist D.N. Majumdar on the basis of his study on the tribe of Kolhan (Jharkhand) has used the term Bonga in place of Mana. He postulated the theory of Bongaism in place of manaism.

Criticism

- This theory does not explain as to why Mana originated.
- This theory has not accepted social facts.
- This theory does not explain difference between sacred and profane.

Naturalism

The theory of naturalism for the origin of religion was propounded by the German Scholar Max Muller. He was a great scholar of Sanskrit and other languages. In his opinion natural events have been responsible for the origin of religion. He had made study of Indian and European myths and arrived at conclusion that natural power have been responsible for the origin of religion. In all myths, powers of sun, moon, stars, rivers, seas, mountain, lake, hills, animals and herds, have appeared like human beings and behaving like human beings. It was quite natural that human beings would have been influenced by the natural objects and beings. They would have become fearful from natural events. This fear would have given birth to religion. In contemporary society, too, the worship of sun, moon, tree, snake, cow, horse, elephant, buffalo, peacock, cock, pigeon, fire, river, sea and earth is still continuing.

- *Evolutionary Theory*: British evolutionist anthropologist Frazer in his book, "Golden Bough" has postulated an evolutionary theory for the origin of religion. According to him, human society has passed through three successive stages of development in unilineal sequence. In the beginning society was controlled and governed by the magic. The head of each band was also a magician. He was possessed by human power. He kept the super human power in his or existence control. He used to get the desired goal fulfilled by the super human power which he possessed and kept under full control. The band leader attempted to make success of the group in food gathering and hunting and to save the group during trouble. This was the form of society in the beginning where magic used to control the behaviour of the people.

But belief in magic got weak when the people observed and experienced that natural events like flood, starvation, earthquakes, fire and many others are not governed by the magician who was possessed by super human power and kept super human power under control. When people experienced the failure of magic, they began to believe in such a super human power or super natural power which cannot be controlled by any individual. But such powers can be pleased by surrendering existence in his shelter, offering worship, singing prayers and so on. This type of thinking of people gave rise to the origin of religion in the second stage of development. Now society was controlled by religion in which super human power was supreme authority, seeing every deeds and omnipresent. Later on super human power was termed as Gods, Goddesses and deities and were termed by different names in different religions. This development was not the final stage of development of society.

The society in the last stage or final stage of development discovered science on the basis of observations, experiences and cause-effect relationship. The inventions made by science has made our life more easy and we have done progress and are also marching towards progress day-by-day. Now we are leading our life in scientific stage.

- *Functional Theory*: Functional theory for the origin of religion was propounded by British functional anthropologist B.K. Malinowski in his book, "Scientific Theory of Culture and Other Essays". According to him, religion satisfied third level of needs known as integrative needs. The religion originated to bring integration in human society. It integrates the people in the name of Gods, Goddesses, festivals and fairs. It controls the behaviour in society and inculcate the social value and quality.
- *Structural-Functional Theory*: Structural-functional theory of origin of religion was propounded by British anthropologist A.R. Radcliffe-Brown in his book, "Structure and Function in Primitive Society". According to him, a special type of social structure is created due to religion. This special social-structure has three important parts—religious specialists, followers, religious centres and religious performances. The religious specialist occupies top most position and performs functions for the society in getting the worship and rituals performed.
- *Sociological Theory*: The sociological theory of origin of religion was propounded by French sociologist and anthropologist Emile Durkheim. He in his book "Elementary Forms of Religious Life" (1912) opined that religion is a social fact for all societies. Therefore, attempts to trace the explanation of origin of religion should be made on the basis of existence of social facts. The social facts related to religion reveal two types of behaviour in society:

- Belief or thought and ritual (action).
- Sacred and profane.
- These became the elementary forms of religious life.

The religion came into existence due to the concepts of sacred and profane. All activities related to religion are perceived with purity and they are isolated from the profane or impure things. The belief in sacred gave rise to belief and action. Belief is thought behind the sacred things and ritual is action part according to belief. Thus, the structure of religion has given birth to two types of behaviour, sacred and profane and belief and ritual. Thus, according to Durkheim, it is society which is responsible for the origin of religion.

- *Structural Theory*: An another French anthropologist Levi-Strauss in his book, "Structural Anthropology" (1963) has attempted to provide structural theory of origin of religion on the basis of linguistic approach. The linguistic approach to the study of religion reveals the dichotomy of nature-culture. The religion originated due to culturalization of natural things. That is why in languages we have structure like Nature *versus* culture. For example, plants, animals, trees, birds, river, mountain, sea and other natural things appear frequently in cultural activities. But when they appear as cultural objects performing cultural activities, they do not remain natural object. The worship of totem is clear example of origin of religion through nature-culture dichotomy.
- *Totemistic Theory*: The totemistic theory of origin of religion was propounded by Emile Durkheim in his book, "Elementary forms of Religious Life" (1912). According to him totem was the first sacred object whose eating and killing was a taboo for clan members. Thus, totem led to the origin of religion.

Science

The present day mankind has not only magic and religion to control the behaviour. Rather mankind has a rich tradition of science by which behaviour of society is controlled. In minimum words, we can define science as systematic knowledge of any things such as God, nature and man. The science is based on facts, observations, experiences, logic and cause-effect relationship. Right from his emergence on this earth during prehistoric period, mankind attempted to acquire knowledge on the basis of observation, experience, logic and cause-effect relationship. As a result, his knowledge tradition went on increasing day-by-day. But mankind reached in historic era of scientific age during fourteenth Century A.D. in Europe when scientific revolution took place and a series of scientific inventions took place. Series of scientific inventions led to the emergence of industries and the process of industrialization began. This process started in England during seventeenth and eighteenth century and were spread in all parts of the globe during British period. With the process of industrialization, the capitalism, democracy and secularism were evolved. The meaning of secularism was not a religion free society. Rather, it is concerned with the equal treat to all religious groups by the state and no discrimination based on religion by the state. Machine, industries and things produced are secular to be consumed by followers of all religious groups. To-day we are living in scientific age. Scientific inventions have made our journey, clothes, food, transport, health, tourism and many other aspects of human life more and more easy and comfortable. Now, science is used in both senses good and bad for the society.

Now, we are going to different planets to explore facts and probability of life there. But we have also made atom bomb and biological weapons to destroy human beings.

Scientific Process

Science begins with observation and ends with observation. In other words, science is dependent upon observation right from initial stage up to arriving at final conclusion. The scientific process involves the following steps:

- Observation, experimentation and experiences with facts.
- Recording the facts.
- Verifying the facts.
- Establishing logic and cause and effect relation.
- Generalising the facts or arriving at conclusion.

Characteristic of Science

The science has following characteristics.

- *Observation and Experimentation*: Science is based on observation and experimentation. Through these the science acquire knowledge about the facts.
- *Recording of Facts*: Recording of fact is another characteristic of science. In science facts are observed again and again and recording is made each time.
- *Verification of Facts*: Verification of facts is a characteristic of science. In science facts are verified again and again. Verifiability is characteristic of science.

- *Logic*: Logic is one of characteristics of science. On the basis of experience and knowledge logic is developed in science. Deduction-induction logic play significant role in science.
- *Cause-effect Relation*: The establishment of cause-effect relation is a characteristic of science. There is a cause behind every effect. In science attempt is made to know the cause of every effect through systematic observation and experimentation of facts.
- *Generalisation*: After establishing cause-effect relation generalization is made in science. Generalization is characteristic of science.
- *Challenge of Super Human Power*: On the basis of systematic knowledge acquired and logical power, the science has started making challenge to the authority of God in many ways and in many directions.
- *Value of Scientists*: The science has been able to provide value to the scientists who have offered and who are offering their lives for simple and complex scientific inventions.
- *Artificial Production*: The science has given us varieties of things which are produced artificially and are used by the mankind.
- *Modern Occupation*: The science has opened a number of areas of modern occupation such as research and scientists.
- *Beneficial for Humanity*: Science is beneficial for humanity and protecting life of human beings at the time of occurrence of natural disaster—flood, epidemic, earthquake, starvation and so on.
- *Destructive for Humanity*: The science is destructive for the humanity, too. It is because atom bombs, hydrogen bombs and biological weapons are all destructive for human beings.
- *New Definition of Time and Space*: The science has given us a new dimension and definition of time.
- *Development of Technology*: The science has been able to develop different types of technologies to be applied in different types of economic and cultural activities.

Similarity between Science and Magic

The magic and science both have some similarities. Main points of similarity between magic and science are as follows:

- Both are means of satisfaction of human needs.
- Both have specialists—magician and scientist.

- In both some experiments are performed.
- Both employ trial and error method.
- Both are used for advantages and disadvantages.
- Both accept natural law.
- Both believe in law of contact.
- In both experiments can bring adverse result, if not performed accurately and properly.

Difference between Magic and Science

In spite of above similarities, both magic and science also have some differences. The main points of differences between magic and science are as follows:

- Magic is based on belief in super human power, but science is based on observation of facts.
- The magic has to pass through mysterious processes, but science passes through observation, recording, verification and generalization processes.
- Magical acts are performed in lonely places, but scientific acts are performed in laboratory.
- If any one else sees the performance of magical experiments, it does not bring desired results. But if any body sees the performance of scientific experiment, it does not effect the desired goal.
- When taboos are not observed, magical acts become unsuccessful. But scientific experiments become unsuccessful due to inadequate knowledge.
- The magic performers are known as magicians, but scientific experiment doers are known as scientists. Black magicians are not regarded in society, but scientists are always regarded by the society.
- Magic is associated more with primitive, folk and peasant societies, but science is more associated with civilized and complex society.

Similarity between Religion and Science

Both religion and science have some similarities. The points of similarities between religion and science are as follows:

- Both religion and science are found in society.
- Both make human beings tension free.
- Both have specialists—priest and scientists.
- In both some kinds of performances are done.
- Both have safety function.
- Both have control function.
- Both have welfare function.

Difference between Religion and Science

Religion and science both have some similarities undoubtedly but this does not mean that they are not different. The main points of differences between religion and science are as follows:

- The religion is related to super human and super natural world. But science is related to human and natural world.
- Religion is based on belief, but science is based on observation of facts.
- Logic or criticism has no place in religion, but logic plays significant role in science.
- The specialist of religion is known as priest, but the specialist of science is known as scientist.
- In religion rituals are performed, but in science experiments are performed.
- Religion is divided into different sects, but scientists are divided on the basis of expertise.
- Fanatics find place in religion, but fanatics have no place in science.
- In religion incidence of religious riots occur, but in science riots have no scope.
- Religion is based on caste and community, but science is above caste and community.
- The benefits of religious performances goes to individual or community concerned, but benefit of science is availed by all individuals, caste and community.
- Religion is related to sacrifice, science is related to facilities.
- Religion is related to welfare, science is related to destruction, too.
- In religion, trial and error method has no place, but trial and error method finds significant place in science.

Difference between Primitive Religion and Modern Religion

Here it will be the fitness of the things to present the differences between primitive religion and modern religion. The religion originated in primitives after magic and since then it has undergone several changes in achieving the present modern status in modern time. The main points of differences between primitive religion and modern religion are as follows:

- Primitive religion originated due to animism, animatism or manaism and naturalism, but modern religion originated due to the initiative taken by states.
- Primitive religion was not divided into different groups and sects, but modern religion is divided into different sects and communities.
- Primitive religion was simple, modern religion is complex.
- In primitive religion sacrifice has great value, but in modern religion *Tantra-Mantra* and *Puja-Path* occupy significant place.
- There was no conversion in primitive religion, but there is scope of conversion in modern religion.
- Each primitive community had its own Priest, but each sect in modern religion has many *Guru* and *Shishya.*
- Primitive religion was acquired through socialization, modern religion is spread through modern religions institutions.
- There is no pomp and show in primitive religion, but there is great pomp and show in modern religion
- There was no texts in primitive religion. But modern religion has texts according to sects and communities.
- Primitive religion was concerned for the welfare of the community, but modern religion has given birth to service, kindness.
- There was no alms-giving and charity in primitive religion, but modern religion has importance of alms-giving and charity.
- In primitive religion there was no concept of begging for the help of others, but in modern religion begging, donation and subscription have significant place.

- Primitive religion originated due to failure of magic, but modern religion appeared with the support of ruling states.
- There was concept of sacred and profane in primitive religion, but in modern religion we find the concept of secularism promoted my modern states.

Totemism

In primitive societies people show mystical genetic relation with flora, fauna, mountain, hills, river, sea and other. This tradition has given birth to belief in super human powers and super natural power. Through this mystical genetic relation, the life of primitives were controlled. Anthropologists have termed such relationship of primitives as totemism. Totem was a unilateral descent group and played significant role in the practice of exogamy.

We may define totemism as a sentiment expressed towards flora, fauna and other natural objects. When the members of a totem express their sentiments and beliefs in the form of institutions, then we may call it as totemism.

Characteristics of Totemism

The totemism has the following characteristics:

- Totem is regarded as sacred.
- Totemic group observes a number of taboos related to its totem.
- Totem is base of clan formation in primitives.
- Totem group observes exogamy.
- Totem leads to formation of descent group.
- Eating and killing of totem is a taboo except on some specific festive occasions.
- The picture of totem is tatooed on body, neck, hands, arms and other parts of body.

Types of Totem

Totem may be divided into following categories:

- *Clan totem*: When formation of clan takes place on the bases of totem, such totem is known as clan totem.

- *Individual totem*: The ruler, priest, magician and physician of primitives had their own totem.
- *Sex totem*: In some primitives, male had a separate totem and female had a separate totem.
- *Part totem*: In some tribals, some parts of a plant, an animal or a bird was treated as totem which gave rise to the concept of part totem.
- *Conception totem*: The totem believed to be responsible for conception, is known as conception totem.
- *Matrilineal Totem*: In matrilineal clan, matrilineal totem is found.
- *Patrilineal Totem*: In patrilineal clan, patritineal totem is found.

Theories Related to the Origin of Totem

A number of theories have been propounded by different scholars regarding the origin of totemism. They are as follows:

- *Nomothetic Theory*: This theory of origin of totem was propounded by Herbert Spencer. According to him, language was not developed in human societies in the early time. In this stage, names of babies were given after plants, animals and other natural things. Later on, people started treating plants and animals as their ancestor. They were treated as sacred and their worship started
- *Belief in Existence of Soul*: This theory of origin of totemism was propounded by Frazer. According to him, primitives believed that soul of deads goes to reside in plants, trees, birds, animals, insects, river, hill and other. They started regarding them pious and sacred.
- *Economic Theory*: This theory was propounded by Herskovits. According to him, primitives had to struggle hard for their existence. In this struggle of existence, the plants, animals, birds, insects would have kept them alive. Gradually, they started treating them sacred and pure.
- *Sociological Theory*: This theory was propounded by French sociologist Emile Durkheim. According to him, totem was the first sacred object regarded and respected by the members of society. Clan organization started in their names.
- *Structural Theory*: This theory was propounded by Levi Strauss, a French anthropologist. According to him, the structure of totemism reveals nature-culture dichotomy. Through totemism culturisation of natural things took place as a result of which nature-

culture dichotomy appeared in social structure. The totemism reveals natural objects transformed into cultural objects through belief and practices.

• *Freudian Theory*: Freud in his book "Totem and Taboo" (1913) has propounded sexual theory for the origin of totemism. According to him, in the beginning men lived in band. Each band had a leader who was the eldest male member of the band. He had full control to have sex with all females of the band. His sons began to hate him. One day they killed him but soon realised their fault. They would have accepted the abode of their father in plants and animals. They began to offer worship to them. Thus, totem originated due to taboo on killing and eating of totems who were representative of their father. The origin of totemism should be explained on the basis of Oedipus complex.

Change in Religion

- There has been decrease in rituals performed in different stages of life such as birth, *Mundan*, earboring, *Janeu*, marriage, birth and death.
- The hold of religion on social life has decreased due to the process of secularization.
- Religion has lost its collective and integrative function.
- To-day a number of societies have religious pluralism–a co-existence of different religions.

Chapter 7
Economic Anthropology

Economic Anthropology is a sub-branch of social-cultural anthropology which deals with study of economic institutions like production, consumption, redistribution, exchange, trade, market, reciprocity and hospitality of tribal societies or simple society.

In primitive or tribal societies or simple societies economic institutions are part and parcel of social-cultural organizations. That is why economic anthropology has been included as a sub-branch of social-cultural anthropology.

You might have seen women cooking food, and men performing outside work in family. You would have seen women and men collecting food materials from the forest, you would have seen cows, goats, buffalos, cocks, hens, ducks, pigs etc. in your house or in neighbourhood. You would have seen people—men and women, exchanging vegetable and other edible or non-edible goods with grains or money taking baskets on heads or on a bicycle, ox and horse. You would have visited village markets where people of neighbouring villages come to sell their goods produced in the hands of local middlemen and purchasing goods and article related to their daily use. You would have seen your relatives bringing goods of different types when they were invited to attend marriage, birth and death rituals. You would have seen serving delicious food materials to your relatives and paying some gifts to them at the time of going back to their respective residences. Have you ever thought what types of these activities are. Such types of activities are termed as economic activities. There are institutions which govern these economic activities. Therefore, they are termed as economic institutions. In simple societies, economic activities are mixed with social-cultural activities and organizations.

The system by which economic institutions like production, consumption, redistribution, exchange, trade market, division of labour, reciprocity and hospitality of primitives are controlled is known as primitive economy.

We have natural resources and human resources. Human resources on the basis of knowledge and science develop technology. Human beings use technology to exploit natural resources for getting production of various things. Thus, economic system consists of human resources, natural resources and technology.

Characteristics of Primitive Economy

The concept of primitive economy is quite different from modern economy. The chief characteristics of primitive economy are as follows:

- *Forest based Economy*: The primitive economy was based on forest. Forest was the centre of economic activities of simple people. They used to do hunting, gathering, and shifting cultivation in the forest. They prepared varieties of baskets, ropes, mats with the help of grass, bark and bamboo. They used to erect house with woods and bamboo available in forest. They used to do barter exchange of things collected from the forest. In reciprocity, they used to exchange roots, shoots, leaves, flowers, fruits, honey and seeds collected from the forest. They used to pay skin, bones, horns, nails of animals and birds trapped as gift to their relatives and guest. They used to serve meat of animals hunted to their guests. They used different parts of flora as folk medicine. They used to meet fuel needs from dry leaves and woods of the forest. Thus, primitive economy was totally forest based.
- *Family as Unit of Production*: In primitive economy family was unit of production. In extended form family included lineage and clan, too. They used to do gathering and hunting collectively. They used to do pastoralism on collective basis and even agriculture on collective basis. Thus family was unit of production.
- *Family as Unit Consumption*: In primitive economy things produced collectively were consumed collectively by the family members.
- *Division of Labour*: The primitive economy was characterized by the division of labour. Women used to do cooking in house and gathering nearby the residence. Men used to do hunting. The aged

used to look after kids, cattle and thrashing field. The children used to assist their parents. They all participated in production process according to their age, sex and efficiency. But they all consumed up to their desire. How much work a member was performing was not taken into consideration in consumption.

- *Lack of Wages*: In primitive economy there was lack of wages. There was no concept of wage payment. All family members participated according to their efficiency in production process and all participated in consumption process. For erection of houses lineage and clan members were requested and they used to erect houses with the help of their relatives. After completion of erection work, a feast was served to lineage and clan members. Thus, for erection of house and work on the occasions of marriage, birth and death, they used to exchange their service and feast. But any kind of wage payment was not made.
- *Lack of Capital*: In primitive economy there was lack of capital. The place of gathering and hunting was forests and hills. In the name of tools, they had stone made simple tools. There was no needs of expertise to handle the tools. Like modern economy, the concept of capital was lacking in primitive economy.
- *Simple Technology*: The technology used for production in primitive economy was very simple. They included only stone tools made by simple techniques. Any member of the family can handle those tools easily. There was no any complexity in building and handling them.
- *Lack of Expert*: In primitive economy there was no expert. All were capable of gathering and hunting and also in using stone tools. All participated in production. Some members did not participate because of some taboos imposed on them particularly some women, children and aged.
- *Subsistence-oriented Economy*: The primitive economy was subsistence-oriented. Primitives used to do production to maintain their survival, not for saving and demand.
- *Barter Exchange*: The primitives had barter exchange system. They used to do exchange of goods with goods. The concept of money was not known.
- *Consumption-oriented Exchange*: The exchange system of primitives was related to consumption. They used to exchange goods with goods for the purpose of consumption.

• *No Concept of Saving*: The primitive did not know the concept of saving. They used to do exchange of goods with goods for consumption, not for profit or saving.

• *Reciprocity*: The primitives had non-market and non-money exchange system between friends and relatives. They used to maintain reciprocal relation with relatives and friends by paying gifts of things produced by them.

• *No Economic Relation*: The concept of master and labour was not known to them and no payment was made for economic activities.

• *Weekly Market*: The primitives had weekly *haat* where they used to do barter exchange of things produced.

• *Production Mixed with Magic*: In primitive society production was mixed with magic. Magical performances were made for the purpose of production.

Primitive Economy—Myth or Real?

Whether Primitive Economy is myth or real, in order to solve this problem, let us make a comparison between the characteristics of primitive economy and modern economy. On the basis of comparison between these two types of economies, we can be able to conclude whether primitive economy is myth or real.

Production: Production is creation of utility. The modern economy is known as industrial economy. For the purpose of industrial production, five factors are important. They are:

- Land
- Labour
- Capital
- Organization
- Entrepreneurship

Land: Land is passive agent of production. Without investing capital and labour, production from land is not possible. For the purpose of industrial establishment, the industrialist acquires land. Either he purchases land or takes land in lease. After acquision of land, capital is required to purchase machines, establish building, and purchase of raw material. When industry is established, experts and labourers are required to run the industries. They create utility through industrial production.

For primitives, the concept of land included not only land, but also rivers, mountains, hills, lakes, seas, plains, forest, flora and fauna. Thus, for them concept of land was not limited to only those parts of earth where houses, buildings, industries and business centres are erected. But among primitive the concept of land was very wide which included all things given to them by nature. They did not require to acquire land. Rather land was given to them by the nature as gift for their survival. The primitives used to create utility in natural things for the production.

Labour: Industrialist has different types of experts and labourers to run the industries properly. The industrialist makes payment of wages to their workers. Expert and labourers perform their special function.

The concept of labour was different in primitive society. There was division of labour to run the family smoothly. But this division was not watertight compartment like usually women perform cooking and men outside work. But males also knew cooking and women also performed outside work.

There was no specialization of work, but few taboos were imposed on certain kinds of work of women. The concept of wages was not known to them. They performed their work with the help of family members or reciprocal exchange of services with their kins. After accomplishment of work, a feast was served to the community member. There was no concept of promotion and demotion.

- *Capital*: The industrialist takes loan from bank to purchase machine and building materials. Capital is a must for industrial production. Primitives were fully dependent on forest. Therefore, they did not require any capital.
- *Organization*: When land, labour and capital are organized properly, modern economic production starts. But in primitive economy there were family organization, clan organization and lineage organization for the purpose of hunting, gathering, fishing, and agriculture.
- *Entrepreneurship*: For establishing and running an industry, the entrepreneurship is a must. Without this courage an industrialist cannot be an industrialist. Because in establishing and running industry, the industrialist may face the situation of loss. He must be ready to face such situation. In primitive economy, there was no need of such entrepreneurship. But primitives were organized for hunting, gathering and fishing.

• *Consumption*: Consumption is destruction of utility. In modern economy, there is a concept of distribution before consumption. The industrialist sends goods produced to markets. From the money received by selling produced goods, he pays loan of bank, rent of land, wages of labourers, transportation cost and raw material cost. After making payment on these, whatever money is left, is termed as profit. From the profit the industrialist meets his own consumption needs.

In primitive society, the production was consumption oriented not profit oriented. Family is unit of production. Family members produce collectively and they consume the produced things collectively.

In primitive economy, there was a concept of redistribution. Primitives used to pay skins, horns, feet of hunted animals to the priest as gift. The priest used to return them to the group members whenever they require them.

• *Exchange*: The modern or economic exchange system is money exchange system. In this system goods produced are sold first to get money. The money, thus, obtained through exchange is used to buy different types of goods and articles according to needs. But primitives had barter system of exchange where goods were exchanged for goods. The exchange system of primitives was consumption-oriented not profit-oriented.

Trade and Market: In modern economy, trade and market play significant role. It is because an industrialist is rationalist. He makes surveys regarding the marketing value of things produced. He produces things keeping demand in mind. He fulfils the demands of market through his production. Modern markets are centre of trade where traders from different parts accumulate for sale and purchase of commodity. Modern market is competitive. There is competition among traders to sale and purchase commodities.

But primitives had their weekly *Haat* where they exchanged their things produced. The medium of exchange was barter. Head load, shoulder load, ox, horse etc. were used for transportation of goods. Buyers and sellers both knew each other by face, name and place. Haggling was also prevalent in weekly *Haat*.

From the above presented account it is clear that primitives had their own system of production, consumption, exchange, trade and market by which they used to meet their economic needs. These economic institutions had kept primitive surving for very long period.

These institutions are still in operation in primitive societies. Therefore, primitive economy was not a myth as modern economists say. Rather primitive economy was a reality for primitives.

Cooperation and Competition in Primitive Society

A question generally appears in our mind whether primitives were cooperative or competitive or both cooperative and competitive. Generally people believe that primitives were cooperative because their social organization was based on collective social and economic activities. But on the basis of empirical evidences, it does not appear true.

In order to understand the cooperation and competition among primitives, Margaret Mead, an American lady anthropologist of culture and personality school, made a study of 13 primitive societies from hunting, gathering to agricultural economic activities. She wrote a book, "Cooperation and Competition among Primitive People" (1937). In this book she has described that cooperative and competitive both types of behaviour were present among the primitive people. These cooperative and competitive behaviours were culturally and environmentally conditioned. For cooperative and competitive behaviour among primitives, their culture and environment were responsible. Her main conclusions were as follows:

- Cooperative and competitive behaviours were integrative parts of their social organization.
- Cooperative and competitive behaviours were related to technological development. As technological development went on developing, more and more competitive behaviour came into existence.
- In building cooperative and competitive behaviour, the role of social structure was of great value. Individuals and social goals are determined by social institutions. For the fulfilment of goal, cooperative and competitive behaviours were determined.
- Information of cooperative and competitive behaviour socialization process and educational system play significant role.

Thus, from the above conclusions of Mead's study, cooperation and competition is not the result of civilization. Rather cooperation and competition are culturally and environmentally conditioned. Due to diversity of culture, cooperation and competition was prevalent even among hunting and gathering societies, though these societies were struggling hard for their existence. She found that Kwakiutl were competitive and Eskimo were individualistic. Arunta of middle Asia were cooperative, Ojibwa were individualistic and Yugo of Philippines were competitive. Kwakiutl and Eskimo were hunter and gatherer, whereas Ojibwa, Arunta and Yugo are agriculturist. Thus, empirical evidences do not support the hypothesis that primitives were cooperative, not competitive. Primitives were cooperative, competitive and individualistic.

Reciprocity

In economic anthropology, non-money and non-market exchange of goods and services between kins and friends is called reciprocity. But in structural anthropology of Levi-Strauss, reciprocity means formation of kinship by exchange of woman between two groups. For organized and collective life reciprocity was essential.

In reciprocity three actions are involved. These are:

- To give
- To take
- To repay

In primitive society, the production was existence and consumption-oriented. They produced such things which were perishable, not durable. In order to save these things from decay, they were sent in the houses of kins, neighbours and friends. Again on the occasion of birth, marriage and death feast, reciprocal exchange of goods produced and services also takes place. The goods received and service rendered are returned essentially on the same type of occasion when they are given. Thus, reciprocity binds relatives and friends more closely. Through reciprocity social relations get strengthen and remains maintained.

Types of Reciprocity: According to Elman Service, reciprocity may be classified into three types on the basis of occasion, quality and amount of goods given, received and repaid.

• *General Reciprocity*: In this type of reciprocity, amount, quality and occasion or give and take are not limited. Here expectation is limitless. Here give and take between two kins or friends may take place at any time. The giver can give any time, taker can take any moment and repayer can repay whenever he desires. It is concerned with good social and economic status.

• *Negative Reciprocity*: In this type of reciprocity expectation of repay remains negative. The quality and amount of repay is not as much as was given and taken in the reciprocity. That is why it is termed as negative reciprocity. Suppose 50 kg. rice was given but 30 kg. rice was repaid. Then, it is an example of negative reciprocity. Negative reciprocity is not considered good. It is taken as bad and it symbolizes low status of a kin. It gradually breaks social relation.

• *Balanced Reciprocity*: In this type of reciprocity the occasion, quality and quantity of things remain same as were given and received. That is why it is termed as balanced reciprocity. It is considered very good for the society. Balanced reciprocity is good for continuation and maintenance of social relationship. Here if 40 kg. golden wheat is given, 40 kg. golden wheat is returned.

• *Occasion of Reciprocal Exchange*: The occasion on which reciprocal exchange of goods and services took place are as follows:

- After harvesting of new crops
- When a cow or buffalo gives calf
- Occasion of birth ritual
- Occasion of *Chhathi* ritual
- Occasion of *Mundan* ritual
- Occasion of Marriage ritual
- Occasion of death ritual
- On receipt of Invitation
- On arrival and departure of guest
- On festivals
- Beginning of agricultural activities
- Agricultural festival celebration

• *Things Exchanged in Reciprocity*: Following types of things are exchanged in reciprocity:

- Rice, Pulse, Vegetables, Goat, Hen, Cock, Chicks, Pig.
- Milk, Curd, Ghee, Oil, Homemade Sweets, Honey, Fruits.

- Baskets, goat, Cow, Ox, Buffalo, Home-made Articles, Home-made Toys.
- Services.

• *Functions of Reciprocity*: Reciprocity performs following important functions:

- Helpful in maintenance of social relation.
- Helpful in identification of status of different kins and friends.
- Helpful in organizing rituals and feasts.

Exchange System

We may define exchange system as a system by which reciprocal transfer of wealth between two sides takes place. The exchange system has following chief elements:

- Wealth is essential for exchange, without wealth exchange cannot take place economically.
- Two sides are also essential for exchange.
- Willingness to exchange between two sides is also a must for exchange.
- Exchange cannot take place under any kind of pressure.
- Exchange of wealth should be legal and reciprocal.
- From the point of view of utility, both sides should have profit.

In the beginning man was parasite on nature. His entire basic needs such as shelter, food, and cloth were fulfilled by nature. He was not a producer. He was consumer of things produced by nature. In those days his wants were very limited. He was self-sufficient. In this period, there was no need of exchange. But as man became producer of varieties of things, he could not remain self-sufficient. The needs also went on increasing. Today he needs food to eat, house to live, cloth to wear, paper, pencil, pen, books and articles to read, medicine to recover from illness, bicycle or scooter, motor-cycle, car, etc. to ride, truck, tractor for transportation, T.V., radio, phone, cell phones, Internet for communication and likewise so many things. Man cannot produce all these things alone. Naturally, he had to depend upon other to get needs fulfilled. Interdependency and specialization of labour gave rise to exchange system.

Types of Exchange: The exchange system may be classified into two categories:

- Barter Exchange System
- Money Exchange System

Barter Exchange System

In the beginning money was not invented. But keeping in mind the essentiality of exchange give and take of goods was started. Gradually, barter exchange system was established and the tradition of exchanging goods with goods began. In this system vegetables, fruits, seeds and other things were exchanged with grains—rice, pulse, maize and so on. Though, money exchange has been established in the market, but the tradition of barter exchange is still prevalent in villages. But this system of exchange has many demerits.

Demerits of Barter Exchange System

The chief demerits of barter exchange system are as follows:

- *Willingness to Exchange*: In this exchange system, it was very difficult to find two persons who were ready to exchange goods with each other. In absence of willingness to exchange, it was very difficult to carry on barter exchange. For example, if an individual has to exchange 40 k.g. of rice with wheat, he will have to find out such an individual who is ready to exchange his wheat with rice. But it is very difficult to find such types of two persons.
- *Lack of Measurement*: In barter exchange, there was no measurement by which goods could be exchanged with goods. This system lacked measurement and value determination. Suppose a man has an ox and he wants to exchange with a horse, how many oxen will be exchanged with horse, there was no fixed measurement for it.
- *Lack of Medium*: In barter exchange system, there was lack of standard medium. In absence of standard medium, problem was faced in barter exchange system. Due to lack of standard medium it was not possible to determine the price of two goods. For example, there was no fixed standard to measure how many goats would be required for an elephant.

• *Problem of Divisibility*: The barter exchange system had to face the problem of divisibility. It was not possible to divide elephant, cow, goat, horse and other animals at the time of exchange.

• *Problem of Transportability*: This system of exchange also faced the problem of transportability. They were carried on head load, shoulder load and walking with them. River, mountain, sea, forest, lake created problem in movements of animals and goods. It was not possible to carry goods on heads or shoulders for a long distance.

• *Problem of Perishability*: The barter exchange system faced the problem of perishability. The things produced were not durable. Rather they were perishable.

• *Problem of Storage*: The barter exchange system has to face the problem of storage. As things produced were not durable, rather they were perishable, so there was a problem to store them for a long period. Due to perishability, the value of things produced was destroyed.

Money Exchange System

Barter exchange system had to suffer from a number of problems mentioned above. In order to get rid of problems associated with barter exchange system, money exchange system was invented. In this system of exchange, goods produced are exchanged with money. With the help of money other commodities and things are purchased. Thus, in this exchange system sale and purchase of goods and commodities take place through the medium of money. Here money is medium through which goods are sold and purchased.

Money: Now-a-days, whatever desires and needs we have, they are fulfilled by money. Now question arises as to what money is? Whenever these questions appear in our mind, we look towards Rupees, notes and coins. But in economic anthropology the term money has been used in special sense. Money is that thing which as a means of exchange passes from one hand to another freely and which is accepted as last payment of loan.

From above definition, it is clear that only those things can be money which is accepted in give and take without any break. Gold, Silver, cheque etc. are not money because they are not accepted by all.

Types of Money: Money can be classified into following categories:

- Metallic Money
- Paper Money
- Plastic Money

- *Metallic Money*: Metallic money or coins occupy significant place in a country. They are made up of metals. The Government of a country makes coins of fixed weight and value. The coins have seal of Government. Previously there existed coins of gold and silver in different countries. But now-a-days, they are not in existence. But in some countries coins of bronze, brass and aluminium are available. The Government makes coins in their own factory and assures guarantee of weight, value and quality.

The coins are divided into two categories:

- Standard Coins
- Symbolic Coins

- *Standard Coins*: Standard coins are those coins whose face value and intrinsic value is same. This is main coin of a country. When these coins are melted, the value of metal obtained is same as the value of the coin.
- *Symbolic Coin*: Symbolic coins are those coins whose face value is more than intrinsic value. Its value is fixed by the Government. For example notes of Rs.2, Rs.5, Rs.10, Rs.20, Rs.50, Rs.100, Rs.500 and Rs.1000.
- *Paper Money*: Today almost all countries of the globe have paper money. The paper money has following characteristics:

- Paper notes are main money of a country.
- The value of a note is not determined as valuable metal.
- Paper note has no its intrinsic value.
- Paper notes are legally accepted.

Plastic Money: Now-a-days, plastic money has come into existence in the form of ATM Card and Debit Card. Payment through these cards can be made anywhere in the globe.

Functions of Money: The main functions of money are as follows:

- Money acts as a medium of exchange.
- Money provides measurement of value.

- Money is standard of give and take.
- Money is a means of value storage.

Thus, money has four functions—medium, standard, storage and payment.

Money among Primitives

Money was not invented in the beginning. In absence of money things were exchanged with things. This system of exchange is known as barter exchange. But barter exchange system had a number of difficulties. To overcome those difficulties, invention of money took place in primitives. In the beginning, there was barter money. For example nail, tooth, hair, feather, skin, horn, shell, glittering stone pieces were made as means of money exchange system. After invention of pottery, seals of terracotta were made. In metal age coins of bronze, brass, copper, aluminium, gold and silver were made. When paper was invented, paper coins were made. Now-a-days, plastic ATM card and Debit card have been invented for global payment.

Impact of Monetization on Tribal Economy and Society

The process of monetization has affected the tribal economy and society to a great extent. The impact of monetization can be discussed under the following headings.

- *Impact on Production*: Monetization has influenced tribal production to a great extent. They now, not only produce for consumption but also produce things to sell them in *Haat*-bazaar and to get money. They can be seen selling roots, shoots, leaves, flowers, fruits, seeds, honey, wax, herbal medicinal plants, brooms, mat, rope, rice, maize, fried grains, rice beer and a number of other articles produced by them for getting money. In order to get money by selling grains and vegetables they are using HYV seeds, chemical fertilizer, pesticides and weedicides. Thus, monetization has resulted in profit oriented production among tribals. Their production is now not only consumption-oriented.
- *Impact on Consumption*: The monetization has also affected consumption pattern of the tribals. For consumption, now, they are not only dependent on things produced by them. Rather they sell their things produced to get money and from the money, thus obtained, they purchase varieties of commodities which they do not produce.

• *Impact on Labour*: The monetization has also brought its impact on labour in tribal societies. Labourers are getting their payment not in kind but in cash. For earning more and more wages tribal labourers are migrating from neighbouring towns to metropolitans. Tribal girls are getting employment as maid servant, Reja and coolie.

• *Impact on Capital*: Under the impact of monetization tribal people have been able to understand the value of capital. The concept of saving has emerged. The amount of saving is used as capital. They treat their land, agricultural implements, cattle, livestocks and saving in cash as capital. They also take loan from bank, cooperative society, and SHGs.

• *Impact on Reciprocal Relation*: Impact of monetization has also influenced the maintenance of reciprocal relation. Now, relatives and friends have started exchanging money on ritualistic and ceremonial occasion to maintain relationship. From the money saved they are buying items of gifts to be presented to guest and kins.

• *Impact on Exchange System*: The impact of monetization has influenced the barter exchange system of tribals. In place of barter exchange, now they prefer money exchange. They, now, exchange their goods for money and from money they buy things of their requirements.

• *Impact on Bazaar*: Monetization has also affected tribal weekly *haat*. Now, the selling and buying goods take place through the medium of money.

• *Impact on Trade*: Monetization has also affected the trade of things gathered and produced by tribals. For example, Honey, Wax, *Biri Patta*, leafmade plates, cups and other things, *mahua* flower, rope, handicrafts and so on. The trade of these things now takes place through the medium of money.

• *Redistribution*: Redistribution is an institution related to exchange of goods and services found among tribal societies. Through the medium of redistribution, transaction of goods produced takes place in tribal society. This was an important institution of band society. In the beginning men used to live in band. Each band had a leader. He was most respectful person. The members of the band used to do gathering and hunting under the guidance of the leader collectively. Things collected and animals hunted were brought before the leader of the band. The leader used to do distribution of goods collected and animal hunted among the members of the group keeping their needs in mind. The members of the band used to pay special portion of animal hunted, skin, nails, hairs, skull and horns of hunted animals to the leader as gift. The leader used to redistribute them among members whenever they need those things.

The institution of redistribution is also found among Uthalu Birhor of Chhotanagpur who leads a life in band wandering from place to place in forest. They call their band as *tanda*.

Economic Goods

All those things by which desires or wants of the people are fulfilled are termed as goods. For example root, shoot, leaves, flower, fruit, seed, light, water, food, cloth, pen, paper etc.

- *Types of Goods*: Goods may be classified into two categories:

- Unlimited or free Goods
- Economic Goods

- *Unlimited or Free Goods*: Those goods whose supply is more than demand are termed as unlimited goods or free goods. These goods are provided to us by nature free of cost. We have not to pay any cost for these goods. For example light of sun and moon, water of river and air. Unlimited goods are gift to us by the nature. Their supply is more than demand.
- *Economic Goods*: Those goods whose supply is less than demands are termed as economic goods. For example—Rice, wheat, flower, fruit, vegetable etc.

Economic goods are result of labour of man. The man creates utility in these goods by applying their labour. These goods have value. That is why their supply is less than the demand. Human beings produce these things by their labour, or purchase them from market by paying money.

It is worth mentioning here that under special circumstances unlimited or free goods also become economic goods. For example, when a dam is built on a river and its water is used for the purpose of irrigation, it becomes economic good. We have to pay for irrigation of crops. Similarly, when we use the sand of river for house construction, it becomes economic goods.

Human beings have indefinite wants. In order to satisfy wants human being perform economic activities. Performance of economic activities give rise to the production of economic goods.

Property in Simple Society

The term property is used even by layman. They term their money earned, rupees, Paisa, ornaments, land, cattle, tree, house etc. as property. But in economic anthropology the term property has been used in special sense. According to the concept of economic anthropology, all economic goods are termed as property. All those things which have value are termed as property.

Types of Property

The property of simple society may be divided into following types:

- Material Property
- Non-material Property

Material Property: The material property can be divided further into two categories:

- Nature gifted material property
- Man-made material property

• *Nature Gifted Material Property*: Right from beginning things given to us by nature have been regarded as property. For example—mountain, hill, river, lake, sea, plants, trees, animals, birds, fishes, forest, pasture land and so on. The abodes of Gods and Goddesses are also known as property.

• *Man-made Property*: In primitive societies things, made by man are also regarded as property. For example—rope, cot, bed, baskets, brooms, mats, cover, hunting implements, gathering tools, agricultural implements, utensils, reading materials, writing materials.

• *Non-material Property*: In primitive society one finds the concept of non-material property. For example—magic, songs, tales, music poems, proverbs, etc. are examples of non-material property.

Property may also be divided into two categories on the basis of ownership in tribal societies. They are as follows:

- Common Property
- Individual Property

• *Common Property*: Among tribals one finds the concept of common property. For example—road, street, drainage, pasture land, forest, mountain, bank of river, pond, cremation ground or graveyard, abode of gods and goddesses, school land, health sub-centre land, community hall land, *Haat* bazaar land, Dhumkhuria land, Sarana land, Sasan land, akhra land and musical instruments.

• *Individual Property*: Tribals also have concept of individual property. For example agricultural land, agricultural implements, household furniture, utensils, safety instruments, musical instruments, poem created by an individual, cattle wealth, tree wealth, magical expertise, knowledge of health and folk medicine.

Characteristics of Property: Property has following characteristics:

- Utility
- Scarcity
- Transferability
- Externality

• *Utility*: Only those things become property which have utility. The meaning of utility here is capable of fulfilling the needs. Those things which have efficiency or capability to fulfil human needs are termed as property. We are ready to purchase only those things which are useful. Thus, utility is a characteristic of property.

• *Scarcity*: Only utility does not assure that a thing is property. Rather along with utility scarcity is also related to property. Property is scarce because they are available in limited quantity. Their supply is less than demands. Air of fan, cooler, water of tap, gold, silver, etc. are property.

• *Transferability*: The property should have the quality of transferability. The property should be such as to pass from one hand to another. Due to the property of transferability, the property can be exchanged. Sun, moon, star, air, etc. are not property because they do not have individual ownership.

• *Externality*: Only those things come under the category of property which are under external right of man. For example—power of singing and creating poems are under internal right of man, so they are not property.

Tribal *Haat* (Market)

In tribal societies, the places where weekly *Haat* takes place once or twice in a week are termed as tribal market or tribal *Haat*. Exchange of goods produced and commodities required are exchanged in these tribal *Haats*.

In day-to-day talk of common people, *Haat* means a place where sale and purchase of things take place once or twice in a week. But in economic anthropology the term *Haat* or *Bazar* is used in special sense. Here the term *Haat* or market is used in wide sense. The meaning of *Haat* or market in economic anthropology is related to entire area where sellers and buyers have such a competitive and free relation that in entire area the value of good is same.

Types of Market: On the basis of place, markets may be divided into three categories:

- Local Market
- National Market
- International Market

• *Local Market*: When buyers and sellers of things go to a local place for selling and buying commodities, we call such market as local market. Tribal societies generally have local markets which take place once or twice or thrice in a week. At some places, market occurs daily, too.

• *National Market*: When sale and purchase of things take place within the country, such type of market is known as national market. For example *Sari*, *dhoti*, bangles, ornaments, rice, wheat, vegetable, spices, oil, *ghee* etc. have national market.

• *International Market*: When buyers and sellers of a thing are spread all-over the globe, we call such market as international market. For example gold and silver.

Characteristics of Tribal Market

Tribal market has following characteristics:

• *Commodity*: In tribal market, things produced by tribals are sold and purchased. From the money obtained, tribals purchase other commodities of their daily use. For example seasonally produced rice and pulses, seasonally available root, shoot, flower, fruits, seeds, fishes caught from local ponds and river, cocks, hens, honey, wax, goat, rope made articles, broom, mat, baskets, hare, parrot, pigeon, partridge etc. are sold by tribals. From money got, they purchase salt, spices, oil, soap, rice, flour, clothes, glass, bronze, steal and thread made ornaments. They also purchase fried grains and sweets in the market. Haria local rice bear is also sold and purchased. Thus, the commodities sold and purchased in the tribal markets are different from other types of market.

- *Buyers and Sellers*: The buyers and sellers of tribal markets are local people of neighbourig villages, who know each other by name, face and place. In these markets men, women, children can be seen selling and purchasing different things. Tribals come to sell things produced by them and to buy day-to-day use commodities from the local traders. Here, buyers and sellers both are local.
- *Weight and Measure*: Now-a-days, tribal markets have weights and measure or balance by which things are weighed or measured. Kilo and quintals are used for measuring the things. Oils are measured in litre. Clothes are measured in metre. Some things are sold per piece. Local measure called Pila is also used. Fried grains are sold by measuring through pila.
- *Means of Exchange*: Majority of goods in tribal market are exchanged through the medium of money. But for some kinds of things tribals also practice barter exchange but only within the community.
- *Price Determination*: The determination of price in tribal markets takes place through the principle of demand and supply. Some commodities like clothes, shoes, oil, spices are sold at price fixed by the trader. But for the commodities produced by tribals, price is determined seeing the supply and demand. When the demand of a thing is less and supply is more, commodities are sold at low price. But when supply is less and demand is more, commodities are sold at high price. In settling price bargaining takes place too.
- *Transport*: Transport used in carrying commodities to the market are head load, shoulder load, bicycle, ox, buffalo, bullockcart, auto-rickshaw, rickshaw and tractor. But majority of sellers and buyers come on foot with head load and shoulder load.
- *Debt and Credit*: Debt and credit facilities are available in tribal markets, The traders or middlemen know tribals by name, face, family and place, so they provide debt and credit facilities to the

tribals. When loans are not repaid timely, interest is charged. Sometimes, tribals have to put ornaments under bondage of middlemen to get money.

• *Place, Day and Time*: The day, place and time of tribal market are prefixed. Market takes place once or twice in a week on fixed day such as Monday and Thursday or every Saturday. The time of market remains usually from 1 PM to 5 PM. The market occurs in afternoon and ends before sunset.

• *Tax payment*: Tax has been imposed by Bazaar Samiti in tribal markets. The tax amount is nominal.

Role of Tribal Market

The role played by tribal markets can be studied under the following headings:

- Social Role of Tribal Market
- Economic Role of Tribal Market
- Cultural Role of Tribal Market
- Religious Role of Tribal Market
- Political Role of Tribal Market

Social Role of Tribal Market

Tribal market also plays social role. Tribal markets are not only centres of economic activities, but they also perform a number of social activities. The tribal market plays following types of social roles:

• *Reciprocal Exchange of Messages*: In tribal markets people from different villages assemble and share messages with each other. They become aware of joys and sorrows of each other.

• *Meeting of Kins and Friends*: Tribal market is also a meeting place of different kins and friends of neighbouring villages. They exchange various kinds of messages, share fried grains and sweets, do marketing and return home after sunset.

• *Selection of Marriage Partner*: Tribal market helps in the selection of marriage partner. Boys and girls of neighbouring villages get occasion to meet with each other and select their marriage partner with the help of their kins, parents or guardian. Knowing the consent of boy and girl, parents allow them to become couple through marriage.

• *Fixation of Marriage Date*: In many cases, fixation of marriage date also takes place with the help of *Pahan* of both families who also visit market and meet with the people of community.

• *Exchange of Invitation*: The exchange of invitation of marriage, birth and death and also of other ceremonial occasions also take place at the tribal market. Because generally kins of all neighbouring villages meet at market place, it becomes easy to extend formal invitation to them at the same place. This saves time and problem associated with journey of different villages of kins.

• *Socialization*: The tribal market also plays significant role in socialization of children. Children accompany their parents up to market place from very beginning of childhood. In the market they meet their different kins who give them sweets to eat. They know how to behave with their kins on meeting and how to seek their blessings. They meet with traders and see how sale and purchase of commodities takes place. The tribal market socializes the tribal boys and girls to behave with buyer and seller of different commodities.

Economic Role of Tribal Market

The economic roles of tribal markets are as follows:

- Sale and purchase of things produced
- Purchase of things according to need
- Money as medium of exchange
- Weights and measure
- Price determination
- Transport used
- Credit and debt

Cultural Role of Tribal Markets

Cultural roles of tribal markets are as follows:

- Singing songs by folk song singers
- Play of flute player
- Play of bear dance
- Play of sheep fight
- Play of cock fight
- Play of monkey dance

- Hand run swings
- Play of biscope

Religious Role of Tribal Market

The religious role of tribal markets are as follows:

- Sale and purchase of goods of worship
- Sale and purchase of religious dresses and clothes
- Sale and purchase of religious symbols
- Meeting *pahans* of different villages
- Date announcement of festivals
- Date and time announcement of special worship
- Date and time announcement of religious meeting
- Date and time announcement of religious procession
- Announcement of religious fairs

Political Role of Tribal Market

The political role of tribal market are as follows:

- Settlement of quarrel between husband and wife
- Settlement of quarrel between two families of different villages
- Settlement of quarrel between two tribes of neighbouring villages
- Settlement of quarrel between two villages
- Settlement of premarital and extra-marital relation cases
- Settlement of divorce cases
- Settlement of inheritance right
- Holding village assembly
- Meeting of political parties

Land Tenure System in Primitive Societies

It is fitness of the thing to present here the land tenure system of primitive societies. In common parlance, land means a particular part of earth where we live and carry out activities. But in economic anthropology, the term land has been used in wider sense. It includes all things provided to us by the nature as gift. For example flora, fauna, river, hill, mountain, fountain, lake, sea, forest, desert, island and so on. Now question arises what was the pattern of land tenure system in primitive society. Whether it was commonistic or individualistic?

According to evolutionist anthropologist, the economy of mankind has passed through the following stages in unilineal sequence:

- Hunting, gathering
- Pastoralism
- Shifting cultivation
- Settled agriculture

It will be the fitness of the thing to present here land tenure system of each economic stages of development.

In the beginning there was collective or common land tenure system. But as we passed towards complexity from simplicity, we became more and more individualistic. This was common hypothesis of economic anthropologists. But empirical experiences do not prove this hypothesis.

In the beginning man was a parasite on nature. He was not a producer. Rather he was consumer of things provided by the nature. In this stage place of hunting and gathering was forest. He did gathering and hunting collectively. On forest, flora, fauna, river, fountain, lake, sea all men possessed equal right. But different bands used to quarrel for gathering and hunting. One band used to make attack on other band. The band stayed at a particular place till the availability of food materials. As soon as the band witnessed shortage of food, it travelled to another suitable place where food materials were available. Although hunting was done collectively, but some special shares were given to captain of the band, the man who attacked first with spear or arrow and the man who killed the animal. The man who saw the hunt first time was also given a special share. The captain of the band was given nail, hair, horn, skull and skin of animals hunted. Those who found the hunted birds lying in the forest, he became the owner of the bird. Thus, even during hunting and gathering stage traits of common land tenure and individual land tenure were present.

In the stage of pastoralism, a band used to lead some kind of wandering life but along with flocks of animals he domesticated. The pasture land was common and all animals of a flock were also common. But in this stage, too, some traits of individual land tenure was in existence. The leader took special share in animals when hunted. He also had a special share in hairs, horns and skin of animals. As pasture land was sufficient, the concept of individual pasture land of each group was not known.

In the stage of shifting cultivation, each group had a common field located in hill slopes where cultivation was done on collective basis by changing sites of cultivation each year. In this stage each group had its own hill sites for shifting cultivation. After harvesting each family got its share in presence of head keeping number of family members in mind. Each family paid some quantity to head as special share. The head used to redistribute them among members during the time of need. Thus, in the stage of shifting cultivation, the concept of common land tenure and individual land tenure was also existing.

In the stage of settled agriculture, each village had its own land, cattle, tree and houses. They were regarded as a common property of a village. The agriculture was done collectively and agricultural produce were distributed among families in presence of village head. Thus, village level individual land tenure system developed. The boundary of each village was demarcated. As man moved towards civilization, the concept of family land within the village came into existence. The concept of inheritance right also came into existence. Thus, individual land tenure system came into existence. In spite of individual land tenure system in village, each village also has some common land tenure system such as mountain, hill, forest, river, fountain, lakes, sea, sarana, sasaun, Akhra and Dhunkhuria. Each village has common street, road and ponds.

From above discussion, it is clear that primitives possessed the concept of common and individual land tenure system from very beginning of hunting-gathering stage. Thus, primitives were not only commonistic, rather they were commonistic and individualistic both.

Economic Grading or Cultural Types

Economic anthropologists have developed the concept of economic grading or cultural types among tribals of our country on the basis of ecology, technology, and social structure. Ecology, technology and social structure form cultural type. It has been observed that man live in different ecology. According to ecology, they develop technology for the purpose of production. To govern production, a social structure is formed. Thus, ecology, technology and social structure form cultural type.

In the context of tribal Bihar, L.P. Vidyarthi in his paper, "Cultural Type in Tribal Bihar" (1958) formulated the concept of cultural types prevalent in tribal. Taking ecology, technology and social structure of tribal Bihar, he postulated the following cultural types in Bihar:

- Food gathering and hunting tribe—Birhor
- Hill cultivation type: Sauria Paharia
- Plain agricultural type: Munda, Oraon, Ho and Santhal
- Artisan type: Lohra, Mahli, Karmali and Chickbaraik.

D.N. Majumdar in his book, "Race and Culture in India" has discussed three types of economic grading prevalent in Indian tribes:

- Food gathering and hunting
- Shifting cultivation
- Settled agriculture

But in his another book, "An Introduction to Social Anthropology" (1978), he mentioned the following types of economic grading:

- Food gathering and hunting
- Pastoralism
- Shifting cultivation
- Settled agriculture
- Artisan
- Labour

S.C. Dube in his Book, "Manav Aur Sanskriti" (1969) has divided Indian tribes into two categories:

- Important grading
- Semi-important grading

Important economic grading: Under important economic grading he placed following types:

- Food gathering and hunting

- Unsettled agriculture
- Settled agriculture
- Pastoralism

Semi-Important economic grading: This grading includes the following cultural types:

- Tribals engaged in artisans and industries
- Tribals earning through crimes.

L.P. Vidyarthi in his book, "Tribal Culture of India" (1976) has mentioned the following cultural types in tribal India:

- Food gathering and hunting type
- Pastoral type
- Hill cultivation type
- Plain agricultural type
- Simple artisan type
- Folk artist type
- Agricultural and non-agricultural labour type
- Skill labour, service and business type.

Now, let us discuss about each cultural type one by one in detail.

• *Food Gathering and Hunting Type*: The tribes whose economic and social organizations are based on food gathering and hunting have been placed under this cultural type. Food gathering and hunting is still practiced by almost all tribes whose residences are on hills, nearby hills or in forest. But there are some tribes whose main means of stay is still food gathering and hunting. They are Birhor, Sauria Paharia, hill Kharia or Savar, Parahiya, Birjia, Binjia and Korwa of Jharkhand, Raja of Himalyan region, Juang of Orissa, Baiga of Madhya Pradesh and Shampen of Andaman and Nicobar Island.

The social organization of these tribes are very simple. Family, lineage or clan is unit of production and consumption. They erect their huts with wood, bamboo and leaves available in the jungle. They do collection of root, shoot, leaves, flower, fruit, seeds, honey, wax, mushrooms and varieties of bulbs. They collect forest grasses to make brooms and baskets and ropes. They collect bark of trees for making ropes. They collect seeds of Mahua, nim, Karanja, sal etc. for getting oil. They also collect medicinal plants to cure diseases. They use foods collected from the forest either raw or cooked. Previously, they used to do food collection with stone tools. But now-a-days, they use iron tool.

They do hunting of hare, mouse, wild goat, bear, dear etc. for meat, skin, horns and skull.

Food gathering and hunting type tribes are facing a number of problems in their economic activities. The forest cover is decreasing day-by-day. As a result, food collection is becoming problem day-by-day. Wildlife Protection Act and Environment Protection Acts are also creating a problem in hunting and gathering. Attempts are being made to make them settled by giving house, land, livestocks. But they are not comfortable in colonies because colonies are not serving their cultural needs.

- *Pastoral type*: The tribes whose economy and social organization are based on cattle rearing have been put under the pastoral cultural type. Cattle rearing along with agriculture is widely practiced by almost all tribes whose main means of livelihood is agriculture. But there are certain tribes whose main means of livelihood is still pastoralism. The Toda of Nilgiri area are still cattle hearder particularly buffalo. Their economy and social organizations are based on buffalo rearing. In Toda society number of buffalo determines the social status of family. The families who have more number of buffaloes enjoy high status, but the families who have less number have low social status. Payment of buffaloes are done in marriages. Thus, economy and social organizations of Toda represent pastoral cultural type.

The Gujar of Himanchal Pradesh do rearing of cow and buffalo. Maldhari of Gujarat are also dependent on animal husbandry. They regard Nandji, the social father of Lord Krishna as their ancestor. Chopana tribe of Ladakh, Leh and Kashmir valley do animal husbandry. Sabari of Gujarat and Rajsthan do rearing of cattle for their stay. Gola of South India and Gareri of North India are sheep herder. They heard flock of sheep and wander from mountain to mountain during rainy and winter seasons. But they come down to plain area during summer season. They manure the farmer's field with the help of sheep flock.

Animal husbandry is done to get milk, meat, hairs, skin, skull and to get money by selling them in cattle market. The cattle hearders know well about the breeding season of the animals domesticated. They know well about their diseases and folk and herbal medicine to cure them. Previously there were some persons who were expert of animals diseases and their treatment with folk and herbal medicine.

Now-a-days, cattle grazers and herders take help of veterinary doctor's services. They are also doing insurance of their cattle. They are rearing high breed animals.

- *Hill Cultivation Type*: The tribes whose economy and social organization are based on shifting cultivation have been included under this cultural type. This type of cultivation is done on hill slopes that is why it is known as hill cultivation type. As in this cultivation, cultivation site is changed each year, that is why it is known as shifting cultivation or wandering cultivation. This cultivation is also known as Swidden cultivation. Hill cultivation or shifting cultivation is known by different names in different parts of our country. In Jharkhand, it is known as Khalu, Korawa, and Behari. In Madhya Pradesh it is known as Penda, Dahi, Daugar, Farha and Marham. In Orissa, it is called as Pondu, Rewa, Dahi and Dahiyha. In North-eastern region, it is called as Jhum cultivation. Garo, Tripuri, Newatia, Riyang, Chakama and Naga of North-eastern region come under this cultural type. Sauria Pahariya, Korawa, hillkharia or Savar and Parahiya of Jharkhand are example of this cultural type. Savar and Kutia Khond of Orissa and Ghora of Andhra Pradesh also come under this cultural type.

For the purpose of shifting cultivation, tools used are spade, digging tool, axe, and sickle. They are made of iron. Previously stone tools were used for digging and cutting bushes.

In North-east this type of cultivation is known as Jhum cultivation. The Jhum cultivators are termed as *Jhumia*.

For the purpose of Jhum cultivation, a proper site in hill valley or hill slopes is selected. Then the site is cleared by cutting small plants and bushes with axes and spade. After felling trees and bushes they are left for drying. After drying, they are burnt into ash. It is believed that ash increases the fertility of the land. It act as manure. In the month of June when rainy season begins, they dig out holes at regular intervals in vertical and horizontal rows. One seed is dropped in each hole. The seeds of Marua, Maize, Kurthi, Bajara etc. are sown. When rain showers seeds are sown. They start germinating and gradually take the shape of a plant. Some weeds also come up along with the seeds sown in the field. With the help of digging instruments they are taken out. The plant soon after germination requires caring. They take every care of the plant. For this purpose, one member of the community always remains in the field. For rest in day and night, a hut is erected with the help of wooden poles thatched with straw.

This hut is known as *Machan* in local term. Sometimes, a *machan* is made on a tree to avoid the attack of wild animals. They have a time to beat and create noise to frighten wild birds and animals. When crops are grown and ripen, the harvesting is done. After harvesting, thrashing and winnowing is done. Yield is distributed by the community head among all families keeping number and need in mind. At last merry making is done. The new grains are cooked and shared after singing and dancing. Thus, shifting cultivations has following processes:

- Selection of site
- Felling of tree, plants, bushes and grasses
- Burning bushes and grasses
- Sowing
- Weeding
- Care taking
- Magical performances for good yield
- Preparation of thrashing fields
- Harvesting
- Making bundles of crops harvested
- Carrying bundles in thrashing field
- Thrashing and winnowing
- Distribution of grains among families
- Merry making

In shifting cultivation, site is changed each year. They have belief that after harvesting the site requires rest for five years. Therefore, they return to the original site after each five years. They maintain this site cycle of shifting cultivation.

In Assam, 90 per cent people are engaged in Jhum cultivation. Attempts were made by the Government to make a ban on Jhum cultivation and to settle the Jhumia at a fixed place. But it was not possible to abandon this cultural type.

Shifting cultivation is facing lots of problems due to Forest Conservation Act and frequent attacks by wild birds and animals on crops. The yield is also very low.

- *Plain Cultivation Type*: In this cultural types those tribes have been included whose economy and social organization are dependent on agriculture in plain area. In this type people live in permanent village and do cultivation. Each village has a boundary and an acreage.

But the village land is distributed among families. Each family has own plough, oxen and digging and spading iron implements. Each village has common means of irrigation like ponds, rivers, lakes etc. Now-a-days, some families have own wells and pumps for irrigation purpose. Government has also made canal for the purpose of irrigation.

The agricultural land can be divided into two categories: Donland and Tanerland. Low lands are termed as Donland where rainwater is stored for a very long period. In this type of land good variety of paddy are transplanted. High lands are known as Tanerland. In this type of land coarse variety of paddy, maize, Marua, Kurathi, Kodo etc. are cultivated. Vegetables are grown in Bariland and uplands. In plain field two to three types of crops can be cultivated. They are locally known as *Bhadai* crops, *Aghani* crops, and *Chaiti* crops.

There are two types of cultivation: Dry cultivation and wet cultivation. Gram, Masoor, Khesari, Pea do not require irrigation after cultivation in a field. They are known as dry cultivation. But mustard, paddy and wheat required regular irrigation after cultivation. They are termed as wet cultivation.

The agricultural processes starts in the month of Asadh (June-July) and continues till Jyestha (May-June). Before starting agriculture, the worship of plough, oxen, spade, and land is made on an auspicious day and on an auspicious time. Processes related to plain agriculture are as follows:

- Worship of land, oxen, plough and agricultural implements
- Manuring the fields
- After first shower of rain sowing paddy seeds
- Irrigating paddy seedlings at regular intervals
- Spreading chemical fertilizer in paddy seedlings
- Preparing fields for transplantation of seedlings
- Transplanting the seedlings
- Weeding
- Sprinkling chemical fertilizers
- Harvesting and making bundles
- Storing bundles in thrashing field
- Thrashing and winnowing
- Carrying grains in house
- Making rice from new paddy
- Merry making

Santhal, Munda, Oraon, Ho, Bhumij are example of plain cultivation type in Jharkhand. Khasi and Jayantia of Meghalaya, Khas and Tharu of Uttrakhand, Kinnaur, Pingla and Swangla of Himachal Pradesh, Gond of Madhya Pradesh, Mina, Garesia, Damaria, Dulsla and Thakur of western India and Warli of Andhra Pradesh are examples of plain cultivation type.

- *Simple Artisan Type*: In this cultural type those tribes have been included whose economy and social organization are based on production of artifacts, handicrafts, potterys, basketry, weaving and iron smithy. These tribes supply their goods produced to agricultural tribes and castes. They have *Jajmani* relations with peasants, too. They sell their goods in local *Haat* Bazaar to get money.

Gujar of Gujarat, Kimaur of Kashmir, Kanjar of Uttar Pradesh, Lohara, Mahli, Karmali and Chick Baraik of Jharkhand, Gohuliya of Rajasthan, Kolam of Maharashtra, Irula of Tamil Nadu, Thoti of Andhra Pradesh and Kota of Tamil Nadu are examples of artisan tribes in India.

In the age of industrialization, these tribes are facing a lot of problems. They are becoming labour from artisan.

- *Folk artist Type*: In this cultural type those tribes come whose economy and social organization are based on folk art. They perform dance, sing song and do plays by moving here and there. In return of singing, dancing and showing play, they are paid in cash and kind. In this type male, female and children are involved. They have their own musical instrument which are very simple like drum, *damaru*, flute and *kartal*. These tribes maintain their stay on the basis of performing art. On the occasion of festivals and fairs, they perform a special dance to earn more and more. Nat and Sapera (snake charmer), of South-East India, Kela and Mandupatta of Orissa, Pradhoeu, Ojha, Madaria, Pancula, Gadadi, Domars, Bachnol of Andhra Pradesh, Kota of Nilgiri area and Kabelia of Rajasthan are examples of this cultural type.

- *Agricultural and Non-agricultural Labour*: In this type those tribes have been included whose main means of stay is earning wages as agricultural and non-agricultural labourers. There is no specific tribe who survive only on wage earning. But some families of all tribes are engaged in earning wages in agricultural fields or in non-agricultural fields.

They migrate from villages to urban areas when agricultural work is over. They are termed as migrant labourers.

- *Skilled Labour, Service and Business Type*: Now-a-days, such a cultural type among tribes has emerged whose economy and social organization are based on skill, service and business. There is no specific tribe under this cultural type, but some families of all tribes are engaged as skilled labour, government servant, private jobs and own small or big business.

Gift and Ceremonial Exchange

The primitives had their own gift and ceremonial exchange. On the occasion of birth, marriage and death they had ceremonial exchange of feast, hospitability and gift. Visit of relatives particularly *Damad* (Son-in-law) and *Samadhi* (father of Son-in-law) and their primary kins were regarded as very significant. Therefore, a grand hospitability was provided to them by serving delicious breakfast, lunch and dinner along with own made rice-beer called *Haria*. They were requested to stay more days. Some member of the community was always with them. At the time of departure they were given some glittering and precious stones, some birds trapped, some animals domesticated as *Vidai*. Receiving these gift, the guest felt honoured.

Gift was also given to sisters and daughters in the form of clothes, ornaments, precious stones, feathers of peacock, parrot, partridge, calf of cow or buffalo at the time of departure for father-in-law's house from own father's house. They were also given shells Corel and Kauri in gift. Sister's son and daughter and daughter's son and daughter were given gift in the form of dresses, ornament, shells, corels, birds, goat and calves of animals domesticated.

On the occasion of birth, marriage and death, there was ceremonial exchange of food materials and feast. Invited guests were given a grand hospitality with delicious breakfast, lunch and dinner. They were also given some gifts according to the occasions on which invited.

Gift and ceremonial exchange was also prevalent for friends. Heads of different villages and communities had friendship relation. They used to pay a visit in the house of each other. When a head went to the head of other village, he was extended a grand hospitality. He was presented a gift of cloth and handicrafts. Sometimes, he was given peacock and duck as gift. Gift and ceremonial exchange are still continuing but its forms have changed. Now things for giving in presentation are purchased from the market. Modern gift items are being exchanged. Some examples of ceremonial exchange prevalent among tribes of the world studied by eminent anthropologists are as follows:

Kula Exchange

The description about Kula exchange appears in the book of B.K. Malinowski, "Argonauts of Western Pacific" (1922) and his article "Kula: the circulating exchanges of valuables in the archipelago of Eastern New Guinea" (1920).

Malinowski had conducted his field researches among Trobriand islanders consisting of four major matrilineal tribes, namely, Papua, Mailu, Massium and Pygmy of New Guinea. Among Trobriand islanders he observed the system of barter exchange known as Kula. Kula barter exchange takes place through gift, hospitality, and trade. This system of exchange was prevalent among Trobriand islanders, aborigines of New Guinea, Amplett island, Loughton island and Dobu. The culture of these aborigins are quite different from one another, but are tied together by Kula gift exchange. Kula has not only economic function, but it is also significant from ceremonial point of view. In fact, it is a complex whole of economic, social, political, cultural, magical, religious, recreational and communicational values.

In this ceremonial exchange system inhabits of a close circle of islands as mentioned above participate. The objects concerned in this exchange are of two types—(i) Red shell necklace and (ii) White armshell bracelets. The first one is locally termed as Soulwa and the second one is known as Mwali. These two valuables rotate in opposite direction. Soulwa always moves in clockwise direction, whereas Mwali always moves in anticlockwise direction. Every participant of Kula has two partners—one from whom he receives Soulwa and one who gives him Mwali, and one whom he gives Mwali and one who gives Soulwa. This can be understood better by the diagram presented below:

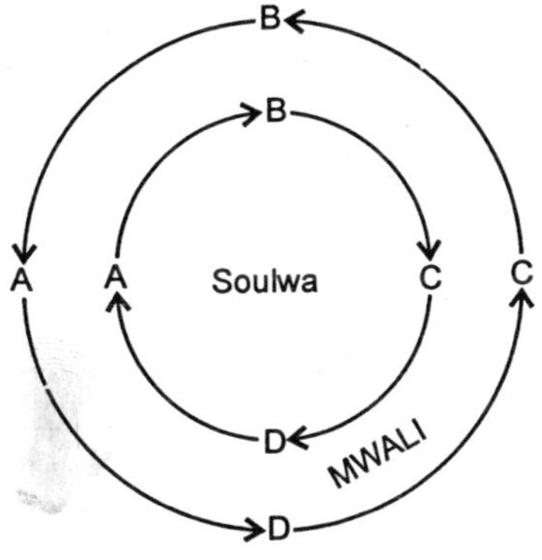

A gives Soulwa to B and receives Mwali from him and again he gives Mwali to D and receives Soulwa from D. In this way exchange takes place between Kula partners. Kula exchange may take place in four ways:

- Between individual of same community
- Between individuals of two neighbouring islands
- Between two neighbouring communities across sea—without organizing ceremonies
- Between two communities across sea by organizing ceremonies.

The Soulwa and Mwali given and taken under Kula system of barter exchange have no commercial value, but having Kula relatives and friends is considered to be prestigious in Trobriand islanders. There is no bargaining or haggling about Kula gift and return of good may or may not take place at once, but after the laps of a year or two they are returned definitely. Kula relationship functions on the principle that once in Kula is always in Kula.

The Kula exchange is not of economic value, but it is related to many other social value and activities. They are as follows:

- Like all ceremonial activities, Kula has participative and expressive value.
- It is related to high social status—Having more Kula partner enhances one's social status in the society.
- Kula system is related to canoe making. Canoe making is related to economic and magical activities. For Kula exchange new canoes are made and old ones are repaired. At the time of beginning of Kula journey religious and magical performances take place in presence of community heads and members. This is celebrated as festive occasions. The Kula exchange journey may be of 100 miles.
- Although objects of Kula are not traded but there is trading on Kula expedition. Malinowski noted the contrast between bargaining and haggling when ordinary goods are bartered in formal Kula ceremony.
- Kula system of exchange performs integrative function. It provides protection to partners in Kula Journey. It brings

people in institutionalized relationship and a feeling of belonging to one society.
- Kula exchange system also reveals the prevalence of taboo in Kula Journey. Women are tabooed from Kula Journey. They are assigned task of rearing and caring children.
- The members who do not have sufficient magical knowledge are also tabooed from Kula Journey.
- Children are also excluded from Kula Journey.
- The community chief bears the expenses of Kula Journey and provides guidance to Kula travellers.
- Occasionally wife of community head participates in Kula Journey.
- As it involves long canoe voyage from one island to another island, Malinowski has termed it as Argonauts of Western Pacific. It is because they set out for a long sea voyage for economically valueless objects.

Wasi Exchange

Malinowski has also explored a system of barter exchange similar to Kula known as Wasi among Trobriand islanders. The Trobriand islanders do barter exchange of fish and yam. This system of barter exchange prevalent among Trobriand islanders is termed locally as Wasi. The Wasi system of barter exchange takes place between inhabitants of coastal villages and inside villages. The inhabitants of coastal villages do not perform agriculture but they produce fish. The inhabitants of inside villages do agriculture, but do not do fishing. There, in there two types of villages engaged in two kinds of economic activities, barter exchange of fish and yam takes place. The fish givers take yam and yam givers take fish.

Wasi exchange system takes place in mock situation. That is why it is known as mock exchange. The fish producers of coastal villages visit along with fish without informing the members of yam producing village silently and place the fish at a safe place at night and come back. In the morning the village head is informed and he distributes fish among all families according to their size and needs. The yam producers visit the village of fish producers and place yam silently at a place at night. In the morning, the village head is informed and he distributes the yam produce among all families of the village according to size and need. As this exchange takes place silently without prior information to surprise the partner village, it is termed as mock barter exchange. In local term, it is also known as Sagali.

Wasi differ from Kula. In Wasi consumable things are exchange but Kula deals with non-consumable things.

- *Urigubu System*: The Urigubu system of exchange is related to transfer of cultural material obtained in Kula relation from one individual and group to another individual and group. Among Trobriand islanders materials obtained in Kula relation are transferred to sister's son from mother's brother. This is a system of gift exchange in which gifts are presented to sister's family by brother's family.

Besides Kula objects, maternal uncle sends one-fourth of agricultural produce to his sister's family. This is termed locally as *Urigubu.*

- *Pokala and Youla System*: This system of exchange includes two things—Pokala and Youla. The gifts presented to the head is known as *Pokala* and services provided by the chief is termed as Youla. Thus, this system of exchange is related to the exchange of gifts and services. The members of Trobriand villages present gifts of Kula valuable to their chief. The chief in turn provides political and religious services.

- *Potlatch System of Exchange*: The potlatch system of exchange is characteristic feature of Kwakiutl, an American Indian Tribes. The Kwakiutl tribe are competitive. In their society there is competition for ceremonial exchange. In this system of exchange, feast is exchanged between kins and relatives. In providing feast wealth determines the prestige and social status. On the occasion of ceremonial feast exchange, every family attempts to spend more and more than it has. Food left after feast are thrown away. But it is shown that the family can spend more for relatives and friends.

Thus, gift and hospitality function on principle of reciprocity and allocation.

Chapter 8
Political Anthropology

Political anthropology is a sub-branch of social-cultural anthropology which deals with the study of political institutions of primitive societies or simple societies. The political institutions of simple society are Primitive Law, Primitive Justice, Primitive Government, Primitive State, village head, Village Panchayat, inter-village Panchayat, leadership pattern, nation building process, and national integration. Political Anthropology is a sub-branch of social-cultural anthropology because in primitive or simple societies political institutions are parts of social-cultural organizations. The system by which the institutions like power, authority, law, justice, Government, leadership, nation-building and national integration are controlled is known as political system. But in case of primitive society, the political system is an integrated part of social organization.

You might have seen people quarrelling in villages or your locality. Such quarrel may be between husband and wife, between two families, between two lineages, between two clans, between two tribes or castes and between two villages. You might have seen some people mediating or a Panchayat sitting or few prominent persons of the community known as Pancha attempting to settle the disputes, conflicts and quarrel. You might have heard the incidence of thefty, dacoity, physical assault, manhandling, abusing, extra-marital relation, premarital relation, rape, gang rape, disputes related to property and inheritance of childless couples. Such type of activities are treated as anti-social activities in society. The society has evolved political system in which crime, justice, punishment, compensation are decided, maintained and controlled by political institutions of the people in which members of the society are involved in maintenance of law and order and Justice. Thus, political system is that system of society which defines the roles which human beings occupy in order to maintain law and order at one hand and supervise the functioning of the society on other hand. The main function of political system is to maintain law and order in simple society. But in complex society along with this function the other functions such as distribution of resources for social and economic development is also associated with political system.

Power and Authority

We may define power as force to exercise legally or illegally for controlling others. The power may be legitimate or illegimate. The meaning of legitimacy is rightfulness, whether one is given right to exercise power. When one is given right to exercise power, it is known as legitimate power. But when one is not given to exercise power, but he exercises his power, it is termed as illegitimate power. For example power is exercised by both—police and dacoit. But power exercised by the police is an example of legitimate power and power exercised by a dacoit is an example of illegitimate power. The concept of power does not tell us whether it is legitimate or illegitimate because here emphasis is on exercise of force and its compliance. The state has power to exercise legitimate power over its territory.

The legitimate power is known as authority. In the concept of authority emphasis is on legitimacy.

Types of Authority

Authority maybe classified into three types which are as follows:

- Traditional authority
- Charismatic authority
- Legal-rational authority

• *Traditional Authority*: When a person becomes head of family, village head, inter-village head, village priest or a king as per tradition, such type of authority is known as traditional authority. Here legitimacy is derived from existing conventions.

• *Charismatic Authority*: When a person occupies a post on the basis of his charisma, it is called a charismatic authority. For example magician, priest, scientist, leader, administrator etc. It emerges in the situation of crisis. In the situation of crisis, which may be natural, social and political, we look towards a person who could solve our crisis. Such a person looks extraordinary and bearing charisma. He possesses such a quality which ordinary people do not have. If a charismatic person occupies power or post, he occupies charismatic authority. It is also quite likely that a charismatic person may remain outside the realm of power. For example our *Rashtrapita* Mahatma Gandhi. Therefore, we may make a difference between a charismatic leader and charismatic authority. A charismatic leader resolves the crisis but may remain outside the political system. Here legitimacy is derived from the charisma of a person.

- ***Legal-rational Authority***: This is characteristic of complex society. Here legitimacy is derived from the legality and rationality. In this type of authority, laws are impersonal and apply equally to all. Individuals have to compete for authority as per rules. Besides impersonal laws, merits and qualification are also important principles.

The traditional authority tries to maintain the system as it is, while legal-rational authority is ideally suited for change. This also explains why simple societies are, relatively conservative and tradition bound, while complex societies are progressive and change-oriented.

Polity and Power

Polity is related to distribution of power in a society. There is no society in the world where there is no power. Society is an abstract system of social relationship. In each relationship, there are some who exercise power over the others. Thus, no relationship is without the exercise of power. Power is universal feature of human society. Even in a group of two individuals, i.e. dyad, one exercises power over the other.

We may define power as ability of a person to exercise his will on the other and seek compliance. It is ability to take decisions for one-self and other decision and to see the compliance of his will by the others. Defined in this way, power is central to every institution and group.

For example the head of household exercises his power by virtue of being head over his members and his decision is binding on all members. Similarly, headmaster is more powerful in school being head and his decision is binding on all teachers and students. Thus, in every institution there are some who exercise power over the others.

• *Social Power and Political Power*: There is difference between social power and political power. The power occupied by a person in social institution is limited only to the institution concerned, but political power cuts across different institutions and groups. It runs the Government which takes major decisions about society and its affairs. For example, the principal of school exercises his power over the running of institution which he heads, but the task of framing educational policy and its implementation is of the Government. Political power is closely connected with governing and administering. But power in social institutions is related to control the activities, but they do not rule and govern. The power holders of social institution are termed as non-governing elite. The political power holders are termed as governing elite. The heads of family and school are non-governing elite, whereas, Prime Minister, Chief Minister, Ministers, President are governing elite.

Primitive Law

We may define primitive law as a law which is observed by primitives or simple societies. Such laws have customary, religious and moral basis and has social sanction. The concept of law in simple society is very simple. It is related to organized and collective life. For leading a collective life concept of taboo or restrictions were formulated. These taboos were related to sex behaviour and kinship. Probably conflict within and between bands was taking place for women and sex behaviour. In order to avoid conflict, the concept of incest was evolved. The taboo on incests was the first primitive law. According to these laws, sex relation of parents with children was banned and group marriage was started in which male members of two groups exchange women with each other. Sex taboo on premarital and extra-marital relation was also prohibited. In this way, the laws related to marriage and kinship began. Rules of endogamy and exogamy were framed. Rules regarding preferential marriage were also developed.

In the beginning there was no concept of property. Gradually, the concept of communal property was developed and finally the concept of inheritance of property and the concept of succession began. The concept of inheritance gave rise to kin groups like siblings, lineage, clan, descent rule, residence rule, authority rule etc. Such laws were essential for maintaining peace, harmony, order and leading a collective or organized social life.

It was collective responsibility to obey the rules formulated by ancestor. But primitives were also aware that some one may break the law and that is why they had evolved the concept of Government and Justice. Through these institutions they brought law breakers under control.

Why Laws are Obeyed in Simple Society?

The laws of simply society are very simple. They are related to common living and leading a collective organized life. The power and authority which forces the observance of laws in simple society are as follows:

- *Social Sanction*: The social sanction includes socially approved and socially disapproved behaviour. The social sanction may be divided into two:

- Positive Social Sanction
- Negative Social Sanction

- *Positive Social Sanction*: The people behave according to the norms and values of the society because they have positive sanction. Those who behave as per positive sanction enjoy high prestige and status. They are praised and rewarded by the people. The most powerful source behind positive sanction is public opinion. In simple society public opinion has special value because each member know each other by name and face. So, one cannot dare to go against public opinion.
- *Negative Social Sanction*: To behave not as per norms and values of the society has negative sanction in simple society. Norms and value breakers are criticized and outcasted from the community. That is why people do not dare to break laws formulated for maintaining order and peace in the society.

The law breakers are not allowed to avail different kinds of facilities provided by the society. When they behave negatively in the society, the society also imposes negative sanction on their social facilities.

- *Fear of Magical and Religious Power*: The people of simple society have deep faith in super human and supernatural power. They have belief that super human powers are omnipresent and have a watch on every activity of a person. For doing good deeds people are rewarded and for doing wrong deeds people are punished by super human power in this life or life after death.

- *Moral Value*: In simple society, laws are closely associated with morality. Those who break laws are treated as immoral and characterless.
- *Pressure of Public Opinion*: The pressure of public opinion forces the people to observe the laws and not to go against them.
- *Reciprocity*: The people observe laws to maintain reciprocal relation with others. The people of simple society are dependent on each other. This dependency forces them to observe laws for maintaining reciprocal social relationship.

Primitive Law: Nature and Characteristics

Primitive law means those laws behind which there are compulsive forces of society. The modern law have compulsive force of state police, lawyer, court, vigilance and Judge are the governmental agencies which forces people to follow laws. But simple society lacks such agencies. Here observance of law is collective and reciprocal responsibility. That is why it is the duty of each member to observe the laws of the society. It is also responsibility of each individuals to observe law. The nature and characteristics of primitive laws are as follows:

- *Customary Basis*: The basis of primitive law is customs which are related to observance by each member in daily life and on different occasions. They are existing traditions from one generation to the next. It is also observed as custom which is above modern law.
- *Religious Basis*: Primitive laws have religious basis because they are believed as formulated by Gods and Goddesses and ancestral deities of the communities concerned. When primitive laws are observed, deities and ancestors become pleased and provide all kinds of blessing.
- *Moral Basis*: Primitive laws have moral basis, too. Observing laws is taken as of high moral value. Those who observe laws are regarded as moral and those who do not observe law are treated as immoral and characterless. They do not enjoy any kind of status in the society.
- *Social Sanction*: The primitive law is related to social sanction. It is associated with public opinion. Sanction imposed on members of the society are of two types—Positive sanction and negative

sanction. Abeyance of law has positive sanction. Such members who observe laws are praised, respected and rewarded by the society. They enjoy high social status in the society. The disobedience of law has negative sanction. Those members who disobey law are declared as criminals. They are punished, criticized and ousted from the community.

- *Cannot be Changed*: As primitive law has customary and religious basis, it cannot be changed. Although few modifications can be made, but cannot be changed totally.
- *Cannot be Challenged*: Primitive law cannot be challenged in the court because it has positive sanction of the society. They are observed as customs and customs are above law. Our modern law has banned the practice of child marriage, dowry and many other customs, but they are still observed as customs.
- *Difference from Society to Society*: All societies do not have same customary laws. They differ from society to society. Even in the same community, they differ from lineage to lineage and clan to clan.
- *Collective Responsibility*: Observance of primitive laws is collective responsibility. Community members obey it and punish them who attempt to break the laws. The maintenance of law in primitive society is responsibility of all.
- *No distinction Between Crime and tort*: The primitive law does not make a distinction between crime and tort. When an individual makes a crime his/her all family and lineage members are treated as criminals. For committing a crime by an individual his any family member can be punished.
- *No difference between Civil Law and Criminal Law*: Primitive law does not make a distinction between Civil Law and Criminal Law. Those who break law of society are treated as criminals.
- *Importance of Kin Group*: In the observance of primitive law kin groups play important role. It is because simple society is kinship based society.
- *No need of Police, Court and Lawyer*: In primitive law there is no need of police, court and lawyer and they are needed in modern law.
- *Determination of Crime by Kin Groups*: For disobeying primitive laws, a Community Panchayat sits and determines the nature of crime. The kin groups decide the punishment imposed on crime doers.

• *Implementation and Compensation by Kin Group*: The crime determined is implemented by the kin groups and for compensation, kin groups join their hands. Thus kin groups are involved in both determination of crime and payment of compensation.

• *No Significance of Intension*: In primitive law intension does not occupy place of significance. Crime is taken as crime, intension of crime doers has no value. They take revenge as blood for blood, hand for hand and head for head.

Difference between Primitive Law and Modern Law

Primitive law differs from modern law. The main points of differences between primitive law and modern law are as follows:

Primitive Law	*Modern Law*
Primitive law has customary basis	Modern law has social justice and welfare basis
It has moral basis	It has evidence basis
It has religious basis	It has secular basis
It is formulated by deities and ancestors	It is formulated by the state
It exists as tradition	It exists as code of conduct
It has social sanction of the community	It has political sanction of the Government of a State
It is obeyed	It is enforced
It is collective responsibility	It is the responsibility of the Government of a State
It does not make a distinction between crime and fort	It makes a distinction between crime and tort
It does not distinguish the social law from criminal law	It distinguishes the social law from criminal law
It is applied only to kin groups	It is applied over the whole territory of the State
It differs from society to society	It is same for all communities in a territory of State
Importance of kin groups	Importance of *thana*—Police, court, lawyer
In primitive law enforcing agency is community	In modern law enforcing agency is Government
Punishment by kin groups	Punishment by Court
Compromise by kin group	Compromise by Court
Compensation by kin group	Compensation by Court
Cannot be changed	Can be changed by the Government
Cannot be challenged	Can be challenged.

Primitive Government

Government is an essential element or agency of a State. Through the Government the State achieves its objectives. It is a machinery by which common policies are determined, common affairs are regulated and common interests are protected.

The Government performs three kinds of functions—executive, legislative and judiciary. The Government formulates laws for citizens. It executes the law and punishes the law breaker through judicial system.

Now, one important question which appears here is that whether primitives had any kind of Government. It is true that primitives lacked Government like modern state. But it is also true that laws were obeyed and law breakers were punished and some new laws were framed and implemented. Thus, all three important functions of a Government—legislative, executive and judiciary were existing in primitive societies in one form or the other. There were some institutions which performed the function of a Government. They were council of elders, village head, village Panchayat, Inter-village Panchayat and Chiefdom or tribal chief. Through these institutions law and order in primitive societies were maintained.

Type of Government in Primitive Societies

Following types of Government were prevailing in Primitive Societies:

- Democracy
- Monarchy
- Gerontocracy
- Oligarchy
- Theocracy

Democracy: Democracy is a form of Government in which people have great say in the formation of Government, it is for the people, by the people and of the people. Example are America and India.

Monarchy: It is a form of the Government in which king is the head of the state and performs all functions of the Government. For example African tribes.

Gerontocracy: It is a form of Government where authority lies in the hand of old persons of the village community, lineage or clan group. Majority of tribes have this form of Government.

Oligarchy: It is a form of a Government found in band society. For example Ulhalu Birhor of Jharkhand.

Theocracy: It is a form of the Government where authority lies in the hand of priest. For example *Pohan* and *Baiga* of Munda and other tribal communities.

Functions of the Government: The main functions of the primitive Government are as follows:

- To protect customary laws.
- To determine the nature of crime and punishment.
- To implement the judgement related to crime and punishment.
- To make rule as per the present need of the society.
- To do welfare activities in the society.
- To settle the cases of dispute between husband and wife.
- To settle the cases of divorce and compensation.
- To settle the cases related to inheritance dispute.
- To declare the disputed property as community property.
- To protect community during war.
- To save the community during spread of epidemic, starvation, flood, and fire.
- To decide the cases of two families.
- To settle dispute between two villages.
- To organize festivals and fairs.
- To organize customary feast.

Judicial System of Primitives: The concept of crime and punishment was prevalent in simple society or primitive society. There was no difference between social laws and criminal laws. But those who violated laws of society, were declared as criminals. Now it became the duty of the primitive Government to decide the nature of crime committed and punishment given. Primitives did not possess the concept of *thana*—police, court and lawyer. But they had their own system by which crime was determined and punishment was given. In deciding the nature of crime community members were involved. When punishment was given with common consensus, it became duty of entire community member to get the judgement of the community executed. Thus in providing judgment and executing the judgement, community members were involved. The determination of crime and punishment was done consensually. In primitives, the following institutions were involved in judiciary:

Council of Elders

- Village head
- Village priest
- Village Panchayat
- Inter Village Panchayat
- Chiefdom or Tribal Chief.

With the help of above political institutions Law and Justice were maintained in simpler societies.

We may discuss the judicial system of simple societies under following headings:

- *Collective Responsibility*: The judicial system of simple society was based on collective responsibility. When a crime was committed, it become the duty of the entire community to identify criminal, to decide nature of crime he committed and to decide the punishment—physical or social or economic nature.
- *Determination of Crime*: The primitive judicial system followed a process to determine the crime. This process provided a person to prove that he/she is not guilty. When a person is proved that he is guilty, only then punishment is given to him/her. Otherwise, no punishment is given and the community seeks excuse for the harassment given.

As soon as a case related to crime comes before village head, inter-village head or a tribal chief, the process of identification of crime starts. A meeting of the Panchayat is called by the village head, inter-village head or a tribal chief. Both parties are given occasion to place their sides. Before putting side, each one is asked to take oath in the name of Bonga, the supreme deity and to touch *Saal* or *Karam* tree which represent a deity. It is believed that before deity a person cannot dare to tell a lie. If he or she tells a lie, the deity will definitely punish physically or economically or both.

In order to determine crime some magical acts are also taken into consideration. For example sacrifice of egg and other such activities. Like fire test and some other kinds of tests are also performed in order to find out the culprit.

- *Evidence*: The primitive judicial system also put special emphasis on evidence. In order to get evidence two kinds of methods were employed:

- Oath
- Ordeal

Oath: In order to prove that he is not criminal, the person concerned is expected to take oath in the name of son, husband, village deity, sing bonga, ancestral spirit, and own health and property. If a person takes fake oath, he or she is punished by the deity and suffers from physical, material and divinal troubles. The person will die suddenly, his son will die, her husband will meet death, his entire property will be damaged. He or she will become mad and die slowly. That is why oath occupies special value in primitive justice. When a person takes oath before the community member, it is believed that the person has not committed crime.

Ordeal: Besides taking oath, a person has to go through ordeal in order to put himself/herself not a criminal. For example, the accused person is asked to put finger in boiling water or oil, or to put fire on palm, to eat twenty one chillies, to stand in water during cold season for whole night, to sit in hot sun for whole day, to stand in rain water for day and night, to jump a well, to have a fight, to climb on long branchless tree etc. If the accused is successful in such an ordeal, he/she is declared non-criminal.

Intension: In the primitive judicial system, the intension of the accused is not taken into consideration. A crime is crime whether committed knowing or unknowingly. For committing unknowingly crime, he is also punished equally. Suppose the dog of an owner kills a hen of a person, the intension of the master is not taken into consideration. Rather he has to pay a hen to the aggrieved person.

Trial: The trial is also an important part of Primitive Judicial System. The village head and village Panchayat sit for trial. Hearing of both sides, evidences, intension and type of crime all are taken into consideration. Witnesses oral statements are also heard. When crime is proved, he/she is declared as a criminal by the community.

Punishment: The primitive judicial system also determines the punishment as soon as crime is fixed. The punishment given by primitive judicial system may be divided into two categories:

- Soft Punishment
- Hard Punishment

- *Soft Punishment*: For example if a boy and a girl of two clans enter in premarital sex relation, they are got married forcefully. It they deny only then hard punishment is imposed. If a man and a woman enters into extra-marital sex relation, then they are asked to spit on land and then leap it from tongue. The hair of women is cut, the head of man is shaved. But even after all such punishment they continue their relationship, they are asked to leave the village forcefully. If two boys and girls of two communities or same clan get themselves married, and come back with kids after a long period of marriage, then society may consider their cases sympathetically. They are advised to go through purificatory ritual, a community feast is organized and persons are readmitted as member of the community. Similarly beating with shoes, sleeping on thorn bed, putting chilly powder in eyes, putting black ointment on face are examples of soft punishment.

Hard Punishment: Hard punishment is related to death sentence. In this case punishment is head for head, hand for hand, life for life and so on. This type of punishment takes place in order to take revenge with enemies.

Compensation or Weregild: In primitive Judicial System, there is also a provision for compensation as punishment. The crime doers have to pay compensation to the affected person or party. In compensation social and economic status of the crime committers is taken into consideration. For example a cow for a cow, a cock for a cock, a goat for a goat, money for treatment in case of injuries, community feast etc.

Compromise: Compromise is also an integral part of primitive judicial system. It is taken as very good if both sides make a compromise. In arriving at compromise, Panchayat plays significant role. The compromise releases tensions of both sides.

Political System of Simple Society in India

Like other simple societies of the world, the Simple Societies of India also have their own political system consisting of different institutions performing the work of the Government, executive, legislative and judiciary.

The simple society has kinship based society. They live in small communities. The members of these communities are tied together through reciprocal rights, duties and responsibilities. Besides reciprocity, they are bound by social sanction, public opinion, divinal fear and morality. But conflict is also true universally in all kinds of societies. The continuity of conflict is not taken good for the community. In order to resolve conflict and maintain law and order in society, political system is a must. The Simple Society of India has the following types of political system:

- Council of elders
- Village head
- Village Panchayat
- Inter Village Panchayat or Union of Villages
- Chiefdom or Tribal Chief.

Council of Elders: The main function of this council is to extend support to village head. This council is temporary group of some selected persons from a tribal village community. The members of this council are selected by the village head and adult members of the community. This council helps the village head in handling village problems and conflicts of various kind.

The council of elders is existing in Luchai and Naga tribe of north-eastern India, Tharu of Himalayan region, Kamar of Madhya Pradesh, Savara of Orissa, Koli Mahadeva of Maharashtra.

The council of elders has a special vigil on the behaviours of adolescents and youths. It protects the adolescents and youth from anti-social behaviours and inculcate social qualities in them. The membership of village council remains changing.

Village head: Each tribal village has a secular head who is known as village head. The post of village head is hereditary. The transfer of this post goes from father to the eldest son. In some tribal communities village heads are elected. But both types of village head has no difference in power and authority. They share the same responsibility.

The village head is termed by different local names in different tribal communities. For example *Khulkpas* in Naga of north-eastern region, Mahto in *Oraon*, Munda in Munda, Manjhi in Santhal of Jharkhand, *Mukhia* in Lodha of West Bengal, Sayana in Baiga, Pendda in Maria Gond, Patel in hill Maria Gond of Bastar, Basau in Bhil of

Rajasthan, *Muppan* in Kadar of Kerala. In Bodo of Orissa, village head is elected, while other tribes have hereditary head.

There are assistants to village head known as Kotwar.

The main functions of village head are as follows:

- To represent his village in Inter-village meeting of Panchayat.
- To maintain law and order in village community.
- To punish the crime doers
- To call meeting of Village Panchayat.
- To settle the husband-wife dispute.
- To settle the inter-family, inter-lineage and inter-clan dispute.
- To settle the inter-tribal dispute
- To participate in inter-village dispute.
- To allot the forest land in families.
- To protect the common property of the village.
- To raise funds for village level worship and festivals.
- To assist village priest in organizing worship and festivals.
- To settle divorce cases.
- To decide the crime and type of punishment.
- To protect the village from other villages.
- To collect taxes from the families of the village for maintenance of tribal chief.

The village head is not a dictator. Rather he is chief of equals. He does not take his own decision. Rather he takes decision on consensus basis. Women have no participation in the village headship.

Village Panchayat: Tribal villages have their own traditional village Panchayat headed by the village head and participation of village officials and heads of all families. Naga of North-east, Khas of Dehradun, Munda, Oraon, Ho, Santhal of Jharkhkand, Hill Bhuiya of Orissa, Lodha of Bengal, Gond of Madhya Pradesh, Bhil of Rajasthan, Dubla and Gaunit of Gujarat and Toda of Nilgiri area have village Panchayat. The meeting of village Panchayat takes place at Sasana, Akhra or under an old tree, or at any common place of the village.

The meeting of the village Panchayat is chaired by the village head. The decisions are taken on consensus basis. The village priest and other village officials participate in the meeting. All heads of families of a village are its members. The decision of village Panchayat is obeyed. Its disobeyance is regarded as disobeyance of entire village.

Union of Villages or Inter-Village Panchayat: Some tribal villages have Union of villages or Inter-Village Panchayat. Through inter-Village Panchayat, tribals solve their inter-Village problems. They also extend cooperation to each other during flood, calamities, epidemic and attack of enemies. Like Village Panchayat, inter-village Panchayat also lacks participation of women. The number of villages in an inter-village Panchayat may vary between three to two hundred depending on the spread of a tribe into different villages.

The post of inter-village Head is generally hereditary. It is inherited by the eldest son of the inter-village head. But in some tribes inter-village head is elected with mutual consent in presence of all heads of villages under an inter-village Panchayat.

The inter-village Panchayat is locally termed by different names. For example the Santhal of Santhal Pargana in Jharkhand call it as Manjhi-Parganait system or Pargana Panchayat. The Oroan of Jharkhand call it as Parha Panchayat and the Munda of Jharkhand call it as Munda-Manki system or Pir Panchayat.

The main functions of inter-village Panchayat are as follows:

- To maintain a tribal unity.
- To provide safety to villages under its jurisdiction.
- To hear the cases of inter-village disputes.
- To settle the inter-village disputes.
- To organize common festivals.
- To organize religious processions.
- To organize religious fairs.
- To send the taxes collected by each village heads from their respective villages to the king or tribal chief.

Chiefdom or Tribal Chief: The tribals also had the concept and practice of chiefdom or tribal chief. Tribal chief was chief of all tribes residing in a region. For example Phani Mukut Roy, a foster son of Madira Munda, was the tribal chief of all tribes residing in Chhotanagpur and Santhal Pargana. He laid the foundation of Nagvanshi Dynasty in Chotanagpur whose descendants ruled the region for many years.

The practice of tribal chief was also prevalent among Naga tribe of Nagaland, Mizo tribe of Mizoram, Gond tribe of Bastar and Madhya Pradesh, Bhil tribe of Rajasthan and Mina tribe of Rajasthan.

The tribal chief was not the owner of land. The owner of lands were the people who had cleared the forest for cultivation. But for the maintenance of expenditure of tribal chief, each family used to contribute their produce according to the acreage held by a family. Tribal chief maintenance expenditure were collected by each village head from each family of the village. All village heads used to deposit the tax collected to inter-village head. The inter-village heads used to deposit all taxes in the treasury of tribal chief. In return tribal chief used to provide protective and administrative services to his people. Thus, tribal chief was not owner of lands of the region ruled by him. He was simply a service provider to his people. Rather he was chief of equals.

The main functions of tribal chief were as follows:

- To provide good administration in the region.
- To provide protection of all kinds to the people.
- To fight a war with those chiefs who wanted to encroach the boundary of primitive state.
- To provide services during flood, starvation and epidemic.
- To control natural resources and forest resources.
- To organize fairs and festivals.
- To organize various kinds of folk plays and folk sports.
- To keep people of the region united.
- To control various kinds of crimes in the region.
- To provide peace and prosperity to the people.

Primitive State

The state is an important component of political system. Political system is that system of the society which defines the roles that human beings occupy in order to maintain law and order on one hand, and supervise the functioning of the society on the other. To maintain legal order is one of functions of the political system. In fact, it is main function of political system in simple societies. Bu in complex society along with this main function, other functions of political system are to distribute resources for social and economic development.

Although state is an important component of political system, but it is worth mentioning here that there are societies in the world which did not have the institution of state. For example hunting and food gathering societies, pastoral societies and peasant societies do not have a king, head or lord who is centre of power. These societies do not have a centralized authority. They do not have Governments and Judicial system. Nor do they have a division of society into classes of rich and poor or privileged and unprivileged. These societies are known as stateless societies. They are different from those societies that have a centralized authority, Government, legal system and classes. They are state societies.

The prominent examples of stateless societies are the Australian aborigines, the Yako and Ibo of Nigeria, the Masai and Nandi of East Africa and the Nuer of Sudan. Uthalu Birhor, Kota, Toda are examples of stateless societies in India.

Some outstanding examples of state in simple societies are Swazi and Ashanti State.

Swazi State: The Swazi primitive state is in South Africa. This primitive state has a Central authority known as King or Raja. In unavoidable situation, the Swazi change their residences, too. This state has a number of villages situated on hills. Each village has a special hut for the stay of great mother or Rani Maa, a big hut for stay of cattle and a big hut for stay of unmarried members. Each village is a matrilineal descent group. Guests stay in huts along with unmarried person. Over all villages, there is a king who have armies to protect the villages and Rani Maa.

This state has two capitals—(i) The house of king, and (ii) house of Rani Maa. There is also a Council of Ministers to advice the king. It was a kinship based state.

Ashanti State: The Ashanti reside in dense forest of Africa. This tribe has a population of nearly 10 lacs or more. Here army is the centre of state activities. Each village has matrilineal descent group. Each village has a head. Over heads of all villages, there is a king. The king is the chief authority of Ashanti. Each village has army organization. Raja is chief of all villages. There is council of ministers to help the king. It is a military based state. Some tribes had priest based state. Example Polynesian tribe and Cheyanne Indians.

Modern State: It is characteristic feature of complex societies. Modern state has following characteristics:

- Definite territory
- Population
- Government

- Sovereignty
- Businessman and trading class
- Producer and consumer class
- Military organizations
- Administrative class.

Definite territory: Definite territory is a must for a state. The boundary of one state differs from the boundaries of neighbouring state.

Population: Each state has a population residing in different territories.

Government: Each state has a Government. The form of Government may be different such as democracy, monarchy, theocracy, oligocracy, gerontocracy. But there is a Government in each state.

Sovereignty: The Government of a state is free to make and implepment laws for its citizens.

Producer and Consumer: The state has classes like producer and consumer.

Businessman: The state has businessman or trader as a special class.

Army: The state has army to control internal and external situation.

Administrator: Each state has administrator.

Difference between State and Stateless Society

Earlier we have discussed that there are societies where there is no state. Such societies are termed as stateless society. For example a number of hunting and gathering societies, pastoral societies and peasant societies. They are examples of simple society. Absence of political state does not imply that these societies lack an orderly existence. They are certainly not in state of anarchy. In such society, elders, priest, secular head extend help in solving conflicting situation. In complex society law and order is maintained by the Government. Besides law and order, distribution of resources for social and economic development is also an important function of modern state. The main points of differences between stateless society and state society are as follows:

- Stateless society is early form of society, state is the most evolved form of society.
- Stateless society has no fixed territory, state has a fixed territory.
- Stateless society is kinship based, state society is class based.
- There is no distinction between rich and poor in stateless society, but there is distinction between rich and poor in state society.
- One does not find privileged and non-privileged class in stateless society but one finds privileged and non-privileged class in state society.
- In stateless society there is no difference between producer and consumer, but in state society one finds the existence of producer and consumer.
- Stateless society has no military organization, but state society has military organization.
- Stateless society does not have businessman and traders, but state society has businessman and traders.
- Each stateless society has its own laws obeyed by its members, each state has its own laws applicable to all societies residing in the territory of a state equally.
- In stateless society law and order is maintained by social sanction, public opinion, morality, fear of magic and religion, but in state society law and order is maintained by the Government.
- The stateless society does not make distinction between civil law and criminal law, but state society makes a distinction between civil law and criminal law.
- In stateless society determination of crime and punishment is done by the kingroup, but in state society the determination of crime and punishment is done by court, Judge, lawyer and *thana*-police.
- The stateless society provides membership, but state society provides citizenship.
- In stateless society laws are obeyed as social and reciprocal, but in state society laws are enforced.
- The law of stateless society cannot be changed and challenged, but the law of state society can be changed and challenged.

- While deciding compensation, the social and economic status is taken into consideration in stateless society, but social and economic status is not taken into consideration in state society while deciding compensation.
- The stateless society serves human needs, whereas state society serves political needs.

Functions of State

The functions of state can be divided into two categories:

- Essential functions
- Optional functions

Essential functions: Essential functions of a state are as follows:

- Protection of boundaries of state
- Establishment of internal peace
- Judicial system
- Rights and duties of citizen
- Legal relation in family
- International relation
- Economic function

Optional functions: The optional functions of the state are as follows:

- Education facility
- Health and sanitation facility
- Establishment of industries
- Agricultural reforms
- Transport and communication
- Control on trade
- Interest of labour
- Banking, currency and money
- Social reform
- Social justice and welfare
- Employment generation

Theory of Origin of State

The main theories propounded for the origin of a state are as follows:

- Divinal Theory
- Power Theory
- Social Contact Theory
- Economic Theory
- Evolutionary Theory

• *Divinal Theory*: According to this theory, each state was created by God with a king to rule it.

• *Power Theory*: According to this theory, state came into existence for achieving more and more power. Some authorities become more and more powerful with their army organization. They increased their territory and led the formation of state.

• *Social Contact Theory*: According to this theory, kinship organization finally led to the formation of state.

• *Economic Theory*: According to this theory, state came into existence when stratification of society on the basis of class, such as rich and poor, privileged and non-privileged, consumer and producer, seller and buyer took place. A central authority was established to control different classes.

• *Evolutionary Theory*: According to this theory, the human society has progressed through three successive-stages—band, tribe and state. The state is most evolved form of society.

Leadership Pattern in Simple Society

Leadership is an individual quality, by which he or she provides guidance to member of the society. In tribal societies, too, there are a number of individuals who possess the quality of leadership.

Professor L.P. Vidyarthi and B.K. Roy in their book, "Tribal Culture of India" (1976) have classified tribal leaders on the basis of four categories:

- Status in Society
- Individual Quality
- Functional achievement
- Influence area

Status in Society: On the basis of status in the society tribal leaders may be classified into three categories:

- Formal leader
- Informal leader
- Exploiter leader

• *Formal leader*: Those leaders who occupy formal position in formal social organization. For example, village head, inter-village Panchayat head, religious head *Pahan* and so on.

• *Informal leader*: Those leaders who do not occupy any formal position in the social organization but provide guidance on many occasions. For example aged persons of the village community.

• *Exploiter leader*: Those leaders who exploit the people at one hand and provide help to people on the other hand. Such leaders are called exploiter leader. For example landlord and Mahajan.

On the basis of individual Quality: On the basis of individual quality, tribal leaders may be classified into following types:

- Ideal leader
- Institutional leader
- Benevolent leader
- Socially privileged leader

• *Ideal leader*: In this category such tribal leaders may be placed who were or are ideals for the society. For example Birsa, Siddo-Kanho, Buddhu Bhagat, etc.

• *Institutional leaders*: In this category those tribal leaders have been placed who are associated with an institution such as family head, village head, inter-village Panchayat head, *Pahan*, Mahato, Mokadam, Patel, Manjhi, sardar, Parharaja, Kotwar etc.

• *Benevolent leader*: In this category those tribal leaders have been placed who are of benevolent character, for example Ojha, medicineman, singer, teacher, priest etc.

• *Socially previleged leader*: Under this category those leaders have been included who are socially previleged such as village head, village priest and inter-village Panchayat head.

On the basis of function: On the basis of function, tribal leaders may be classified into following categories:

- Traditional leader
- Modern leader

• *Traditional leader*: Traditional leaders are those who perform traditional function such as *Pahan*, Munda, Baiga, Mahto, Sayan, Manjhi, Sardar etc.

• *Modern leader*: Modern leader perform modern functions such as Mukhia, Ward member, Panchayat Samiti member, Zila Parishad member, MLA, M.P., Councillor, Mayor etc.

On the basis of influence area: On the basis of influence area tribal leaders may be divided into following categories:

- Village level leader—Village head
- Inter-village level leader—Manaki
- Panchayat level leader—Mukhia
- Block level leader—Panchayat Samiti member
- District level leader—Zila Parishad member
- Region level leader—Santhal leader, Oraon leader, Munda leader
- State level leader—Babulal Marandi, Shibu Soren and others
- Country level leader—Jaipal Singh, Ramdayal Munda.
- Urban leader, Doctor, Engineer, Professor, etc.

Nation-building in Independent State

When a state becomes independent, the first task of the Government is nation-building. But before dealing with the process of nation-building, it will be the fitness of the thing to present here the difference between a state or country and Nation.

State or Country: A state or country is a geographical entity having a territory, the people living throughout the territory, a Government to establish the rule of law, i.e. to maintain law and order in the State and the Government should be free to formulate and implement law.

Nation: A nation is a body of sentiments and feelings of the people living throughout the length and breadth of territory of belonging together. The common feeling of ownness and togetherness is the chief feature of the nation. For example the feeling of Indianness prevalent among population throughout the length and breadth of the country reveals our national feeling that we all are Indians.

Nation Building Process

In an independent state, the nation building process includes the following steps to inculcate national feeling among the people across region, religion, language, caste, creed, race and so on:

- Teaching of national cultural history and national leaders.
- Making people aware of national boundary and its protection.
- Celebration of national festivals.
- Inculcating the feeling of safety and protection to all.
- Providing social justice and empowerment to all.
- Making arrangement of livelihood to all.
- Providing special protection to deprived sections of the society such as PTGs, Minorities, SCs, STs, OBCs, women and children.
- Initiating welfare measures for exploited, oppressed and depressed classes.
- Providing reservational facilities to deprived lot to bring them all in the mainstream of development.
- Promoting national anthem, national heritage, national bird and national animal.
- Promotion of national games and sports.
- Promoting educational facilities to all classes and areas—rural and urban.
- To assure balanced development and sustainable development.
- To establish communication between the Government and the people.
- Enhancing the principle of democracy and secularism.
- Building a constitution to rule the people and protect their interest.
- Development of social peace and prosperity.

By observing the above steps, the Government can do nation building in the mind of people.

National Integration

In our country India, there is plurality of region, religion, language, caste, creed, race, ethnic group and culture. But in spite of all such diversities, we all are united as Indians. Why? It is because we all are bound together by a common sentiment and we feeling. Economic and political freedom enhance our we feeling.

We may define national integration as a political approach by which discriminatory behaviour is banned and unity among all citizens is created. Thus, national integration is a political concept. It removes social, cultural and economic inequality prevalent among the people of the country and brings unity and integrity by creating national feeling. It creates a feeling of unity amidst diversity among the people. The national feeling is above caste, creed, race, region, religion, culture and language. Creation of national constitution, national cultural history, life sketch of national leaders, national games, national sports, national anthem, national bird, national animal and national heritage, national language, livelihood to all, protection to all and welfare measures for disabled and deprived sections of the society enhance the feeling of national integration among the masses.

National integration had to face the situation of impediments created by casteism, communalism, regionalism and lingualism. Such elements create hindrance in the maintenance of national integration. It will be worthmentioning here about the elements which create national disintegration. Elements creating national disintegration are as follows:

Casteism: In the context of national integration, casteism has been defined negatively. It places emphasis on favouring members of own caste at the cost of other castes. In casteism one forgets his national feeling and begain to behave with his caste feeling. His caste identity supersedes his national identity. The worst victim of casteism is occurrence of caste riots. In the situation of caste riots, we begin to behave as a member of our caste group and forget our national identity as Indian. We become so prejudiced and biased against the other castes that we do not hesitate in looting their property and murdering them. The occurrence of riots and blood shed between different caste groups put a question upon us. Are we really Indians. It puts a black spot on our national feeling and national integration. One cannot say that members of one caste are more nationalist, and other castes are less nationalists. Members of all castes are nationalist equally. They have contributed significantly in freedom struggle and maintenance of national integration. But unfortunately incidence of caste riots have abandoned our national feeling time to time in which many people have been killed. Thus, being fanatics in the name of caste and behaving as enemy with the members of other castes is very dangerous for the national integration.

***Communalism*:** So far as national integration is concerned, communalism is also a negative concept. Its meaning is to favour the members of own community at the cost of other communities. In communalism we forget our national identity and start behaving as per our communal identity. In our country there is plurality of religion. Such as Hinduism, Jainism, Buddhism, Islam, Christianity, Sikhism, and so on. We have temples, mosques, churches and Gurudwaras throughout the length and breadth of the country. We all visit our religious centres and offer worship to our deities. We all celebrate our festivals. The main festivals of all major religions are celebrated as national festival. National holidays are declared on these occasions.

There is no national harm in offering worships to deities and celebrating festivals of our own religions. Rather it reveals our national culture. Offering *Puja-path,* to deities and celebrating festivals of own religion do not reveal that the person concerned is less nationalist. The harm is in giving up own national identity and behaving as per own communal identity. It is because of this reason that the term communalism is always defined as negative, destructive and harmful concept.

Unfortunately, our country has witnessed ugly scene of communal riots on many occasions such as in 1946-1947 at the time of division of country. In this riot thousands and thousands of Muslims and Hindus were made lifeless, homeless and propertyless by violent attack on each other.

In 1984, thousand of Sikhs and Hindus were murdered, their properties were looted and their houses were abandoned in Hindu-Sikh riot after assassination of the then Prime Minister Smt. Indira Gandhi. Again 1992 Hindu Muslim riots had taken place throughout the length and breadth of the country in which lacs of people were killed, their properties were looted and their houses were abandoned after demolition of Babari mosque at Ayodhya in U.P. Again in 2002 Gujarat Hindu-Muslim riot played an ugly game making thousands of people homeless, propertyless and lifeless. Besides, these major riots, a number of minor riots have taken place here and there on religious and other occasions. Thus, communalism has always a negative impact.

In communal riots, we forget our national feeling and identity. We begin to behave as per our religious feeling and identity. We become fanatics towards the followers of other religious group. Jealousy and hatred develop in our heart towards the other. We begin to harm lives and properties of others. We forget that we are Indians and they are also Indians. An Indian is going to cause harm of property and life to another Indian. Occurance of communal riots has put a question on our nationality as Indian and our secular Constitution. In this way, communalism creates a great hindrance in maintaining the spirit of national integration.

***Regionalism*:** Like casteism and communalism, regionalism is also defined negatively in the context of national integration. Regionalism is favouring the people of own region at the cost of other regions of the country. People belonging to a region show special honesty, pride and feeling for their own region. There is no harm in showing honesty and respect to a region in which people are born and brought up. But the harm is when we favour the people of our region at the cost of people of other regions of the same country. Such behaviour and feelings are against the spirit of national integration. People of one region develop jealousy and hatred against the people of other regions of the same nation. On many occasions situation of regional riots have also emerged in our country. In Maharashtra and Assam, Biharis are killed, looted and abused on different occasions. Such behaviours in the name of region is harmful for the national integration.

***Linguism*:** Like casteism, communalism and regionalism, linguism has also been defined negatively in the context of national integration. It is because lingual riots have tarnished our image of secular and democratic nation. It puts a question are we really Indians? Linguism is favouring the people who speak same language or dialect at the cost of other linguistic groups of the same nation. Our nation is of plural languages. In Eighth Schedule of our Constitution 22 languages have been included, besides these Government recognized languages hundred of dialects are spoken. Unity among linguistic variability is principle of our national integration. But unfortunately in our country, lingual riots have occurred damaging our secular image and spirit of national integration.

In 1964, Tamil Nadu has witnessed ugly scene of lingual riots. In 1998, 2000, 2003 and even in 2015, Assam has witnessed cruel scene of lingual riots in which non-Assamese speakers were brutally murdered, made homeless and their properties were looted. These behaviours are enemies of our national integration.

From the above account, it becomes clear that for maintaining national integration it is essential to curb the caste, communal, regional and lingual riots.

Chapter 9
Linguistic Anthropology

You might have seen people producing sounds to tell, to ask, and to do something. You might have also seen people shaking hands, meeting shoulder to shoulder and also turning their face to see someone also. Have you ever thought what kind of these behaviours are? These are our linguistic behaviours through which we say something to someone else and get something from someone else. Through linguistic behaviour, we communicate with others and other communicate with us. Thus, for the purpose of communication between two or more persons a medium is required and that medium is our language or linguistic behaviour.

For the purpose of communication, each community has a language. That is why a community speaking the same language is termed as speech community. Language is such a means by which we talk to each other not only in family and neighbourhood but also with other communities. It is language which has made us social being. We acquire language in society. Through language we acquire culture in society. Thus, language and culture both are social heritage, inseparable and inter-dependent.

Meaning of Language

The simple meaning of language is a means by which we communicate with our other fellows for satisfaction and fulfilment of our various needs. But in language we do not produce meaningless sounds. Rather we produce sounds according to our needs and which have social-cultural meaning. Thus, language is not our natural rather artificial behaviour. It is because we produce sound according to our needs. We pronounce only those sounds which we need in our need fulfilment at a particular time. For the purpose of communication each speech community has its own lexicon and each word has a particular social-cultural meaning. The language in which we produce sound is known as verbal language. But we also have an another form of language known as body language. The body language includes our facial expression, gesture, eye contact, handshake, shoulder shake, lip movement, teeth movement, tongue movement, nose movement, mouth expression, neck and head movement, finger movement and so on.

The verbal language is expressed in many forms such as oral, written, visual and audio-visual.

Definition of Language

Famous American cultural linguist and pupil of Franz Boas, Edward Sapir in his book, "Language" (1921) has attempted to provide a definition of language. According to him, language is purely human and non-instinctive method of communicating ideas, emotions and desire by means of a system of voluntarily produced symbols.

From the above definition of language provided by Sapir, it is quite clear that language is a method of communication. But this method is purely human and non-instinctive. Through language communication takes place by means of a system of voluntarily produced symbols.

Characteristics of Human Language

Human language has following characteristics:

Language is a method of communication: This is one of the characteristics of human language. Human beings employ language as a method to convey and receive messages of various kinds. Without application of this method communication is impossible.

Language is purely human: Language is one of characteristics of human beings. Although birds and animals also produce sound symbols to attract their fellows and to convey some messages. But yet language is quality of human beings. It is because birds and animals use limited number of sound symbols and they repeat the same sounds again and again. They use limited symbols to attract fellow of opposite sex, to send messages of fear and to communicate the existence of food at particular place. But human beings can create thousands of symbols and can attribute social-cultural meaning to them. That is why language is regarded as human quality.

Language is non-instinctive: Language is not natural or instinctive, rather it is artificial or non-instinctive. We create language artificially in order to convey and receive messages of various kind.

Language is Social Heritage: We do not inherit language genetically. We acquire or learn language as a member of society. At the time of birth a human child is just like a mass of bone and flesh. But gradually he is made a social being. In making him social being language plays significant roles. Through the process of socialization, human beings acquire or learn language. In this way language is social heritage.

Language has arbitrary created symbols: In language one finds artificially created sound symbols whose answer cannot be given why those symbols are used for a particular thing. For example why father is called father, why mango is called mango, why cow is called cow? Answer of all these questions are impossible to get.

Language is Verbal and Non-verbal Both: Language has not only verbal sound symbols. It has also non-verbal symbols. The verbal symbols are oral, written, visual and audio-visual. The non-verbal language is known as body language and is expressed through gesture, facial expression, eye contact, and movements of other body parts.

Language is Local as well as Universal: There is no society in the world without using any language. Thus, language is universal in human society. But the form of language is not same all-over the world. The form of language differs from society to society. Thus, language is local as well as universal both.

Language is Transferred: As language is a social heritage so it is transferred from one generation to the next. Every individual acquires language from older generation and transfers it to the younger generation. Thus, language is transferred from one generation to next, from one place to another, from one community to the another.

Language has the Quality of Creativity: Language deals with creativity. There are folklorists who create poems, songs, *Bhajan*, *Kirtan*, *Geet*, Legends, Stories, proverbs, idioms and tales. Thus, language has the quality of creativity.

Quality of Displacement: The language possesses the quality of displacement. Through human language past, present and future events can be described, analysed and explained. Thus, it has the quality of displacement.

Double Articulation: The language has the quality of double articulation. The human beings are in advantageous position to use the same basic sound units twice to create symbols. For example, good, book, look, took, goose, choose, better, utter, butter etc. Thus, the language has the quality of double articulation.

Human language shows variation: Human language shows variation not only on the basis of region and community, but also on the basis of age, sex, caste and occupation. The pronounciation of male and female varies, the pronounciation of children, young and old varies. Similarly, the style of pronounciation varies according to caste, region and occupation. Thus, human language shows variation.

Human language shows multilinguism and Diglossia: Language shows the quality of multilinguism and diglosia. The same individual may be speaker of different languages. This shows the quality of multilinguism in language. The same language used by children, aged, male, female shows variation based on age, sex, caste, occupation etc. This shows the quality of diglossia in language.

Rule Governed: Human language is rule governed. In language sounds are produced not in haphazard manner but they are arranged according to rule. The rule governed sounds reveal meaning in social-cultural context and communication goes on.

Why Human Beings could become Speaking Animal?

Now question arises as to why human beings could become speaking animal? In order to answer this question we will have to look at the physical changes which took place in man in course of evolution. These changes were as follows:

- Erect posture
- Bipedal walk
- Freely opposable thumbs
- Stereoscopic vision
- Developed brain and creation of symbols

Erect posture: Due to the evolution of erect posture man could stand erectly. This adaptation made the skull to establish on neck vertically. As a result larynx and pharynx were pushed downwards. They began to work as a first resonator. Mouth cavity became the second resonator and nasal cavity became the third resonator. Evolution of these three resonators made the man a speaking animal. Because with the adaptation of these resonators man could pronounciate.

Bipedal Walk: Bipedal walk make the upper arm free to work as hand. With the help of hands he was able to do a number of works related to gathering, hunting, protecting and tool-making. Not only this he began to send symbols to his fellows with the help of fingers and hands. Bipedal walk was related also to the development of body language. Such as gesture, facial expression, eye contact, movements of head and hand.

Freely opposable thumbs: This adaptation in man made him not only to perform varieties of works but also to communicate with body language with his fellows.

Stereoscopic Vision: This adaptation made man to see in all directions such as forward, backward, upward and downward. As a result he could experience things and events around him. This adaptation help in expression power.

Developed Brain and Creation of Symbols: The man is born with a small skull but gradually it assumes big size. The brain of man is developed than other animals particularly primates. The developed brain size made to think and develop symbols. The symbols led to the development of language.

Thus, the above evolutionary changes in man developed in him work power, speaking power and expression power and man could become a speaking animal.

Theories of Human Language Origin

A number of theories have been propounded to know the origin of human language. These theories are as follows:

Divinal Theory: According to this theory language is a boon given to man by God. God has made us not only as speaking animals, but he has also given a well structured language for communication. But on the basis of empirical facts this theory of origin of language cannot be accepted.

Natural Sound Theory: According to this theory language in human being would have emerged by hearing. The natural sounds such as flowing of water, blowing of wind, chirping of birds, roaring of animals and other natural events. These sounds were followed by man and used in course of communication. In this way language would have emerged.

Body Language Theory: According to this theory sound language developed from the body language. While communicating through body language some sounds would have emerged. These sounds gradually led to the development of sound language.

Interjectional Theory: According to this theory sound language would have emerged in order to express emotions and feeling such as joy, sorrow, hatred, jealousy, surprise and so on. Such emotional sounds would have led to the development of language.

Functional Theory: This theory emphasizes that language emerged in course of performing work individually or collectively. The farmers make special type of sound at the time of ploughing. The blacksmith, washerman, carpenter, potter and labourers produce special sounds while they perform work. Thus, language would have emerged due to functions performed by human beings.

Sociological Theory: According to this theory language originated because of social interactions. Man is a social animal. For the fulfilment of his various kinds of need, he is dependent upon the fellows of the society. For need fulfilment he has to communicate with his fellows. The communication sounds led to the origin of language. Thus, language originated because man is a social animal.

Evolutionary Theory: About this theory a detailed description has been made while describing as to why man became a speaking animal. Therefore, to avoid repetition, the same description is not being presented here. The adaptation of lungs, larynx and pharyx as first resonator, mouth cavity as second resonator and nasal cavity as third resonator led to the origin of sound language in man. This is most accepted theory of origin of human language.

Relation between Speech and Mind

Man is a speaking animal and he gives speech, but it is essential here to understand the relation between speech and mind. Some scholars especially physical psychologists believe that speech is located in mind. As all observed things find a place in mind, similarly language also makes its place in mind through hearing organs. It is because hearing organs are extension of brain. But in reality, the speech does not find morphological shape in mind by hearing. In order to acquire a real shape, the speech has to be associated with a morphology. The meaning of speech units appear from the morphology. From this point of view speech is quite an external tradition. It has no relation with body, the speech is quite away from body and mind. It is related to mind only as consciousness. Like other human activities, speech also assumes consciousness in mind.

The Process of Language Acquisition

Language is a social heritage. It is acquired in the society as its member. Each older generation transmits language to its younger generation. In this way, language continues from one generation to the next generation.

It is worth mentioning here the processes through which a child acquires the language of the community in which he is born. The acquisition of language in child passes through the following stages:

- Babbling stage
- Holophrastic or one word stage
- Two word stage
- Telegraphic stage

Babbling Stage: When the child is between 5 and 6 months of age, he or she starts babbling. In this stage the child attempts to utter some kind of sounds and sound sequence which are quite different from their cry and gurgles. These sounds are meaningless to large extent. Even deaf children are found babbling in this age like normal children. Some scholars do not consider babbling as prerequisite for later development of language. But some other scholar consider babbling as necessary prerequisite for later development of language. As both normal and deaf children pass through the stage of babbling, it is presumed that human child is biologically predisposed to babble.

Holophrastic or one word stage: When a child attains an age around one year he/she enters into holophrastic stage or one word stage. In this stage the child starts using one word sentences to express himself. These words are limited in number. They may be related to the family members like Mummy, Daddy, or animals like cow, dog, cat and things like paddy, ball, cup etc. He also utters some words related to action or demands. For example, no or more. He also calls all men as Papa and all women as Mama.

Two-word stage: When the child is of around two years of age he starts uttering two words at a time. This stage is known as two word stage of language. In this stage, there is absence of syntactic or morphological markers. For example Papa-toffe, Mama-cat, Bhaiya-shoe, cow-calf, fat-bad, cat-rat etc. In this stage a child learns about 50 different words and become a conversation partner of speech community.

Telegraphic stage: In this stage of language acquisition, the child begin to utter two, three, four, and five or more words together. The child starts expressing the words in telegraphic manner. For example come here, go there, Mama is cooking, Papa is doing work, uncle is sleeping, dog is barking, cat is mewing etc. The most significant feature of this stage is that the children grasps the principle of sentence formation. Gradually, he picks up grammatical or syntactical rules of language. By the age of three years, the child acquires about 100 words easily and his pronounciation becomes closer to the adult language. When the child acquires 4 to 5 years of age he is fully capable of acquiring adult language and becomes a part of his linguistic community or speech community.

Theory of Acquiring Adult Language

In order to explain as to how the child manages to acquire the adult language, two theories have been propounded. These are as follows:

- Imitation Theory
- Reinforcement Theory

Imitation Theory: According to this theory, a child acquires adult language by imitating the language of adult person around him. By imitating the language of adult persons, he is able to know the intricacies of syntax and sentence formation.

Reinforcement Theory: This theory lays emphasis on the correction in mistakes which a child commits during imitation of adult language. In spite of hearing several times, the child commits mistake. Therefore, in order to make the child utter correctly the adult members force the children to utter correctly and to avoid uttering incorrect words. Thus, positive reinforcement for uttering correct words and negative reinforcement for non-uttering incorrect words forces the children to pick up adult language.

This theory of adult language acquisition by children is not true on the basis of empirical evidences. Empirical evidences reveal that the incorrect utterances of the children are enjoyed in place of putting reinforcement. It also appears that children formulate its own rules for the purpose of sentence making.

Methods of Acquisition of other Language

In a linguistic community there are some persons who have acquired other languages, too. Such persons are multilingual persons. When the child grows up in multilingual environment, he starts speaking other languages. But an adult person may take his whole lifetime to speak a second language. Difficulty here is in the distinction between the process of acquisition and learning. Acquisition is a process of gradual development of using a language in communicative situation. But learning is conscious process of mastering the vocabulary and grammar of a language. That is why an adult person learns language rather than he acquires a language. Empirical evidences indicate that even in an ideal acquisition situation, an adult can very rarely acquire native like proficiency in using a second language. It is also observed that after the critical period of acquisition, i.e. puberty it becomes difficult to learn another language. But some other opinions are that optimum age of language acquisition is between 11 to 16 years of age and not the early teens. However, in order to learn second language some methods have been devised which are as follows:

- Grammar-Translation Method
- Direct Method
- Audio-lingual Method
- Communicative Method

Grammar-Translation Method (Written Method): This is the most traditional method to learn a second language. In this method, an emphasis is placed on the written rather than spoken language. In this process, the learner has to memorise a long list of words and a set of grammatical rules. This method equips a person to write another languages fluently but not to communicate the second language fluently.

Direct Method (Spoken Method): This method is quite contrast to grammar translation method. In this method emphasis is on spoken language not on written language. This method is commonly known as direct method. Here learners are left to think and express the second language and pick up words and sentences for spoken purposes.

Audio-lingual Method: In this method emphasis is more on structured materials for the learners. It starts from much simple and gradually moves towards more complex grammatical compositions. It places emphasis on more and more repeated practice of learning. Although it appears monotonous and boring, but helps the child in picking up the language mechanically.

Communicative Method: This method of learning the second language has come into existence recently. This method emphasises upon the learning of function of the language rather than its forms. The learning in this method is organized around activities on various social contexts, not on giving a high degree of grammatical input.

Evolution of Writing

Man emerged on this earth as a speaking being in Pleistocene period nearly 3-4 million years ago. But when he became a writing being is a matter of debate among the scholars. The first evidence of writing left by our ancestors are cave paintings and drawings which suggest that Cro-Magnon man, Chancelade man and Grimaldi man had developed some kind of writing in the form of paintings and drawings. This was probably the first stage of writing evolved by upper Paleolithic man nearly 35,000 to 40,000 years ago. The present-day form of alphabetic writing system was evolved in the stage of prehistoric civilization nearly 5,000 to 7,000 years ago from drawing stage to present day alphabetic stage. Writing of human language has passed through the following main stages:

Cave drawings: It was probably the first stage of writing evolved by our upper Paleolithic ancestors—Cro-Magnon man, Grimaldi man and Chancelade man. In India the evidences of cave drawings have been gathered from a cave site Bhimbetka in Madhya Pradesh belonging to Mesolithic period. From these evidences, it is clear that man left the survivals of writing in the form of cave drawings that are found in several parts of the world. It may be possible that he would have started drawing on earth and sands with the help of fingers and wooden sticks but we do not have any evidence in this regard.

Picture Writing: This was probably the second stage of writing represented by pictograms or writing through pictures. Contrary to modern writing system, each picture represents the direct image of the object seen. This form of writing shows a non-arbitrary relationship between the form and meaning. It indicates a high degree of consistency. Infact it does not represent any language except reference. It was used by our prehistoric ancestors, but it is still very much in use in simple to complex, rural to urban, traditional to modern societies of the world. Pictographic writings are in use to represent the signs of aerodrome, railway station, bus stand, public toilet, hotels, hostels, parking places, restricted areas, family welfare, theatres, petrol pumps and so on. The advantage of this form of writing is that it can be understood by anyone by any linguistic background.

Ideographic Writing: This was probably the third stage of writing. In this form of writing, the picture represents not exactly the object but its attributes. For example the picture of a sun could also represent warmth, heat, light, day, brilliance, and so on. These ideas are associated with sun and a picture of sun could represent anyone from the list given above.

Cuneiform Writing: This form of writing was evolved by Sumerians, who had built a civilization in Southern Mesopotamia, the south of modern Iraq nearly 5,000 years ago. Sumerian pictogram is known as cuneiform writing by using a wedge shaped stylus. In this system of writing symbols represent not the actual thing but the name of the thing. The inscriptions used by Sumerians were produced by pressing a wedge shaped implement into soft clay tablets resulting in ▼ ▼ ▲ forms. It is believed that Sumerians had true word writing system.

Rebus Writing: Gradually, a single sign was increasingly used to represent all words with the same sound. This principle was named as rebus writing system. For example the sign of an eye could represent pronoun I. The sign of sun could represent son. The sign of bee and leaf were represented by belief. Although this system of writing was not very effective, but it led to the evolution of syllabic writing system later on.

Syllabic Writing: This form of writing has evolved from the cuneiform writing of ancient Sumerians. The ancient Babylonians and Persians had adopted cuneiform of writing from ancient Sumerians. But they had used them to represent the sounds of syllables in their writing. Thus, the system of syllabic writing was evolved. In syllabic writing system, each syllable in the language is represented by its own symbol. Words are written by juxtaposing the symbols of their individual syllables. By 5000 BC, the Persians had devised a simplified syllabic alphabet for their language.

Hieroglyphic Writing: When Sumerian syllabic writing was at peak around 4000 BC, a similar system of writing was evolved in Egypt. This system of writing is known as hieroglyphic writing.

Alphabetic Writing: This system of writing was evolved by the Greeks. The word alphabet is derived from the first two letters of Greek alphabet, alpha and beta. The alphabetic system became the system of writing where each symbol represented one phoneme or the sound unit. This system of writing was passed to the Italians who in turn passed it to Romans. The Christian missionaries used alphabetic system for translating the Holy Bible into many languages for the benefit of many preliterate people of the world. Another line of development brought the alphabetic system of writing to East-Europe where Slavic languages were spoken. Modification there is known as Cyrillic alphabet, which is the basis of modern Russian system of writing.

Structure of Human Language

As already discussed human beings use two kinds of languages to send and receive messages from their fellows and other members of the society. They are as follows:

- Body Language or Non-verbal language
- Verbal language

Structure of Non-verbal or Body Language

There is no doubt that verbal language has certainly immense power. But sometimes non-verbal language can tell us more than the verbal language. There should also be similarity in behavoiur of verbal and non-verbal language to make the expressions more clear and impressive. On many occasions non-verbal languages are used as a substitute of verbal languages. In many speech situations verbal and non-verbal languages go together. Thus, non-verbal language accompany, modify, enrich and energise the verbal language.

The significance of non-verbal language such as gestures, facial expression, postures and tone of voice was recognized since classical times. Classical Greek and Roman scholars had attempted to codify the non-verbal languages mentioned above. The codification of non-verbal languages was significant feature of Bharat's *Natyashastra* or

Bharat Natyam between fourth and first century B.C. *Bharat Natyam* has left before us many dance poses or *Mudras*. These *Mudras* express human emotion in a subtle way without using any spoken language. The same is also true for many classical dances prevalent all-over the world where emotions have been expressed through poses, gestures, facial expression, voice tone and body parts movement. During 19th century, non-verbal language got established status of linguistic research with publications of conversational niceties. It got scientific status with implementation of experiments and rigorous documentation using charts, graphs, formulae, sketches, to record varieties of hand gestures, facial movements, eye movements, teeth movements, tongue and lip movements, eyebrow movement, head and neck movements. In fact non-verbal language is an integral part of our communicative behaviour. Whistling, hissing, murmuring, clapping, finger gesturing, bowing, shaking hands, shaking chest, meeting shoulder to shoulder, smiling, sitting with crossed legs, contacting eyes, turning face, putting finger on lips and a number of non-verbal languages very well indicate love, hatred, jealousy, happiness, frustrations, greeting, command and other feelings. These feelings can also be expressed by spoken languages.

Thus, the study of non-verbal languages is of great importance and an interesting area of research in linguistic anthropology. Now, it will be the fitness of the thing to present here some of the modes of non-verbal languages which either supplement or substitute the spoken languages in human communication.

Paralinguistics: It deals with association between vocal patterns and emotional expressions. Under paralanguage come all extra speech sounds such as hissing, shushing, whistling and imitating sounds. It also includes quality of voice (Sepulchral, whiny, giggling) hesitation very high speech and rate of taking. The idea of paralinguistic goes back to the writings of Charles Darwin, "Expression of Emotions in Man and Animal" (1865). But scientific advances in this regard took place in 1950s. Now-a-days, Paralanguages are being studied with the help of sophisticated machines. It has developed into two major directions:

- Voice as an indicator of personality
- Voice as an indicator of state of human interaction

But both these areas depend upon voice as a conveyor of emotion.

Kinesics: The term Kinesics was introduced in 1950s to designate the articulation of body or movements resulting from muscular and skeletal shifts in the process of communication. This includes all actions—physical or physiological, automatic reflexes, posture, facial expression, gesture and other kinds of body movements. It was Bird Whistill who initiated the study of body movements in 1946 while he was undertaking anthropological field-work in 1946 among the Kutenai Indians of western Canada. In 1952, he had begun a model of organizing Kinesic behaviour taking verbal and non-verbal aspect together. He had favoured contextual approach in place of clinical approach to the study of Kinesics.

Prosemics: Non-verbal behaviours which use space as their channel of communication are linked together and termed as prosemic behaviour. One cannot see space in the same way as facial expressions, body movements or voice tone, but it is a vital part of every social encounter. The root of Prosemic study like Kinesic study is also seen in Anthropology. Edward Hall in his book, "Hidden Dimension" (1966) marked the beginning of systematic study into prosemic behaviours. According to him prosemics is study of man's perception and use of space in conversation and talking. In fact, it is a human non-verbal communication using space for conveying some messages to another. He pointed out four major cultural space—intimate, personal, social and public.

Chronemics: It deals with the study of non-verbal language using time in talking and conversation.

American Sign Language (ASL)

As discussed earlier that it is speech faculty which distinguished man with other non-human animals. Man is endowed with the faculty of speech uniquely. He can create different words and shades of different meaning with the help of verbal language. But it has been observed that deaf children cannot speak. But deaf children are equally capable of acquiring and creating language to express themselves as efficiently as normal children with the help of sign languages. Thus, it is quite clear that human language can be acquired other than verbal or sound language, too. The hand and body movement of deaf carry definite meanings. The deaf speakers are capable of creating new sentences in their gestural languages as normal children. The deaf children learn the sign language in the same way as normal children learn to speak their language in their own linguistic environment. In America deaf children acquire sign language with the help of American Sign Language (ASL). France has French Sign Language (FSL). British has British Sign Language (BSL). Thus different countries have evolved different sign languages according to their linguistic requirements.

Structure of Verbal or Sound Language

There is no doubt that human language is a two way process. It involves both production and reception of sounds. So far as process of speech is concerned, it involves associating sounds with meaning and meaning with sounds. It is different from writing where meaning is associated with a sign or a visual symbol. Therefore, the structure of verbal or sound language requires the understanding of followings:

- Language
- Phonology — Sounds
- Morphology — (Meaningful Combinations of Sounds)
  ↕
- Syntax — (Meaningful Combinations of Words)
  ↕
- Semantics — (Meaning)

From the perusal of above presentation it is clear that in order to understand the verbal or sound language, we need to understand how sound is produced, how sounds are combined meaningfully to form words and how words are combined meaningfully to form sentences and how meaning is attached to words and sentences. Thus, phonology, morphology, syntax and semantics are the basics of verbal or sound languages.

Phonology: It deals with study of sounds. It is divided into two categories:

- Phonetics
- Phonemics

Phonetics: It deals with the study of production, transmission and reception of speech sounds.

Phonemics: It deals with the study of sound and sound patterns of a specific language.

Phonetics is again divided into three such as articulatory phonetics, acoustic phonetics and auditory phonetics.

Articulatory Phonetics: It deals with the study of mechanism of production or articulation of sounds.

Acoustic Phonetics: It deals with the study of physical properties of sound themselves.

Auditory Phonetics: The study of perception of speech sounds through ear is known as auditory phonetics.

In speech, the air of elementary canal passes through larynx, pharynx and vocalsac. These acts as first resonator. The second resonator where the speech sounds get shape is mouth cavity which includes lips, tongue, teeth and palate. The third resonator where the speech sounds get shape is nose and its regions known as nasal cavity. Through these resonators speech sounds are produced. But in human speech, sounds are produced for the purpose of communication of messages of various kinds. Sounds are not produced here meaninglessly. Human speech associates sounds with meaning and meaning with sounds.

The smallest unit of sound is called phonemes. Phonemes do not have social and cultural meaning. But they are valuable from the point of view of linguistics and morphology. Phonemes are pronounced as a pair of contrast sounds.

Morphology: From the point of view of speech, morphology is of great value. Under morphology come those words which are created by combing two or more phonemes. For example Go, Do, God, Dog, Man, Woman, Cow, Cat etc. These phonemes combined words are known as morphenes. They have social and cultural meaning. So they are used frequently in speech sounds or verbal languages. Morphenes are of various types about which we are concerned here.

Syntax: It is a combination of words to form sentences and sentences to form stanza or paragraph and stanza or paragraph tells us meaning. Thus, words, grammars, poetry, story, riddles, idioms, proverbs, sayings, jokes and many other come together under syntax.

Semantics: It is concerned with the study of meaning of words, riddles, idioms, phrases, poems, songs, sayings, jokes, grammar and so on. But understanding meaning is not an easy task. Without understanding meaning how two or more persons can communicate. Meaning is essential for speakers and hearers.

The meaning may be divided into two:

- Linguistic Meaning
- Speaker's Meaning

Linguistic Meaning may be divided again into two types:

- Dialectical
- Idiolectical

Speaker's Language may also be divided into two types:

- Literal
- Non-literal

For example:

What a beautiful dress?
What a beautiful dress?

Both above sentences are same but its speaker meaning and linguistic meaning may remain different. Similarly, its literal and non-literal meaning may be different. In case of above cited both sentences anyone of them can be used teasingly or satirically. Similarly, any one of them could be used as admiring expression.

The meaning also varies across dialects and between persons. The meaning of same words varies from dialect to dialect and person to person.

Lexical Relation: Meaning also have lexical relationship between words. It can also be understood by analyzing the relationship between words which is commonly known as lexical relation. Lexical relations can be understood by the following types:

Synonymy: When two or more words have very closely related meaning, they are termed as Synonymic terms. For example apathetic/passive/indifferent or Pedigree, ancestry/descent.

Antonomy: The words which have opposite meaning are termed as antonymous. For example: Good-bad, Hot-cold, Up-down, Pass-fail, Come-go, Man-woman, Boy-girl and so on.

Hyponymy: When two or more words are in hierarchical relationship and the meaning of one is included in other, such words are known as hyponyms. For example: cow/animal, apple/fruit, brinjal/vegetable, *Dhoti*/cloth.

Homophony: When two or more written words have the same pronounciation, they are termed as homophones. For example: floor/flour, to/two, meat/meet, and so on.

Homonomy: Words with same written and spoken forms but with very unrelated meaning are termed as homonyms. For example bank/bank, pupil/pupil/ mole/mole.

Polysemy: It refers to identical words with related multiple meaning. For example head/head, run/run,

Metanomy: When two or more words manifest a very close connection like whole-part relationship, they are termed as metanyms. For example bottle/wine, house/verandah, Governor/Raj Bhawan.

Language and Society

There is universal truth that language varies with its speakers. There is no doubt that two speakers of the same language have many similarities in their respective ways of speaking. No two speakers of the same language speak in an individual way. The modern linguistics are mostly concerned with the pattern of language commonly shared by its speakers. The focus on variation of speaking is marginalized which distinguishes one speaker from the other. But in understanding the language difference in variation of speaker is equally important. The study of language variation is a fascinating subfield of linguistics called as socio-linguistics. Socio-linguistics study language variation in social context. Speakers of language not differ only in physical features and appearances, but they also differ on the basis of age, sex, education, occupation, religion, place of residence, caste, class, ethnicity and so on.

Speech Community

Speech community is basic unit of analysis in socio-linguistics rather than a language. A speech community is the social unit in which speakers share the same words and cultural meanings unique to a particular community.

The speech community may exclude one or several languages. It is very difficult to delineate the boundaries of a speech community. But relative degree of sharing rules and usages of language among a group of speakers with mutual communicative capability may be taken as criterion for delimiting the boundaries of different speech communities.

Idiolects: Each individual has a distinct style of speaking. The individual style of speaking is known as *idiolect*. It is very easy to recognize familiar voices on the telephone, even though the speaker does not reveal his identity. Similarly, familiar voices are also easily recognizable. The voice of a popular news reader, announcer or an advertiser on the telephone can also be recognized without watching the screen. It is because the speech of an individual is characteristically unique. But this cannot be concluded that the voice of an individual does not change. The voice of an individual also changes according to age and disease in life time. The quality of voice of an individual also changes like other biological processes. But variation of an individual speech variety is termed as idiolect.

All individual speakers use several idiolect on several occasions and in several situations. For example, the idiolect of an individual in home is quite different from his idiolect as advertiser, announcer, teacher, priest, leader, buyer, seller, administrator etc. Again the idiolect of a politician with wife and children in the home is quite different from his idiolect in public meeting, Assembly, Parliament etc. Thus idiolect is concerned mainly with speech variety of an individual.

Dialect: When we try to find out something common from the idiolects of a group of individuals by means of abstraction, we call it dialect. The term dialect refers to a form of speech used by the members of a social, ethnic or regional group having something in common.

Dialect is spoken by a small localized group of individuals, which is intelligible to all its members. It is considered as intelligible variation of the same language. Dialects do not have scripts of their own. They use the common script of the language.

Style: The speech variation does not only depend upon the place of habitation of an individual or his social standing in his society, but also according to the context in which he speaks. The special manner in which people speak in particular situations is referred to as a style. As appropriate dresses are required for every specific situations such as wedding dress, morning dress, war dress and so on, so speech styles are also required on different occasions. Formal and informal situations demand stylistic variation of speech. Deviation from this is considered bad manners on the part of speakers.

Stylistic variations of speech are not only lexical but also phonological, morphological, syntactical and semantic.

Standard Dialect: A stylistical variety of speech which is formal used by leaders and upper socio-economic classes, used for literature or printed documents, taught in school and used in mass media is termed as dominant dialect or standard dialect. For example standard British English, standard American English, standard Hindi etc. The standard dialect serves more of a social function. It does not necessarily mean that it is linguistically super or better than other dialect. Its popularity or superiority could only be judged by using purely social considerations.

Idiolect, Dialect and Language

It is fitness of the thing to present here the distinction between language, dialect and idiolect.

Idiolect is individual variation of speech. If the number of speaker of a language or dialect is 300, then there will be 300 dialects. It is because speech of each individual varies from other individuals.

The speakers of a dialect do not have their own scripts. They use the common script of the language. They do not have patronage of state. The individuals acquire them as mother-tongue. A region may have a dialect boundary.

Language is promoted by the state for business transactions. It has own script and the patronage of the Government. There are schools, colleges and universities where languages are taught.

Register and Jargon

The register and Jargon are helpful in understanding variation of the dialect according to use in very specific situation. We have varieties of registers such as religious, legal and professional registers. The expressions found in one register cannot be found in another register.

What makes a special kind of register so special is the use of special Jargons. Jargons are technical vocabulary associated with a special activity of a group. As every specialized trade and profession uses its own Jargon, their special register bear testimony of dialectical variation.

Social Class and Dialectical Variation

A relationship has been observed in socio-economic status of a person and variation in pronounciation or speech sound. Labov (1972) studied dialectical variation between sale persons in three city departmental stores in New York. They were Saks, Macy and Klenin and they represented high, middle and low status respectively. He was interested to know the pronounication of '*r*' sound after the vowel. He asked questions to answer sales persons that elicited the expression fourth floor. He observed that the sales persons with high socio-economic status were using more '*r*' sound. The use of '*r*' sound was reduced in middle socio-economic status. It was very low in low socio-economic status. The study reveals clearly that people belonging to different socio-economic status bear difference in dialect.

A similar study in Reading was conducted by Trudgil (1974) in England which gave an opposite result. Trudgil observed that upper middle class English speakers tended to pronounciate less 'r' sound than their lower-middle counterparts. This study reveals clearly the differential social values associated with same pronounication at different places.

The occurrence of more 'n' sound like talkin, rendin, goin, comin, speakin, writin are more associated with lower social class throughout English speaking world. But the higher social class English speakers pronounciate more 'ng' sound such as talking, reading, going, coming, eating, writing, walking, waiting etc.

The developing of 'h' sound in the word like 'ello' is an another social marker which indicated lower social status and less education in contemporary English as revealed by the Study of Yule (1996).

Age, Sex, and Dialectical Variation

The age of speaker belonging to the same social class also reveals speech variation. This difference can easily be noticed among speakers of different generations of same social class. The use of words like bicycle, radio, ice box, wireless and so on used by grand parent's generation are considered unfashionable in speech by younger generations. Similarly, the use of words like T.V., Internet, Cell phone,

Satellite, digital, space etc. are considered unfashionable in speech of grand parent's generation.

A number of studies have been conducted on correlation between gender and speech variation. John Fishcher study (1958) reveals the frequent use of— 'ing' of such as reading, eating, putting, searching, finding etc. as characteristic of female speech and frequent use of— 'in' such as playin, goin, comin etc. as male characteristic when he had interviewed a group of school children of both sexes. Out of 24 children, 21 children alternated frequently between both forms 'durin' the interview. Fischer came to the conclusion that sex, class, personality, aggressive/submissive and mood (tense relaxed) of the speakers jointly determine the choice of pronounication. He observed that children were apt to say singing, playing, dancing, reading or interesting if they were girls, if their families were above median income, if they had dominating or assertive personality and if they were tense.

Yule in his study (1996) found that female speakers used more prestigious forms of speech than male speakers of the same social background.

Dialectical variations in terms of gender also appear through speech. In every dialect, there is a different vocabulary for men and women. For example boy-girl, men-women, uncle-aunt, male-female etc. In Hindi a separate Grammar is also used for male and female. The different vocabularies for men and women is not a choice but is prescriptive.

Some psychologists are of the opinion that females are more talkative than males and female speech is less forceful than males. When there is a conversation in a marked group of men and women, men interrupting women is far greater than *vice-versa*. Women are also reported to use more expressions associated with tentativeness and use more qualifiers before expressing an opinion.

In English we have many gender based terms and usages whose bias is predominantly masculine. In English and many other languages, masculine terms are considered to be grammatically basic and feminine terms are generally derived from their masculine terms. For example Goddess, princess, lioness, heroine terms have been derived from God, prince, lion and hero. Masculine terms are also used to include female, too, for example men, chairman, mailman, fireman, watchman, etc. Now-a-days, gender neutral terms have come into existence. For example chair person, mail person, fire person, watch person etc. Similarly, pronouns like they, them and there are applied for both sexes. In spite of all such attempts linguistic sexism is still continuing.

Ethic Background and Dialectical Variation

In multi-ethnic society, different ethnic groups use their variant of the standard dialect which contains the identifying features of their original language. For example Afro-Americans in USA have a different social dialect. This is known as black English which is considered as bad speech in America. The black English is characterized by frequent absent of the copula (form of verb to be) resulting in expression like you crazy or they mine. This does not confirm to the rule of standard English as the verb is missing in both the cases. Black English also reveals double negative construction which is considered illogical. For example I do not-know nothing.

Multilinguism and Diglossia

In most parts of the globe different ethnic groups speaking different languages live side by side. They have contact and communication with each other. As a result they learn to speak language other than their own mother-tongue. This is a typical situation of multi-lingualism. Thus, multilinguism refers to the use or ability to use two or more languages by the people of a community. The most common form of multilinguism is bilingualism. Bilingualism is ability of a group of people to speak two languages including their mother-tongue. Theoretically speaking bilingualism refers to the acquisition of complete and equal command over both languages in question. But in practice, the term is applied more loosely for those who communicate in both languages.

Bilingualism is very common in multilingual nation. In our nation states have been organized on the basis of languages spoken over a territory. For example Bengal, Orissa, Andhra Pradesh, Tamil Nadu, Karnataka, Punjab, Gujarat, Chhattisgarh and so on. Each state is bounded by another states. The people of bordering areas have frequent contact and communication. As a result bilingualism is very common in bordering areas.

In state capitals where people speaking of different languages reside for business, service, study and other kinds of modern occupation, one finds stable bilingualism and possibly multilingualism.

Multilingualism is also a common practice in many countries of the world. For example language teaching in India. In schools Hindi, English, Sanskrit and regional languages are taught. Thus, the student has to learn four languages. This is a good example of multilingualism. An interesting example of multilingualism is Native Americans of North-western Brazil and the adjoining part of Columbia. This is a culturally homogeneous area inhabited by at least twenty different types who are fluent in three, four or more regional languages. Because of strict tribal exogamy rule, a child has to learn additional languages of neighbouring tribes to look for a marital partner in adolescence. Thus, multilingualism is a cultural necessity there.

Diglossia: In a multilinguistic situation it is quite possible that different forms of same languages are being used for different purposes. When members of a speech community use two or more varieties of same language under different conditions and for different functions it is known as diglossia. The term diglossia was used by Charles A. Ferguson. Ferguson found that the speakers of same language speak two types of languages—high variety language and low variety language. High variety language is spoken in formal situation. It is associated with education and literacy. Low variety language is spoken for ordinary conversation with friends and relatives. Joking relatives cut jokes in a very loose language, but as parents, elder brothers, elder sisters, younger brothers, younger sisters, their language of conversation is not loose. Again angry persons use abusive language, which differs from their linguistic behaviour in normal situation. In Hindi speaking areas, people use standard Hindi or standard Urdu when they make formal speech on specific occasions. For example in classroom, lecture, seminar, symposium, assembly, Parliament, public address and so on. But in family, friends group, and with relative they use simple Hindi language. Diglossic variety of speech is prevalent throughout the globe. For example classical and formal Arabic of Holy *Quran* such as Arabic of Bagdad, Cairo or Tunis, standard German as formal variety and Swiss German as ordinary variety, Classical and colloquial Greek. But it is very difficult to maintain the superability of two different languages or two varieties of same language by a bilingual. Therefore, a shift from one to the other in speaking occurs which is termed as code switching.

India is an excellent example of diglossic situation. In the state of Bihar, certain local dialects are used with family members and elders, but a particular sub-dialect of western Hindi is used with friends and youngers. In South India where Dravidian languages have been spoken since centuries, the Brahmins and non-Brahmins speech varieties are spoken by different caste affiliations. In North India High forms of Hindi and Urdu are spoken on formal occasions and local Hindustani in day to day conversation. Indian villagers communicate in local dialects with fellow villagers and neighbouring villagers, but they use Hindi on formal occasions. The language of same people speaking a particular dialect varied with elders, youngers, friends and animals or birds. This foretold division has subsequently called *double-nested-diglossia*. In our country despite the spread of education and the impact of popular mass media, dialectical variation associated with castes and caste hierarchy is still a challenge for language planning.

Lingua Franca

In a multilingual area, where people speak divergent languages, there is strong desire among the groups to arrive at some common agreement in using common language for the purpose of social and commercial communication. This commonly agreed language of communication is known as lingua franca. For example, English is considered as Lingua Franca of the whole world. In the United States of America, English has been the Lingua Franca for communication between many different speakers of different native American languages. Hindi and Urdu are Lingua Francas of India and Pakistan respectively where people speak many varieties of dialects in their own regions, but for inter-dialectical communication they use Hindi or Urdu respectively. Different tribal languages are spoken in East Africa, but Swahili is their Lingua Franca for social and commercial purposes. Hausa is a Lingua Franca spoken in West Africa which makes easy for speakers of different tribal dialects to communicate in market places and also for social purposes. In the State of Jharkhand, Nagpuri is a Lingua Franca spoken at markets by tribal and other people speaking different dialects such as Pancha Pargania, Sadari, Khortha, Sadani and so on. In some places a lingua franca develops naturally, but at other places it takes shape due to intervention of state.

Pidgin

When the speakers of two or more unintelligible languages develop a need to communicate with each other for some specific purpose such as trade a pidgin is developed. A pidgin is different from a lingua franca. A lingua franca has a broad base of native speakers, pidgin does not have native speakers of its own. In pidgin two or more groups use their native languages and draw essential elements from them in developing a marginal language. Since pidgin serves a limited purpose, it possesses minimum vocabulary and a reduced grammatical structure. It develops when speakers of different languages have been in regular but limited contact. A good example of pidgin is Tok Pisin or Malenesian Pidgin English widely used in Papua New-guinea. It has 1500 lexical terms, 80 per cent terms have been derived from English. It is known as neo-Malenesian. It is Lingua Franca of about one million people who speak about 700 native languages of Papua Newguinea. It is first language of about 2,00,000 households. It has acquired so much prestige that even Parliament debates are conducted in Tok Pisin rather than in English. The English based China coast pidgin, English based Maroni Pidgin, Navajo based pidgin of American South-West, Cango pidgin in Cango river basin are some of other examples of pidgin developed mostly as a result of British colonialism and expansion of trades in different parts of the world.

Pidgin develops suddenly as per the need arises, and disappears suddenly when it is of no use. Thus, pidgin is a transitary product of course of history. The history of Vietnam is a good example of it. When Vietnam was ruled by French as a part of French Indochina, a French based pidgin came into existence which disappeared due to evacuation of French defence forces after defeat in 1954. With coming of USA combat forces in 1960, an English based pidgin developed which again disappeared as soon as US forces was withdrawn in 1973. Pidgin is simple with fewer items of vocabulary to cater to the immediate need of the communicating groups. It has a structure of its own and is readily adaptable to changing circumstances.

Creole

As referred to earlier pidgin has not a native speaker. But under some pressing circumstances a pidgin may be adopted by a speech community as its native or first language. Pidgin adopted by a speech community as its native language or first language is known as Creole. But realization of pidgin and pidginisation of Creole are also in existence. These processes are opposite to each other. Some examples of Creole are Haitian French based Creole, English spoken in some parts of Jamaica, Gullah—an English based Creole is spoken by descendants of American slaves on the islands of Coast of Georgia and South Carolina, Louisiana spoken by whites and blacks in Louisiana, Krio spoken by Sierra Leoneans are good examples of Creole. Pidgins and creoles are found in costal areas of the equatorial belt. With the spread of education greater social prestige has been attached to the standard language. As a result, the process of decreolisation has come into existence. It has given rise to the use of fewer forms and structure of the creoles than the standard language. Since the use of the language ultimately depends upon the speaker, one may find three possible varieties in these situations. It may be *basilect* closer to the basic variety or an *aerolect* with more feature of external model. Sometimes, one may encounter a *mesolect* which presents a range of different varieties. The range of varieties which evolves after creation of Creole is known as post Creole continuum.

Linguistic Families in India

In India nearly 500 dialects are spoken by the people throughout the length and breadth of our country. All dialects and languages spoken in our country have been classified into four linguistic families which are as follows:

- Austric or Austro-Asiatic family
- Tibbeto-Chinese or Sino-Tibbetan Family
- Dravidian family
- Indo-European Language Family

Austric or Austro-Asiatic Family: This family is also known as Nishad family. The austric family is divided into two sub families—(i) Austro-Asiatic, and (ii) Austronesian. In India we find only speakers of Austro-Asiatic sub-family. The Austro-Asiatic family is again divided into two branches —

- Mon-khmer branch
- Munda branch

The mon-khmer speakers are confined to two groups–Khasi of Khasi hills and Jayantia of Jayantia hills of Meghalaya and Nicobarese of Andaman and Nicobar Islands of Bay of Bengal.

The speakers of Munda family spread across a large number of tribal groups in Central and Eastern India such as Jharkhand, Orissa, Bengal and Assam. The main Munda branch of languages are Santhali, Mundari, Ho, Kharia, Asuri, Birhori, Kharwari, Kora, Birjhia, Binjhia, Korku, Juang, Koudhi, Savara, Godba. Among all these Santhal speakers are more in number than other groups. In ancient times they were known as Nishadas.

Tibbeto-Chinese or Sino-Tibbetan

The Tibbeto-Chinese family was also known as Kirat in ancient time. This family is divided into two sub-families:

- Tibbeto-Burmese
- Siamese-Chinese

The speakers of Siamese-Chinese languages are not found in India. The Tibbeto-Burmese speakers, known as Kirat spread over a large area starting from Ladakh in west to the State of Arunanchal Pradesh in north-east frontiers and down to the Southern most tip of State of Tripura. The Tibbeto-Burmese sub-family is divided into three branches:

- Tibbeto-Himalayan
- North Assamese
- Assamese-Burmese

The Tibbeto-Himalayan branch has two components—Tibbetan or Bhotia group which consists of Tibbetan, Balti, Ladakhi, Lahuli, Sherpa and Sikkim Bhotia. The Tibbetan speakers are spread over Jammu and Kashmir, while the Lahuli inhabit the Punjab. The Sherpa have confined in Darjeeling and Bhotia in Sikkim. The Himalayan group of Tibbeto-Himalayan branch consists of Kanauri of Himachal Pradesh and Lepcha of Sikkim and Darjeeling.

The north-Assam or North-east frontier branch is represented by the member of Aka, Dafla, Abor, Adi, Miri, Mishmi and the missing communities of Arunachal Pradesh.

The Assamese-Burmese branch is again divided into five groups such as Bodo, Naga, Kachin, Kukichin and Burma. Each of these groups consist of a number of languages spoken by the people of Assam and North-eastern states of India making a real linguistic mosaic of India.

Dravidian Family

The Dravidian Language Family in India is divided into three groups on the basis of geographical areas. They are as follows:

- South Dravidian
- Central Dravidian
- North Dravidian

South Dravidian: The speakers of South Dravidian groups are Tamil, Malayalam, Kannada, Yerukula, Yerava, Kuruba, Kurumba, Coorgi, Tulu, Toda and Kota languages. They are distributed in the Southern part of the Deccan Plateau

Central Dravidian: The speakers of Central Dravidian are represented by Telugu, Kui, Kolami, Gondi, Panje, Khond/Kandh languages. Telugu speakers are more in number. They are mostly tribals scattered over States of Andhra Pradesh and adjoining South Orissa.

North Dravidian: The north Dravidian speakers are mainly distributed in Jharkhand, adjoining Orissa and West Bengal. They are represented by Kurukh of Oraon and Malto of Sauria Paharia and Malpaharia.

It is important to mention here that an important Dravidian language Barhui is spoken in Baluchistan far away from the Deccan Plateau of India. This language has the highest concentration of Dravidian speakers. It is believed that the Barhui is remnant of Dravidian language once spoken in Sind, Punjab and eastern Iran.

Indo-European Language Family

Aryan language family is the major linguistic family in India. It is divided into three groups which are as follows:

- Iranian

- Dardic
- Indo-Aryan

Iranian branch of languages are not spoken in India so we are not going to discuss it here.

Dardic language: In this branch the only language is Kashmiri which is spoken by the people of State of Jammu & Kashmir.

Indo-Aryan: Indo-Aryan languages are divided into six groups which are spoken in various parts of our country. They are as follows:

North-Western Group: This group includes Sindhi and Kachhi spoken in Gujarat, Maharashtra, Rajasthan and Uttar Pradesh.

Southern Group: This group consists of Marathi and Konkani. While Marathi is spoken in Maharashtra, and Konkani is spoken in Goa, Karnataka and Maharashtra.

Eastern Group: Eastern group consists of Oriya in Orissa, Maithili, Maghi and Bhojpuri in Bihar, Bengali in Bengal and Assamese in Assam, Sadani in Jharkhand, Nagpuria in Jharkhand.

East-Central Group: This group consists of Chhattisgarhi in Chhattisgarh and Madhya Pradesh, Awadhi in U.P. and Bagheli in U.P.

The Central Group: It is represented by Braj, Bundeli, Hindustani, Kanauji, Punjabi, Rajasthani, Haryanavi, and Gujarati.

Northern or Himalayan Group: It consists of Nepali, Kumauni, Garhwali, Jaunsari, Siramauri, Kului, Mandeali, Gaddi, Churahi languages which are spoken in Uttarakhand.

Besides these a number of dialects are spoken within each group known by separate terms. Their names have not been mentioned here.

Language Change

Like cultures languages are subject to change. No language of the world is static rather it is dynamic. Change in language takes place according to time, need and function. This is also true for English language, which is international Lingua Franca spoken in all countries of the world. The English language has passed through three stages which are as follows:

- Old English Period (5th Century A.D.–11th Century A.D.)
- Middle English Period (11th Century A.D.–15th Century A.D.)

- Modern English Period (15th Century onwards)

The changes which have taken place in English language can be discussed under the following headings:

- Phonological change
- Morphological change
- Syntactical change
- Semantic change
- Lexical change

Phonological change: Between middle and modern English periods a change in quality of vowel sounds had taken place. The general form of words remained the same, but vowel sounds had undergone change considerably. For example:

Earlier English	*Modern English*
Mi:s	Mays (Mice)
Hu:s	Haws (House)
Ge:s	Gi:s (Geese)
Spo:n	Spu:n (Spoon)
Bre:ken	Bre:k (Break)

This process of change in English had started in 1400 A.D. at the time of death of Chaucer and was still taking place when Shakespeare died in 1616 A.D. This is known as *great vowel shift* in English language.

In this period an another phonological change accrued with loss of [X] sound in some words in English language. For example:

Middle English	*Modern English*
Nixt	Night
Druxe	Drought
Saux	Saw

In some words phonological change was brought by pronouncing [gh] as [F]. For example Rough and Tough. In some other cases, it was vocalized to become a vowel. For example holx to hollow and sorx to sorrow respectfully.

An another phonological change from middle to modern English language was in sound with addition of a new sound to the middle of word. This type of change in English language is known as *Epenthesis*. For example:

Aemety	Empty
Spinel	Spindel
Timr	Timber

Phonological changes in English language have also been brought by adding a word at the beginning. This process is known as *Prothesis*. For example—

Schola	escuela (school)
Spiritus	espiritu (Spirit)
Estory	Story

Phonological change in English has also been brought by reversal in position of two adjoining sounds. This change is known as *Metathesis*—

Middle English	*Modern English*
Bridd	Bird
Frist	First
Hros	Horse
Acsian	Ask

Morphological Change

Like phonological changes English language has also witnessed remarkable changes in morphological rules.

By adding 'able': Morphological changes in English language have taken place by adding the word 'able' in another word. For example—readable, doable, washable, eatable, workable, suitable.

By adding a suffix/'yan'/and/'en': Morphological change in English language has been brought by adding suffix 'yan' and 'en'. For example–sweetyan—sweet and–Redyan–Red. Redden-Red, Blueen-Blue, Red–Redden, Sweet-sweeten etc.

This rule has been changed now-a-days.

By adding/'ing'/: Morphological change has also been brought by adding/'ing': For example–read–reading, go-going, come-coming, sing-singing, eat-eating and so on.

In place of adding/'ing' in verb words morphological change has also been brought by adding 'ing' in nouns. For example–roof–-roofing, floor-flooring and so on.

Syntactical change: In English language syntactic change has been brought by *negative construction* through not, do not, never and no. For example—

I am not writing
I do not write
I never write
I deserve no thanks

By adding 'not' after auxiliary words:

Can	can't
Could	couldn't
Should	shouldn't
May	mayn't
Would	wouldn't
Had	hadn't
Have	haven't

By adding double superlative and double comparative. For example more lower and most tallest.

This rule was prevalent in old English, but it has been changed in modern English by single comparative and superlative construction. For example more low and most tall.

Semantic Change

Semantic change in a language takes place by gain or loss of semantic elements. Sometimes, a particular lexical item stands for a different meaning. As a result change in language takes place. There are three ways by which semantic changes take place. They are as follows:

- Broadening of Meaning
- Narrowing of Meaning

- Shifting of Meaning

Broadening of Meaning: In English language some such terms appear which have broader meaning and which include many words of the same semantic field. For example the word Holiday originally meant Holy day or day of religious significance. But gradually its meaning was broaden. Now-a-days, the word includes meaning of all kinds of Holidays or days without work.

Similarly, the word picture was originally used for painted representation. But gradually its meaning was broaden and now-a-days, it is used for all kinds of pictures drawn by a camera.

Originally, the term bird was used only for young birds but gradually its meaning was broaden and now-a-days, it is used for all kinds of birds.

Narrowing the Meaning: Semantic change in English language has also taken place by narrowing the meaning.

For example the term meat was originally meant for all kinds of flesh. But gradually its meaning was narrowed and now-a-days, the term meat is used only for the flesh of goat.

The word deer originally was used for all any kind of animal. But gradually its meaning was narrowed and now-a-days, it is used for a particular kind of animal.

The word liquor was used for all kinds of liquid in the beginning. But gradually its meaning was narrowed and now-a-days, it is used for only wine.

The word girl was used for young person of either sex, but gradually its meaning was narrowed to use only for young female.

Shifting of Meaning: Semantic change has taken place in English language with the help of shifting of meaning.

In middle period English language, the term lust was used for pleasure and did not include sexual pleasure as in modern English.

The term immoral was used for something uncustomary and did not have anything to do with morality as understood now.

The meaning of the word silly in old English was happy. But its meaning was changes as naive in middle period and as foolish in modern period.

The shift in meaning is not only restricted to lexical items, but it includes also changes in entire semantic field.

For example when goose was metaphorically used for foolishness, the same meaning was extended to terms like cukoo, pigeon, coot and turkey.

Sometimes semantic changes in English language have been brought by being opposite terms. For example Hot news–Cold news, Hot war–Cold war, Hot water–Cold water, Red light–Green light.

Lexical Changes

Vocabulary or lexicon of a language is enriched by the process of adding new items from within the language or outside the language. It is also true a language looses its terms, too. But the loss of terms is much less than the items being added. Lexical change in English language has taken place by the following processes:

- Compounding Process
- Blending Process
- Acronymic Process
- Word Coinage Process
- Abbreviation Process
- Borrowing Process

Compounding Process: It is also known as the process of recombining the old words to form new words with new meanings. In this way thousands of new words have entered into English language. For example—maid-servant, chairman, chairperson, fire-fighter, icecap, afternoon, chicken hearted, big mouth, moreover, takeover, undergo, water cooler and so on. In this way, a good number of words have been created in English language through the process of compounding.

Blending Process: The lexicon of English language has also been enriched by the process of blending. Through this process words are also recombined to give a new meaning. Increase in lexicon by blending is less than the compounding. In the process of blending some parts from one word and some parts from other terms are combined to form a third term with a different meaning. For example Smoke+Fog → Smog, Motor+hotel → Motel, Urin+analysis → Urinalysis, Boiled+roasted → Broasted.

Acronymic Process: In this process, new terms are created from the initials of several terms. For example:

VC	— Vice Chancellor
PVC	— Pro Vice–Chancellor
DR	— Deputy Registrar
AR	— Assistant Registrar
CE	— Controller of Examination
DO	— Development Officer
CCDC	— Coordinator Council for Development of Colleges
DSW	— Dean Student Welfare
F.O.	— Finance Officer
F.A.	— Financial Adviser
R.U.	— Ranchi University
DU	— Delhi University
UGC	— University Grants Commission
VCR	— Video Cassette Recorder
VCD	— Video Cassette Disc
CD	— Compact Disc
UNESCO	— United Nations Educational Social Cultural Organisation
IPR	— Intellectual Property Rights
NATO	— North Atlantic Treaty Organisation
WTO	— World Trade Organisation
IMA	— International Monetary Funds
W.B.	— World Bank
WHO	— World Health Organisation
RADAR	— Radio Detecting and Ranging
ATM	— Automatic Teller Machine
PIN	— Personal Identification Number, Postal Index Number.

Like above terms a number of acronymic terms are used as single word.

Word Coinage Process: Lexicon of a language is increased by word coinage process. For example—Kodak Camera, Raymond Suiting and Shirting, Bata Shoe, Tata Iron and Steel, Birla Cement, Sudha Dairy, Elephant brand Mustard Oil, Palm brand Dalda, Sweekar Refine, Nylon Bed, Xerox Machine, Cold Cream. These terms are used as brand names.

Abbreviation Process: Lexicon of a language is increased by abbreviation process. In this process words are made by abbreviations of original longer terms. For example—

Biology	—	Bio
Mathematics	—	Math
Botany	—	Bot
Zoology	—	Zool
Chemistry	—	Chem
Physics	—	Phy
Anthropology	—	Anth
Political Science	—	Pol. Sc.
History	—	Hist
Economics	—	Eco
Advertisement	—	Ad

Like above abbreviation process, a number of abbreviate words can be made by writing the full terms in short form.

Back Formation Process: In English language lexicon has been enriched by the process of back formation. In this process affix of the old words have been deleted. For example:

Swindler	—	Swindle
Peddler	—	Peddle
Hawker	—	Hawk
Editor	—	Edit

Borrowing Process: The lexicon of English language has been enriched by the process of borrowing terms from another languages. In English nearly three-fifth of the nearly 20,000 words have been borrowed from other languages of the world.

The English term drama, comedy, tragedy, physics and zoology have been taken from Greek. The Greek root can also be noticed in the words like acrophobia and Thermometer.

Latin language has contributed a number of terms in English language. For example exit, scientific, advantage, bonus, quorum and describe.

Dutch language has also contributed in the lexicon of English language. For example—freight, leak, pump and yacht.

Italian language has contributed much in musical lexicon of English language. For example—opera, piano, balcony.

Arabic language has also made contribution in lexicon of English language. For example—alcohol, algebra and zero.

Spanish language has also contributed in enriching the lexicon of English language. For example—Harbecue, cockroach, guitar, and ranch.

Some Hindi terms have also been included in the lexicon of English language. For example—Raj, Raja, Maharaja, *bandobust*.

Germanic, Scandinavian, and French elements have also contributed in the lexicon of English language.

Loss of Words: In the lexicon of English language some words have also become extinct or meaningless. For example—

Be seem—Suitable
Mammit —doll, puppet
Wherefore—why

Such words are no more in use now-a-days.

Like English language, other languages of the world have also undergone change. Linguists are trying to understand the historical and genetic relationship among different languages of the world. Like culture, change in language is inevitable.

Language and Culture Similarity

Language and culture have a number of similarities which are as follows:

- Both are social heritage
- Both are acquired
- Both are man-made
- Both are transferred
- Both make man a social being
- Both show continuity and change
- Both are universal as well as local
- Both are material as well as non-material
- Both are rule governed
- Both shift their attention from unconscious to conscious.

Can Language be Isolated from the Culture?

Language and culture are interdependent, interrelated, and interwoven. To think isolating language from culture or culture from the language is like keeping fish out of water. Language is vehicle of culture. Language is transferred from one generation to the next, from one group to another, from one individual to other and from one place to another. In order to make such a travelling, culture requires a vehicle or medium. The language works as the vehicle of culture.

Culture is promoter of language. It provides a special form, meaning and vocabulary to a language. Thus, culture plays a significant role in phonology, morphology, syntax, semantics and lexican of a language spoken by speech community. It adds new words and eliminates old terms. Thus, culture makes language dynamic and maintain its existence even in changed situation by the process of adaptation.

From the above explanation, it is quite clear that culture and language are inseparable. They maintain their co-existence.

Linguistic Approaches for Analysis of Culture

Seeing culture and language are so interdependent, cultural anthropologists and linguists have started exchanging their techniques, methods and approaches for the analysis of culture and language respectively. The following linguistic approaches have been adopted in anthropology for the analysis of culture:

- Etic and Emic approach
- Structural approach
- Semantic approach
- Cognitive approach
- Componential analysis or Distinctive feature analysis
- Phenomenological Analysis
- Symbolic analysis
- Interpretive analysis

Emic and Etic approach

The terms emic and etic were used for the first time by a linguist Kenneth Pike in his book, "Language in Relation to United Theory of Structure of Human Behaviour" (1954). Pike had isolated the parts etic from the terms phonetic and emic from the term phonemic to use as an approach for the analysis of linguistic behaviour. As culture and language are very closely related, cultural anthropologists also started using etic and emic approaches of linguistics for the analysis of cultural behaviour.

In linguistics etic presents the views of the linguist. Here linguist is not a speaker of the language, he is a researcher who studies the language. He is neither a speaker of a language nor a member of the speech community. He is an outsider for the speech community. For a linguist the speech community provides study materials. The linguist observes the linguistic behaviours of the members of speech community. He observes speech organs, movements of body parts and associated production of sound. Here the linguist as an observer and is outsider. If one attempts to describe a language from etic perspective, i.e., from the position of an observer rather than participant, one is free to use diachronic and synchronic approaches both. Like linguists, cultural anthropologists also apply etic perspective for the description and analysis of cultural data diachronically and synchronically. But here researcher is always an outsider not participant of the community whom he wants to study.

In linguistics phonemics present the viewpoint of speech community. In this approach a linguist studies the language of a speech community as an insider with the help of his participation as community member. Here a linguist is not an outsider rather he is an insider. He is not an observer here, rather he is a participant of the speech community. As an participant and insider, the linguist attempts to know the structure and linguistic field of the language of the speech community. As an insider and participant, the linguist is bound to look at language synchronically. He has no time extension here, except its present form of systematic structure. Like linguist, the cultural anthropologist also applies emic approach for systematic structural and synchronic analysis of cultural data and to know the semantic field of cultural behaviour.

Pike had attempted to explain the participant observation technique of Anthropology on the basis of etic and emic techniques of linguistics. According to him, participant technique may be correlated with emic technique of language. It is because, its main aim is to make the researcher to think and behave like local community. The observation technique may be correlated to etic technique of linguistics which attempts to keep a researcher away from the community so that he could make his free observation.

According to Pike, emic technique is helpful in understanding cultural behaviour cross-culturally. It reduces ethnocentrism. Culture cannot be judged by one value.

Structural Approach

Structural approach for the analysis of culture has been taken from the linguistics. The structure of language reveals binary oppositions which appear frequently in linguistic behaviour. Binary opposition is a property of human mind to think in opposite direction. This binary opposition is prevalent in all languages of the world. Taking this technique from the structure of language, cultural anthropologists have also attempted to analyse cultural behaviour on the basis of binary opposition or dichotomy.

The first attempt to analyse social and cultural phenomena on the basis of binary opposition was made by Emile Durkheim, a cotemporary of Farden and Saussure in his book, "Elementary Form of Religious Life" (1912). While discussing the elementary form of religious life he came across binary oppositions of sacred and profane and belief and rituals. According to him, religion is a social fact practiced by the people. It distinguishes sacred from the profane and associates belief and rituals with sacred things. Thus, binary opposition's sacred and profane associated beliefs and rituals provide the elementary form of religious life.

The structural approach of linguistics has also played a significant role in the development of structural analysis of culture and social structure of Levi-Strauss. He was greatly influenced by Emile Durkheim and his pupil and nephew Marcel Mauss. Being influenced by Durkheim's "Elementary Forms of Religious Life" (1912), Mauss postulated the Structural Theory of Gift in his book, "The Gift". Like his mentor Durkheim he also viewed social facts as Elementary Structure. But he changed the Durkheim's collective mind concept into individual mind concept.

According to him, the elementary structure of individual mind comes into existence much before the existence of elementary structure of group mind or collective mind. The elementary structure of collective mind comes into existence much before than—elementary structure of world mind. From the point of view of linguistics, the custom of gift involves three types of action—to give, to receive and to repay. In culture and society these three actions reveal reciprocity. Reciprocity is a deep mental structure and all community members share this deep mental structure. Reciprocity is a universal theory of controlling social organization and kinship.

Levi-Strauss is regarded as founder of French Structural Anthropology. He was greatly influenced by Emile Durkheim, and Marcel Mauss. He had pushed the tradition of French ethnography and Marcel Mauss traditions ahead.

Like Mauss he also concentrated his attention on structure of gift. He also took into account the concept of binary opposition as developed by linguist to understand the structure of language. But Levi Strauss attempted to understand social structure with the help of binary oppositions. His concept of social structure is known as structuralism. It was quite different from the concept of structural-functionalism developed by Radciffe-Brown. Levi-Strauss concept of structuralism is based on linguistic model and Radciffe-Brown concept of structural functionalism is based on organic model.

The theory of structuralism propounded by Levi-Strauss appears in his books, "Elementary Structure of Kinship" (1949), "Structural Anthropology" (1963), "Mythologies" (1969), "Raw and Cooked" (1969).

Taking clues from the concept of phonemes of language, i.e., a pair of contrasting sounds, Levi-Strauss applied the concept of binary opposition in Social-Cultural Anthropology. According to him, the structural anthropology has binary opposition in mental construction. Human mind has a property to think in opposite direction. Because of this binary opposition in mental construction social meanings and semantic fields are created. The binary opposition has a mediator, too. Expressing his opinion in "Elementary Structure of Kinship" (1949), Levi-Strauss said that elementary structure of kinship has binary oppositions and a mediator. They are to give, to receive and to repay. In kinship system, its structure reveals reciprocal exchange of women as gifts between human groups. Here like gift women are given, received and repaid. Here to give and to receive are binary oppositions and to repay is mediator. Reciprocal exchange of women promotes alliance in social groups and brings integration in the community. The structure of reciprocal exchange of women as gift remains in the mental construction of human mind. In kinship system one also finds binary opposition as self *versus* others.

Levi-Strauss has proposed two types of exchange of women in kinship system—(1) restricted exchange and generalized exchange. In restricted exchange only restricted groups are involved in exchange of women. For example cross-cousin marriage. In generalized exchange more than two groups are involved in exchange of women.

Generalized exchange is also of two types—Matrilineal cross-cousin marriage and Patrilineal cross-cousin marriage.

Like kinship, Levi-Strauss has attempted to provide structural analysis of a number of cultural areas. Such as mythology and raw and cooked food. He has described the structural feature of mythology through binary oppositions of nature *versus* culture. In mythology objects like snake, dog, buffalo, lion, elephant, peacock, parrot, mountain, river, seas, forest etc. appear as cultural objects which reveals the nature-culture dichotomy. Sex and blood are natural objects but establishing social-cultural rule on sex taboo which are related through blood is a cultural perspective. This is semantic and emic perspective of mythology. In each mythology one finds nature-culture dichotomy.

In his book, "Raw and Cooked" (1969) Levi-Strauss has attempted to present the structure of food from the point of view of culture. Raw food and cooked food are binary oppositions. This can also be understood as nature *vs.* culture. It is because boiled foods are served to relatives and baked food or raw foods are served to others. Relatives show cultural group, but others show natural group.

Leach has attempted to provide structural analysis of religion. In religion one finds life and death as binary oppositions and rebirth acts as mediator.

Semantic Approach

Semantic approach of culture has also been borrowed from the language. In language phonemes make words, words or morphenes make sentences and sentences make paragraph and paragraph reveals meaning. Likewise linguist, cultural anthropologist also tries to understand the cultural meaning of things and events in emic context. This approach is used in cognitive anthropology about which we are going to discuss below.

Cognitive Approach

Cognitive approach in anthropology for the analysis of cultural context has been adopted in anthropology from the language. This approach is closely related to folk classification and semantic field. This approach in anthropology developed as a reaction about the concept of historical particularism developed by Franz Boas. The approach prefers emic context in place of etic context of culture.

The cognitive approach has two significant fields:

- Etic *vs*. Emic
- Sapir-Whorf Hypothesis

About etic and emic approaches a detailed description has already been provided. Hence, we are not going to repeat them.

Sapir-Whorf Hypothesis: Besides preference of emic over etic, the another important area of cognitive anthropology is Sapir-Whorf Hypothesis. The full name of Whorf was Benjzamin Lee Whorf. He was a close associate of Edward Sapir. Edward Sapir was a pupil of Franz Boas who decided to work on language under the guidance of Franz Boas. He wrote a book "Language" (1921). When Whorf was working in an Insurance Company of High Food, he got a chance to meet with Edward Sapir, because this place was not very far from Yale. Sapir was an anthropological linguist at Yale University. Like Sapir, Whorf was also interested in knowing the relation between culture and language. The interest in same field of study brought the two scholars together–Sapir and Whorf. They had postulated. hypothesis regarding relation between culture and language. Their hypothesis is known as Sapir-Whorf hypothesis. This hypothesis is also known as linguistic relativism.

In order to show the relation between culture and language, Sapir and Whorf cited the example of Hopi language and Standard Average European Language. When they made a comparative study of these two languages, they came to know that people express about things and events differently in both these languages. Both languages had their own vocabulary, classificatory terms and semantic fields. The people of same speech communities were communicating with their fellow members fluently through own language. Thus, no language is less important in comparison to other. Each language has its own importance for the speech community. One cannot divide language as poor-rich, high-low, undeveloped-developed, unpolished-polished and so on. On the basis of comparison Sapir and Whorf developed the concept of linguistic relativism. Hopi and SAE languages both were of equal importance for their speech community. This hypothesis is known as Sapir-Whorf Hypothesis.

Sapir and Whorf found that in SAE languages concept of time was viewed as objective. It was expressed quantitatively such as 10 days, 15 days, 20 days, one month, 2 months, 2 yrs and so on. But in

Hopi language concept of time is viewed subjectively. It lacks quantitative expression. Here the concept of time is taken as late such—He came late, when will he come, when will he go. In SAE languages qualitative nouns are more used such as water, oil, food etc., but in Hopi languages each noun is used for individual specific such as serve food, bring water, rub oil and so on. Here objective is made without quantity. In SAE language, the concept of space is objective, but in Hopi language the concept of space is subjective. Thus, one finds objectivity in SAE languages and subjectivity in Hopi languages. The structure of both these languages is different. But both are of equal value for their speech communities.

Componential Analysis

Componential analysis is also related closely to cognitive anthropology. The cognitive anthropology came into existence with the attempt of those anthropologists who wanted to make anthropology free from the tradition of Franz Boas, particularly historical particularism. They placed emphasis on substantivity, objectivity and emic approach and laid the foundation of cognitive anthropology. This school of anthropology is also known as ethno-science. Ethno-linguistics and new ethnography. The scholars of this school were greatly influenced by methods, techniques and approaches of linguistics. They took into consideration the folk knowledge, concept and semantic field for analysis of culture. The scholars like Harald Koklin, Ward Good enough and Charles Frake of this school occupy special position. It is because they developed componential analysis technique. With the help of this technique folk classification of meaning was attempted. The folk classification of meaning was similar to Linnaean classification. In Linnaean classification living beings are classified on the basis of biology. This system was evolved in western biology. But in folk classification things and events are classified on the basis of culture. The main aim of componential analysis is to find out those classifications and semantics meaning hidden behind them. In componential analysis technique mapping of cultural grammar or semantic field is done by taking interviews of folk informants. Like cultural anthropologists linguists also use opposite sounds to know whether they are meaningful.

Cognitive anthropologists unanimously were of opinion that culture is a formal system of views and behaviours. Like cultural materialistc and neo-cultural evolutionists cognitive anthropologists do not explain culture as a material events. They place emphasis on the ways by which they are organized in the mind of folk people. They attempt to explore the knowledge behind categorization or classification of things and events. This approach keeps the researcher free from biasness. Since, cognitive anthropology believes that different cultures categorize their things and events differently, therefore, each culture has its own cognitive organization and structure. A cross-cultural comparison is also possible.

S. Telor in his book "Concept and Theory of Knowledge" (1966), has revealed the cognitive behaviour of American people and Koya tribe of South India. He found that for Americans drops, fogs and ice have different meaning, but the Koya tribe do not have the different meanings for drop, fog and ice. They use a common term Mank, which includes all drop, fog, and ice. The Koya tribe classifies bamboo into eight category, but American use a common term bamboo for all types of bamboo. The Koya use different terms for different cousins, but Americans use only one term cousins which includes all types of cousin. Thus, each culture, is a mental organization of each things and events.

An another cognitive anthropologist Harald Koklin who made a study of colour categorisation in Hanunoo (1955). When he was making an ethno-botanical study in Hanunoo, he found that Hanunoo categorize colour into four types:

- Ma-biru–Dark or blackness
- Ma-lagati–Lightness or whiteness
- Ma-rara–Redness
- Ma-latu–Greenness

These colour terms of Hanunoo are termed as red, yellow, black, white, green.

An another important study in cognitive anthropology was made by Charles Frake among Subanum of Philippines. Subanum of Philippines categorize disease in their own terms. In the terms of Subanum *Nuka* (skin disease), *Samad* (wound) and *Pasur* (Swellen skin with water after burnt) terms have different meaning. *Nuka* (skin disease) is of various types such as *Pugu* (scabies), *Menge weg* (burnt), *Beldut* (swollen after burnt) and *Buni* (Ringworm). For an external observer, all these terms carry the same meaning of skin disease, but for Subanum these terms carry different meaning. For western society the categorization of diseases and treatment may be a research paper, but for Subanum they are cognitive basis and semantic field.

George Goodenough (1956) included semantic analysis in the study of folk culture pattern. For this he developed a method which is known as componential analysis method. It is also known as Distinctive Feature Analysis. With the help of this method componential analysis of kinship terms are made. For example if age and sex are selected for semantic analysis of kinship terminology, then grand father represents an old man and grand daughter a young woman. Grand father and grand daughter are opposite to each other in age (old-young) and sex (male-female). Thus, kinship terminology shows binary opposition. Such type of analysis is very unique for a culture.

Cognitive anthropology does not accept anthropology as natural science, rather it accepts anthropology as a formal science. According to cognitive anthropologists, culture is not a natural phenomenon, it is a mental phenomenon. It emphasizes on cross-cultural analysis and universal theory of cognition.

Phenomenological Analysis

In the decades of 1960 and 1970 anthropologists had rediscovered Max Weber's theory. According to Max Weber's theory, individual plays important role in origin, creation and renovation of culture. Therefore; culture is not objective, it is subjective. Following this approach anthropologists considered culture as formal system. They have shown it embedded in mental structure. After establishment of Max Weber theory, importance of meaning and creative behaviour got attention in anthropology.

According to Neo-Kant Philosophy of Wilhelms and others, natural science is different from social science. Natural science is based on objectivity and generalization, but social science is subjective. One universal law cannot be discovered in social science like natural science.

Founder of American anthropology Franz Boas was of opinion that contrary to natural science, social science has a mental existence. This mental existence is unique for individual and group. In this difference between natural and social science, phenomenologist and philosopher Harcell added his own observation. According to his observation, natural science is not useful for the study of cultural life. It is because cultural life has a meaning which can be understood as shared experience by subjectivity. Social and cultural world are inter-connected through symbolic network. Each symbol is vehicle of cultural meaning. Thus, in phenomenological analysis emphasis is placed on cultural meaning. Culture is a social phenomenology. It is a lived experience of inter-subjective symbols and meaning.

Symbolic Analysis of Culture

The symbolic analysis of culture is also based on linguistic approach. The founder of symbolic school of anthropology was Victor Turner of Great Britain. According to symbolic anthropology, the cause of social integration is logical system which keeps people united on the occasion of rituals through symbols. Victor Turner was greatly influenced by Emile Durkheim's concept of social solidarity. He attempted to know as to how symbols remain active in society. Structural functionalists attempted to show that organic solidarity is maintained through institutions. Institutions give rise to formal relation. Contrary to structural functionists, Victor Turner accepted the concept of social solidarity propounded by Durkheim. According to Durkheim social solidarity is a function of logical system which maintains solidarity among people of society. Turner was also influenced by Levi-Strauss. According to Levi-Strauss, structuralism, cultural contrast and adaptability are universal mental structure. The building of culture is based on it. But according to Turner social solidarity is ambiguous and it cannot be taken as permanent. Symbols are primary vehicles through which social solidarity is organized. People use symbols as a tool for the fulfilment of their needs. Symbols give rise to social system.

Interpretive Analysis of Culture

The school of interpretive anthropology was founded in America by Clifford Greetz. According to this school culture is an experience of lived life of community. This experience connects people of the community through symbols and makes the world cognizable. Thus, interpretation of culture can be made on the basis of symbols. The scholars of this school are of opinion that interpretation of culture should be made on the basis of meaning embedded in symbols. It is because culture is expressed through external symbols. It is society which makes use of these symbols. Symbols are not closed in mind.

Greetz was influenced by Max Weber and like Weber he emphasized upon *social meaning* in place of *social structure*. According to him, social meaning should be used as explanatory tool of culture in place of social structure. He placed his attention on vehicle of culture. For him, symbols are vehicle of culture not operator of culture as propounded by his British counterpart Victor Turner. Symbols keep culture in motion. The symbols are also transferred from one generation to the next. Society uses symbols for expressing its moral, world-view, value, norms and other aspects of culture. Thus, symbols tell us what culture is. Symbols make individuals capable of leading a life as a social worker and seeing, thinking and experiencing own world. Thus, culture is social phenomenology. It is a lived experience of inter-subjective symbols and meaning.

In his book, "Interpretation of Culture" (1973), Greetz has developed ethnographic method for interpretation of culture. He evolved the thick description technique and their description technique under ethnographic method for interpretation of culture.

According to him, thick technique and thin technique give unique contribution in the explanation of culture. Through these techniques original text of culture can be obtained. This technique provides us those informations which make the world cognizable.

According to thick description technique, interpretive anthropology has following objectives:

- Social-cultural Anthropology is based on ethnography.
- Ethnography is nothing but recording of culture.
- Culture is based on symbols.
- Symbols control social behaviour.
- Symbols get meaning from their roles they play in society.
- Symbols give significant contribution in maintaining social life system.
- Since culture and behaviour are closely related, they cannot be studied in isolation.
- From above technique thick description of culture can be obtained.
- Thick description technique is an explanatory tool to produce ethnography.

Citing an example of Blink and Wink, he attempted to make a distinction between thin and thick description. Blink is an example of thin description and Wink is an example of thick description. In both these behvaiour, the movements of eye is same but meaning is different. Blink is opening and closing eyes frequently unknowing. But Wink is opening and closing of eyes for a love and friendship symbols. Such type of behaviour can be studied only by an observer. This makes difference between observation and observed.

Ethnography of Communication

The science which deals with systematic recording of culture of a community is known as ethnography. The ethnography of communication is systematic recording of culture of communication of a speech community.

A speech community is a community whose members have conversation and communication through same dialect or language. As soon as a researcher visits a speech community for the purpose of recording ethnography of communication, he or she comes across three important things, which are as follows:

- Speech Situation
- Speech Act
- Speech Event

Speech Situation: Speech situation is a situation or context in which speech between persons take place. The situation may be at the time of sharing breakfast, lunch or dinner in family, community feast, visiting temple, singing *Bhajan* and *Kirtan*, village Panchayat, working in field, thrashing field, sitting around fire during winter, playing games, staging drama, performing dance, birth, marriage, death and so on. Such context make people to communicate their views, ideas, feelings, emotions and other kinds of messages among themselves.

Speech Act: It may be defined as minimum speech unit by which analysis of communication is made. For example, asking questions, answering questions, seeking blessings, providing blessings, acceptance, non-acceptance, forgiveness, pity and so on. Speech act may be related to an individual or a group. For example prayer in temple by an individual is example of individual speech act, but prayer in school is an example of group speech act. Speech act may be of a single word or it may be of a number of sentences.

Speech Event: When speech acts are organized in a definite order and are governed by the rule of society, it is known as speech event. For example interview, conversation, telephonic talk, telephonic interview, enquiry and so on. High pitch, low pitch, keeping mum, crying, laughing and so on are also included under speech event.

In some special situation some speech acts become speech event. For example shouting fire-fire, thief-thief, Tiger-Tiger, Snake-Snake etc. They are speech act, but become speech event. As it is expected from the speaker of a language to speak correctly using grammar and meaningful sentence. Similarly, he is expected to follow suitable speech act in a special speech event. If the speaker of a language does not follow the above norms, he is treated as an outsider from the context, mad and foolish.

In anthropology it was Dells Hyms who initiated the study of ethnography of communication in 1962 in his research paper, 'Ethnography of Speaking'. He selected a new area for investigation in anthropology upon which no much research was done. He was of opinion that such type of knowledge can bridge up the gap between grammar of community and ethnography. The traditional fields of linguists were in structural differences and historical development of languages. Similarly, in traditional anthropology nature and function of culture were studied under the ethnography. Later on linguists and anthropologists developed interdisciplinary approach and recognized the importance of each other for their fields of exploration. It was because culture and language were interdependent, interrelated and maintaining co-existence. People achieve cultural goods through language. The members of a society should have linguistic efficiency. To follow the grammatical rules of mother-tongue communicational efficiency are must for working of the society. People learn all these before the adulthood. Ethnography of communication means those behaviours of people whom they achieve in communication. Field-work is an essential part of ethnography of communication. Through field-work comparison between ethnography of communication of two communities can be done.

According to Hyms, each speech event has several elements and their analysis should be made in the study of ethnography of communication. The main seven elements of ethnography of communication are as follows:

- Addresser

- Addressee
- Message form
- Channel
- Code
- Topic
- Scene

Addresser: In the ethnography of communication, addresser is known as participant of communication. It is he who addresses something to the others or for communicating various types of messages. He is also known as sender of message.

Addressee: Like addresser, addressee is also known as participant of communication. It is he who receives the messages. As he receives the messages, he is also known as receiver.

As communication takes place between addresser and addressee, therefore both are senders as well as receivers. Thus, communication takes place reciprocally. Man is such a being who makes communication not only with man, but with animals, birds, spirits, and deities. People make communication with their cattle and birds domesticated. In dream people make conversation with different birds, animals and spirits. Through prayers, priest and rituals communication between deities and people takes place. In some special situation, the participants of communication may be man, animal, bird, spirit and deities.

But when participants of communication are people, then communication depends upon age, sex, education, occupation, caste, class avoiding and joking relatives of the participants. When joking relatives meet, they cut jokes. But making fun and laugh is not allowed at death. Making fun is taken good at the time of 1st April.

Message Form: In communication, message are conveyed in different forms. The forms of communication may be different in different cultures. The message forms may be descriptive, aesthetic or stylistic. It may be of one word, one sentence, one paragraph, in poems, story, proverbs, riddles, idioms, phrases, music, clapping and symbolic.

Channel: In communication generally both types of channels are used. They are as follows:

- Verbal channel
- Nor-verbal channel

Verbal channel: Verbal channel may be divided into following:

- Oral
- Written
- Visual
- Audio-visual

Non-verbal channel: Non-verbal channels are as follows:

- Gesture
- Facial expression
- Eye contact
- Movement of different body parts
- Poses
- Non-verbal symbols
- Hands hake and shoulder meet
- Kissing

Code: Each culture has its own codes of languages. Each language or dialect has its own dialectical and linguistic lexicon and semantic fields. Therefore, linguistic or dialectical codes occupy significant place in communication. Besides verbal codes, there are also non-verbal codes such as Temple, Church, Gurudwara, Mosque, flag, bell, drum, whistling, clapping, whispering, etc.

Topic: The communication, revolves round a topic. Therefore, topic plays significant role in communication. All message forms revolve round the same topic such as song, *bhajan*, *Kirtan*, tales, experiences, incidence, riddles and so on.

The method of communication study is field-work. With the field-work all elements of communication can be explored, analysed and described systematically.

Linguistic: The science which deals with the study of origin, nature, structure, function and change regarding languages is known as linguistics. It makes diachronic as well as synchronic study of languages prevalent in the world.

Branches of Linguistics: Linguistics may be divided into following branches:

- Pre-linguistics
- Micro-linguistics

- Meta linguistics

Pre-linguistics: It makes study of speech and hearing organs and their actions in speech. It consists of speech organs, hearing organs and physical psychology.

Micro-linguistics: This is the pure form of linguistics. It has three parts:

- Phonology
- Morphology
- Semantics

Phonology: It makes study of all sounds produced by speech organs. These sounds have linguistic value. It is divided into two:

Phonetics: It studies all sounds produced by human speech organs which have linguistic value. It can be observed.

Phonemics: It deals with sorting out of sounds for specific purposes. It can be understood by participation.

Morphology: The basic sound units are known as phonemes. They have linguistic meaning but not social-cultural meaning. When two or more phonemes are combined they make morphemes or words. Morphemes have social-cultural meaning. There are series of phonemes in a language. For example vowels, consonant, high-low pitch, and combinations of words. Phonemes play significant role not only in making more and more words and sentences, but they also play significant role in providing grammatical form to language. The morphology has three directive duties which are as follows:

- It makes study of organization of sounds in a word and its grammatical forms.
- It makes self analysis of grammatical forms and words which have been composed from morphemes.
- It is duty of morphology to organize words in sentences and sentences into paragraphs.

Types of Morphemes: There are three types of morphemes. They are as follows:

- Base morpheme
- Inflectional morpheme

- Derivational morpheme

Sometimes suffix and prefix are added to make morphemes.

Semantics: It makes study of meaning expressed through words, combinations of words, and combination of sentences. It makes study to know what message is being conveyed through a paragraph.

Meta Linguistics: Meta linguistics make study of phonemes, morphemes and semantics of languages spoken by a community.

Linguistic Anthropology: A branch of anthropology which studies origin, nature, history, structure, function and change of human languages spoken over the world. It covers the entire linguistic aspects prevalent in societies and cultures.

Applied Linguistic Anthropology: Linguistic Anthropology has applied value. Its knowledge is valuable for the society from different point of views. We can discuss the applied value of linguistic anthropology under following headings:

- Applied value in literacy and education
- Applied value in medicine
- Applied value in law
- Applied value for administration
- Applied value in trade and business
- Applied value in communication development
- Applied value in development communication
- Applied value in language planning
- Applied value in research
- Applied value in linguistic relativism.

Bibliography

Atal, Yogesh, 1965: *Adivasi Bharat*. Delhi: Raj Kamal Prakashan.

Benedict, R., 1934: *Patterns of Culture*. New York: Mifflin Houghton.

——— 1946: *The Chrysanthemum and the Sword*. Boston: Houghton Mifflin.

Boas, F., 1988: *The Central Eskimo*. Washington: Smithonian Institute.

—— 1897: *The Social Organisation and Secret Society of Kwakiutl Indians*. Washington.

—— 1911: *Mind of Primitive Man*. New York: McMillan.

—— 1927: *Primitive Art. OSIO*: Aschelhoung and Company.

—— 1928: *Anthropology and Modern Life*. W.W. Norton and Company.

—— 1940: *Race, Language and Culture*, New York: McMillan and Company.

Bose, N.K., 1929: *Cultural Anthropology*. Bombay: Asia Publishing House.

—— 1932: *Canons of Orissan Architecture*. Calcutta: Ramananda Chatterjee.

—— 1948: *Excavations in Mayurbhanj*. Calcutta: University of Calcutta.

—— 1967: *Culture and Society in India*. Bombay: Asia Publishing House.

Child, V.G., 1925: *The Dawn of Western Civilization*. New York: Knopf.

Child, V.G., 1946: *What Happened in History*. New York: Pelicon.

Child, V.G. 1951(a): *Social Evolution*. New York: Henry Schuman.

Child, V.G., 1951(b): *Man Makes Himself*. New York: New American Library, Mentor.

Child, V.G., 1953: *What is History*. New York: Henry Schuman.

Child, V.G., 1958: *The Dawn of European Civilization*. New York: Knopf.

Darwin, C., 1859: *Origin of Species*. New York, American Library, Mentor.

Darwin, C., 1871: *Descent of Man and Selection in Relation to Man*.

Dube, S.C., 1954: *The Kamar*. Lucknow: Universal Publication.

Dube, S.C., 1955: *Indian Village*. London: Cornell University Press.

Dube, S.C., 1958(a) *India's Changing Villages: Human Factors in Community Development*, London: Cornell University Press.

Dube, S.C., 1958(b): *Power and Conflict in Village India*. London: Cornell University Press.

Dube, S.C. (ed), 1968: *Institution Building for Community Development*. Hawai: East-West Centre Press.

Dube, S.C., 1960: *Manav Aur Sanskriti*. Delhi: Raj Mahal Prakashan.

Dube, S.C., 1962: *Bhartiya Samaj Parichaymala*. Delhi: Rajmahal Prakashan.

Dube, S.C. (ed.) 1971: *Essays on Modernisation*. Delhi: Vikas Publishing House.

Dube, S.C., 1973: *Contemporary India and its Modernisation*. Delhi: Vikas Publishing House.

Dube, S.C. (ed.) 1977: *Tribal Heritage of India*. Delhi: Vikas Publishing House.

Dube, S.C., 1990: *Tradition and Development*. Delhi: Vikas Publishing House.

Du-Bois, C., 1946: *The People of Alor: A Social Psychological Study of an East Indian Island*. Mineapolish: University of Minneasota Press.

Durkheim, E., 1893: *Division of Labour in Society*. New York: MacMillan.

Durkheim, E., 1895: *The Rules of Sociological Method*. New York: Free Press.

Durkheim, E., 1897: *Suicid*, New York: Free Press.

Durkheim, E., 1912: *Elementary Forms of Religious Life*. New York: Allen and Unwin.

Evance-Pritchard, E.E., 1940: *Nuer*. London: Oxford University Press.

Evance-Pritchard, E.E., 1949: *The Sansui Cyrenaica*. London: Oxford University Press.

Evance-Pritchard, E.E., 1951: *Social Anthropology*. New York: Free Press.

Firth, R., 1921: *Primitive Economics of New Zealand Maori*. London: George Routledge.

Firth, R., 1957: *Man and Culture: An Evaluation of Work of Malinowski*. London: Routledge and Kegan Paul.

Firth, R., 1963: *We the Tikopia*, Boston: Beacon Press.

Firth, R., 1964: *Essays on Social Organisation and Value*. London: Routledge and Kegan Paul.

Fortes, M., 1945: *The Dynamics of Clanship among Tallency*. London: Oxford University Press.

Fortes, M., 1949: *The Web of Kinship among Tallency*. London: Oxford University Press.

Fortes, M. and E.E. Evance Pritchard (eds.) 1940: *African Political System*. London: Oxford University Press.

Frake, C.O., 1961: "Diagnosis of Disease among Subanum of Mindanao". *American Anthropologist*. 63, 113-132.

Frake, C.O., 1964: "How to ask for a Drink in Subanum". *American Anthropologist*. 66(b), 127-132.

Frazer, J.C., 1887: *Totemism*. Edinburg: Adams and Charles.

Frazer, J.C., 1911-15: *The Golden Bough*. 3rd ed. London: MacMillan.

Freud, S., 1913: *Totem and Taboo*. London: Penguin Books.

Freud, S., 1928: *Future of an Illusion*. London: School of Psychoanalysis.

Freud, S., 1930: *Civilization and its Discontents*. New York: Jonathan Cape and Harrison Smith.

Giglioli, P.P., 1972 (ed.): *Language and Social Context*. Baltimore: Penguin Books.

Gluckman, M., 1949: *Malinowski's Sociological Theory*. New York: Oxford University Press.

Gluckman, M., 1955(a): *Custom and Conflict in Africa*. Oxford: Bosil Blackwell.

Gluckman, M., 1955(b): *Judicial Process among Baroste of Northern Nigeria*. Manchester: Manchester University Press.

Gluckman, M., 1962: *Essays on the Rituals of Social Relations*. Manchester. Manchester University Press.

Gluckman, M., 1963: *Order and Rebellion in Tribal Africa*. New York: Free Press.

Golden Weiser, A., 1933: *History, Philosophy and Culture*. New York: Knopf.

Goodenough, W.H., 1957: *Cultural Anthropology and Linguistics*, Washington: George Town University Press.

Greetz, Clifford, 1973: *Interpretation of Culture*. New York: Basic Books.

Gumperz, J.J., 1964: "Linguistics and Social Interactions in Two Communities". *American Anthropologist*. 66(6), 137-153.

Gumperz, J.J. and Dell Hymes (ed.) 1972: *Directions in Socio-linguistics*. New York: Holt, Rinehart and Winston.

Haddon, A.C., 1895: *Evolution in Art*. London: W. Scot.

Haddon, A.C., 1908: *The Study of Man*. London: J. Murray.

Haddon, A.C., 1910: *History of Anthropology*. New York: Patnam.

Haddon, A.C., 1927: *The Wanderings of People*. Cambridge: Cambridge University Press.

Haddon, A.C., 1934: *History of Anthropology*. London: Warrs.

Hall, E.T., 1966: *The Hidden Dimension*. New York: Doubleday.

Harris, M., 1964(a): *The Nature of Cultural Things*. New York: Random House.

Harris, M., 1964(b): *Patterns of Race in America*. New York: Walker.

Harris, M., 1968: *Rise of Anthropological Theory*. New York: Knopf.

Harris, M., 1971: *Cultural Materialism*. New York: Knopf.

Herskovits, M., 1948: *Man and His Work*. New York: Knopf.

Hickerson, N.P., 1980: *Linguistics Anthropology*. New York: Hall, Rinehaart & Winston.

Hoebel, E.A., 1949: *Man in Primitive World*. New York: McGraw Hill.

Honigmann, J.J., 1954: *Culture and Personality*. New York: Harper & Row.

Honigmann, J.J., 1963: *Understanding Culture*. New York: Harper & Row.

Hymes, Dell (ed.) 1964: *Language in Culture and Society*. New York: Harper & Row.

Hymes, Dell, 1974: *Reinventing Anthropology*. New York: Vintage Books.

Jakobson, R. and Moristalle 1956: *Fundamentals of Language*. The Hauge: Mouton.

Kalpan, B., 1961: *Studying Personality Cross Culturally*. Evanston: Raw Peterson.

Kardiner, A., 1935 (ed.): *The Individual and His Society*. New York: Columbia University Press.

Kardiner, A. and Ralph Linton, 1945: *Psychological Frontiers of Society*. New York: British Columbia Press.

Kardiner, A. and Prevel, E., 1961: *They Studied Man*. Cleveland: World Publishing Company.

Kluckhohn, C., 1949: *The Mirror for Man*. New York: MacGraw-Hill.

Kroeber, A., 1923: *Anthropology*. New York: Harcourt Brace.

Kroeber, A. (ed.), 1925: *Handbooks of Indians of California*. New York: Harcourt Braci.

Kroeber. A., 1939: *Cultural and Natural Areas of Native North America*. Berkley: California University Press.

Kroeber, A., 1944: *Configuration of Culture Growth*. Berkley: California University Press.

Kroeber, A., 1952: *The Nature of Culture*. Chicago: University of Chicago Press.

Kroeber, A., 1957: *Style and Civilization*. Ithaca: Cornell University.

Kroeber, A., 1963: *An Anthropologist Looks at America*. Berkley: University of California Press.

Lavob, William, 1972: *Socio-linguistic Pattern*. Philadelphia: University of Pennsylvania.

Leach, E., 1954: *Political System of Highland Burma*. Boston: Beacon Press.

Leach, E., 1961(a): *Rethinking Anthropology*. London: Athlove Press.

Leach, E., 1961(b): *A Village in Ceylone*. New York: Cambridge University Press.

Leach, E., 1983: *Language: An Introduction*. New York: Random House.

Levi-Strauss, C., 1949: *Elementary Structure of Kinship*. Paris: Plon.

Levi-Strauss, C., 1963(a): *Structural Anthropology*, Harmondsworth: Penguin Books.

Levi-Strauss, C., 1963(b): *Totemism*. Boston. Beacon: Basic Book.

Levi-Strauss, C., 1964: *Mythologies*. Paris: Plon.

Levi-Strauss, C., 1966: *The Savage Mind*. Chicago: Chicago University Press.

Lewis, O., 1951: *Life in a Mexican Village*. Urbana: University of Illinois Press.

Lewis, O., 1961: *The Children of Sanchez*. New York: Random House.

Lewis, O., 1966(a): *The Culture of Poverty*. Scientific American.

Lewis, O., 1966(b): *Lavida*, New York: Random House.

Linton, R., 1936: *The Study of Man*. New York: Appleton Century.

Linton, R., 1945: *The Cultural Background of Personality*. New York: Appleton.

Linton, R., 1917: *Culture and Ethnology*. New York DC.: McMurtrie.

Lowie, R., 1920: *Primitive Culture*. New York: Bone and Liverite.

Lowie, R., 1927: *Origin of State*. New York: Harcourt Braci.

Lowie, R., 1937: *History of Ethnological Theory*. New York: Farrer and Rine-hart.

Malinowski, B., 1913: *Family among Australian Aborigines: A Sociological Study*. London: University of London Press.

Malinowski, B.K., 1922: *Argonauts of Western Pacific*. New York: Duttan.

Malinowski, B.K., 1926: *Crime and Custom in Savage Society*. London: Kegan Paul.

Malinowski, B.K. *Sex and Repression in Savage Society*. London: Routledge and Kegan Paul.

Malinowski, B.K., 1935: *Coral Garden and their Magic*. London: Routledge and Kegan Paul.

Malinowski, B.K., 1945: *Dynamics of Culture Change*. London: Routledge and Kegan Paul.

Malinowski, B.K., 1944: *Scientific Theory of Culture and Other Essays*. London: Routledge and Kegan Paul.

Malinowski, B.K., 1947: *Freedom and Civilization*. London: Routledge and Kegan Paul.

Maine, H.J.S., 1883: *Early Law and Customs*. London: J. Murray.

Maine, H.J.S., 1983: *Early History of Institutions*. New York: Halt.

Maine, H.J.S., 1861: *Ancient Law*. London: J. Murray.

Majumdar, D.N., 1936: *A Tribe in Transition Study in Culture Pattern*. London: Longmans Green and Company.

Majumdar, D.N., 1944: *Fortunes of Primitive Tribes*. Lucknow: Universal Publisher.

Majumdar, D.N., 1946: *Races and Cultures of India*. Allahabad: Kitabistan.

Majumdar, D.N., 1950: *Affairs of a Tribe: A Study in Tribal Dynamics*. Lucknow: Universal Publisher.

Majumdar, D.N., 1958: *Caste and Communication in an Indian Village*. Bombay: Asia Publishing House.

Majumdar, D.N., 1960: *Social Contours of an Industrial City*. Bombay: Asia Publishing House.

Marret, R.R., 1909: *The Threshold of Religion*. London: Methuen.

Marret, R.R., 1927: *The Diffusion of Culture*: Cambridge: Cambridge University Press.

McLennan, J.F., 1865: *Primitive Marriage*. Edinburg: Farrer and Rinehart.

McLennan, J.F., 1876: *Studies in Ancient History*. London: McMillan.

Mead, M., 1928: *Coming of Age in Samoa*. New York: Morrow.

Mead, M., 1930: *Growing up in New Guinea*. New York: Blue Ribbon.

Mead, M., 1935: *Sex and Temperament in three Primitive Societies of New Guinea*. New York: Morrow.

Mead, M., 1937: *Cooperation and Competition among Primitive People*. New York: McGraw Hills.

Mead, M., 1939: *From South Sea*. New York: Morrow.

Mead, M., 1942: *And Keep Your Power Dry: An Anthropologist Look at America*. New York: Morrow.

Mead, M., 1949: *Male and Female*. New York: Morrow.

Mead, M., 1955: *Cultural Patterns and Technical Change*. New York: Mentor.

Mead, M., 1964: *Continuity in Culture Evolution*. New Heaven: Yale University Press.

Mead, M.R. Bunze (ed.) 1960: *The Golden Age of Anthropology*. New York: George Braziler.

Mead, M. and M.C. MacGeorge, 1951: *Growth and Culture: A Photographic Study of Balanese Childhood*. New York: Putnam.

Mead, M. and Rodha Metraux. 1953: *The Study of Culture at a Distance*. Chicago: University of Chicago Press.

Misra, K.K., 2000 : *A Text Book of Anthroplogical Linguistics*. New Delhi: Concept Publishing Company (P) Ltd.

Morgan, L.H., 1851: *League of Iroquis*. Rochester: Sage and Bora.

Morgan, L.H., 1877: *Ancient Society*. New York: World Publishing.

Morgan, L.H., 1870: *System of Consanguinity and Affinity of Human Family*. Washington: Swithonian Institute.

Morgan, L.H., 1881: *Houses and Housewife of American Aborigines*.

Murdock, G.P., 1937: *Statistical Correlations in Science of Society*. New Heaven: Yale University Press.

Nadel, S.F., 1951: *The Foundation of Social Anthropology*. New York: Free Press.

Nadel, S.F., 1957: *The Theory of Social Structure*. New York: Free Press.

Opler, M., 1951: *Village Life in North India*. Chicago: Dolphian Society.

Opler, M., 1952: "Extension of an Indian Village". *Journal of Asian Study*.

Parsons, T., 1937: *Structure of Social Action*. New York: Free Press.

Pike, K., 1954: *Language in Relation to Unified Theory of Structure of Human Behaviour*. Gleandale: Summer Institute of Linguistics.

Radcliffe-Brown, A.R., 1922: *The Andaman Islanders*. Cambridge: Cambridge University Press.

Radcliffe-Brown, A.R., 1948: *Natural Science of Society*. New York: Free Press.

Radcliffe-Brown, A.R., 1950 (ed.): *African System of Marriage and Family*. London: Oxford University Press.

Radcliffe-Brown, A.R., 1952: *Structure and Function of Primitive Societies*. London: Oxford University Press.

Radcliffe-Brown, A.R. and M.N. Srinivas 1958 (ed.): *Method in Social Anthropology*. Chicago: University of Chicago Press.

Rafzel, F., 1882: *Anthropo-Geographic*. Stuttgart: J. Engel Horn.

Redfield, R., 1930: *Topeztlan: A Mexican Village*. Chicago: Chicago University Press.

Redfield, R., 1934: *Chancom*. Chicago: Chicago University Press.

Redfield, R., 1941: *Folk Culture of Ucatam* Chicago: Chicago University Press.

Redfield, R., 1953: *Primitive World and its Transformation*. Chicago: Chicago University Press.

Redfield, R., 1955: *The Little Community: Viewpoint for the Study of Human Whole*. Chicago: Chicago University Press.

Redfield, R., 1955: *Thinking about Civilization*. Chicago: Chicago University Press.

Redfield, R., 1956: *Peasant Society and Culture*. Chicago: Chicago University Press.

Rivers, W.H.R., 1906: *The Toda*. New York: MacMillan.

Rivers, W.H.R., 1914(a): *History of Melanesian Society*. Cambridge: Cambridge University Press.

Rivers, W.H.R., 1914(b): *Kinship and Social Organisation*. London: Constable.

Rivers, W.H.R., 1922: *History and Ethnology*. New York: MacMillan.

Rivers, W.H.R., 1923: *Conflict and Dream*. New York: Harcourt Brace.

Roy, S.C., 1912: *Munda and their Country*. Calcutta: Church Press.

Roy, S.C., 1914: *The Oraon of Chotanagpur*, Ranchi: Church Press.

Roy, S.C., 1925: *The Birhor: Little Known Jungle Tribe*. Ranchi: Church Press.

Roy, S.C., 1928: *Oraon Religion and Custom*. Ranchi: Church Press.

Roy, S.C., 1935: *The Hill Bhuiyas of Orissa*. Ranchi: Church Press.

Roy, S.C., 1937: *The Kharia*. Two Volumes. Ranchi: Church Press.

Shahlins, M. and E. Service 1960: *Evolution and Culture*. Ann Arbor: University of Michigan Press.

Sapir, E., 1921: *Language*. New York: Harcourt Brace.

Schapera, I., 1947: *Migrant Labour and Tribal Life*. London: Oxford University Press.

Schmidt, W., 1933: *High Gods in North America*. Oxford: Clerendon Press.

Schmidt, W., 1939: *The Culture Historical Method of Ethnology*. New York: Fortunys.

Seligman, C.C. and B. Seligman. 1911: *The Veda*. Cambridge: Cambridge University Press.

Singer, M., 1972: *When a Great Tradition Modernises*? Chicago: Chicago University Press.

Singer, M., 1975 (ed.): *Traditional India: Structure and Change*. Chicago: Chicago University Press.

Srinivas, M.N., 1942: *Marriage and Family in Mysore*. Bombay: Asia Publishing House.

Srinivas, M.N., 1952: *Religion and Society among Coorgs of South India*. Bombay: Asia Publishing House.

Srinivas, M.N., 1962(a): *Caste in Modern India*. Berkley: University of California.

Srinivas, M.N., 1962: *Caste in Modern India and other Essays*. Bombay: Asia Publishing House.

Srinivas, M.N., 1966: *Social Change in Modern India*. California: University of California Press.

Srinivas, M.N., 1976(a): *The Remembered Village*. Berkley: University of California.

Srinivas, M.N., 1976(b): *Nation Building in Independent India*. New Delhi: Oxford University Press.

Srinivas, M.N., 1986: *Dominant Caste and other Essays*. New Delhi: Oxford University Press.

Srinivas, M.N., 1989: *The Cohesive Role of Sanskritisation*. New Delhi: Oxford University Press.

Srinivas, M.N., 1992: *On Living in a Revolution*. New Delhi: Oxford University Press.

Srinivas, M.N., 1996: *Village, Caste, Gender and Method*. New Delhi: Oxford University Press.

Srinivas, M.N., 1997: *Caste: Its Twentieth Century Awatar*. New Delhi: Oxford University Press.

Srinivas, M.N., 1969 (ed.): *India's Social Structure*. New Delhi: Oxford University Press.

Srinivas, M.N., 1977 (ed.): *Dynamics of Social Change in India*. New Delhi: Oxford University Press.

Steward, J., 1955: *The Theory of Culture*. Urbana: University of Illinois.

Tarker, Frank, 1986: *Linguistics for Non-linguistics*. Boston: Little Brown.

Tax, S., 1964 (ed.): *Horizons of Anthropology*. Chicago: Aldine.

Turner, Victor, *The Forest of Symbols: Aspects of Andembu Ritual*. Ithaca: Cornell University Press.

Turner, Victor, 1969: *The Ritual Process: Structure and Anti-structure*. New York: University Press.

Tyler, S.A., 1956: *Conceptions and Theory of Knowledge*. New Heaven: Bookman Associate.

Tyler, S.A., 1969 (ed.): *Cognitive Anthropology*. New York: Holt, Rineheart of Winston Inc.

Tylor, E.B., 1861: *Anahuac, Mexico and Mexicans: Ancient and Modern*. London: Longmans, Green, Longman and Robert.

Tylor, E.B., 1865: *Researches into Early History of Mankind and the Development of Civilization*.

Tylor, E.B., 1871: *Primitive Culture: Researches into the Development of Mythology, Philosophy, Religian, Language, Art and Custom*. London: J. Murray.

Tylor, E.B., 1881: *Anthropology: An Introduction to the Study of Man and Civilization*. New York: D. Appleton.

Upadhyay, V.S. and Gaya Pandey, 1993: *History of Anthropological Thought*, New Delhi: Concept Publishing Company.

________ 2001: *Manav Shastriya Vicharak Ewam Vichar Dharayen*. Delhi: Directorate, Hindi Medium Implementation, Delhi University.

_______ 2001: *Jana Jatiya Vikas*. Bhopal: Madhya Pradesh Hindi Grantha Academy.

_______ 2001: *Vikasatmak Manav Vigyan*. Bhopal: Madhya Pradesh Grantha Academy.

_______ 2002: *Tribal Development in India*, Ranchi: Crown Publications.

_______ 2003: *Samajik Sanskritik Manavshastra*. Ranchi: Crown Publications.

Vidyarthi, L.P., 1961: *Sacred Complex in Hindu Gaya*. Bombay: Asia Publishing House.

Vidyarthi, L.P., 1963: *The Maler: Nature-Man-Spirit Complex in a Hill Tribe of Bihar*. Calcutta: Bookland Private Limited.

Vidyarthi, L.P., 1964: *Cultural Contours of Tribal Bihar*. Calcutta: Punthi Pustak.

Vidyarthi, L.P. and B.K. Rai (1976): *Tribal Culture of India*. New Delhi: Concept Publishing Company.

Vidyarthi, L.P., 1977: *Rise of Indian Anthropology*. Two Volumes. New Delhi: Concept Publishing Company.

Vidyarthi, L.P., 1980: *Trends in World Anthropology*. New Delhi: Concept Publishing Company.

Wester Marck, E., 1981: *The History of Human Marriage*. New Delhi: Concept Publishing Company.

White, Leslie A., 1949: *The Science of Culture*. New York: Grow Press.

White, Leslie A., 1959: *The Evolution of Culture*. New York: McGraw Hill.

Wister, C., 1917: *The American India: An Introduction to the Anthropology New World*. New York DC.: McMurtri.

Wissler, C., 1926: *The Relation of Nature to Manin Aboriginal America*. New York: Oxford University Press.

Wissler, C., 1929: *An Introduction to Social Anthropology*. New York: Halt.

Index